A NATION WHOLLY FREE

A NATION WHOLLY FREE

THE ELIMINATION *of the* NATIONAL DEBT *in the* AGE OF JACKSON

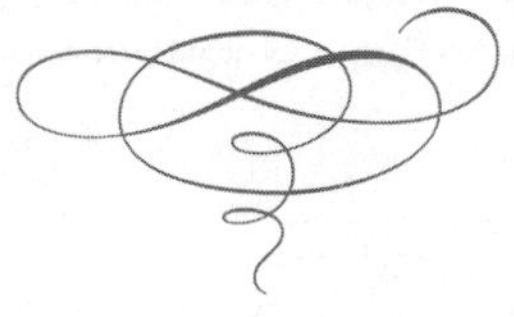

· CARL LANE ·

WESTHOLME
Yardley

Westholme Publishing, LLC
904 Edgewood Road
Yardley, Pennsylvania 19067
Visit our Web site at www.westholmepublishing.com

First Printing October 2014
10 9 8 7 6 5 4 3 2 1
ISBN: 978-1-59416-209-1
Also available as an eBook.

Printed in the United States of America.

For Lizzy,
With the laughing face

CONTENTS

INTRODUCTION

After the attacks of 9/11, the United States went to war against Al Qaeda and the Taliban in Afghanistan and, in 2003, against Iraq. Many American lives were lost and military personnel maimed. To sustain these military operations, the government borrowed billions of dollars. These obligations, together with the Bush tax cuts, the 2008 economic meltdown, and the Obama administration's stimulus program, have created a national debt that now exceeds $17 trillion, an amount greater than our Gross Domestic Product. Many Americans are left wondering: Can such a huge debt ever be paid off—and, if so, how? And, if not, *then* what?

Anguish over the national debt, exacerbated by bitter political partisanship, underpins our current drift from one crisis to another. In the summer of 2011, the House of Representatives flirted with defaulting on our debt obligations, and the nation's credit rating was downgraded for the first time ever. On January 1, 2013, Congress allowed the country to dip briefly over the so-called "fiscal cliff." The so-called "sequester," imposing huge across-the-board cuts in federal expenditures, took effect on March 1, 2013, but did not stop debt growth. In October, Congress again toyed with default on the debt and shut the government down for sixteen days. Despite enactment of a bipartisan budget deal in January 2014, the future remains unclear. One thing, however, is certain: How to address the debt issue will remain a matter of contention.

Yet anguish over our national indebtedness is not a twenty-first century novelty. It characterized our politics for two decades following 1815. The same concerns arose then as today. How could the debt inherited from the War for Independence, the Louisiana Purchase, and the War of 1812—peaking at more than $127 million in 1816 (a tremendous sum in that era)—ever be paid off? Yet it was, and its extinction marks the only period in our entire history (two years and ten months, from January 1835 to October 1837) when the United States was debt free. Most Americans are unaware of this episode. It has been largely erased from our national memory.

One purpose of this book is to rekindle that memory by telling the story of how debt freedom was secured. It takes its title from the memoir of Missouri senator Thomas Hart Benton, who remarked that after the War of 1812 the question was whether the United States could pay down its national debt and become "a nation wholly free." Indeed, eliminating the national debt became a post-1815 priority. The book argues that after President James Monroe announced in late 1824 that the public debt would be extinguished on January 1, 1835, securing debt freedom underpinned much of the politics and policies pursued at the national level. The circumstances surrounding John Quincy Adams's election to the presidency by the House of Representatives in 1825, together with his programmatic agenda, raised doubts about his commitment to debt freedom and doomed his administration to failure. Andrew Jackson, on the other hand, elected president in 1828, was dedicated to national debt freedom, and his determination to achieve it factored into all the major policy decisions of his two administrations. Viewing Jacksonianism from the perspective of debt freedom unifies issues as diverse as internal improvements, the Bank War, the Nullification Crisis of 1832-33, and others that dominated the era. The pursuit of national debt freedom was, in fact, a core element of what is often called Jacksonian Democracy. This story is, accordingly, traditional political and policy history, not economic or financial history. It tells a familiar story, but from a new vantage point.

This thesis is not intended to challenge any of the rival schools of thought concerning the Age of Jackson. Rather, it aims to call attention to a common factor in Jacksonian public policy that has been largely overlooked. Remarkably little has been written about the elimination of the national debt in 1835. In addition, this book aims at encouraging further research into the relationship between debt freedom and Jacksonian Democracy. Throughout the text the terms "national debt" and "public debt" are used interchangeably.

Moreover, since today we confront a national debt of extraordinary magnitude, I hope that this story will shed light on our current situation. For this reason the book is intended for a general as well as an academic audience. The securing of our debt freedom in 1835 is an interesting story, and I hope that I have told it well. Furthermore, especially in view of our current debt crisis, I also hope that this study will, at the very least, inspire confidence that we can solve our fiscal problems and ensure a prosperous future for our children, grandchildren, and great-grandchildren. We have lived with public debt for more than 235 years, and obviously we have survived. This study may even offer some guidance on how to address our present debt problem. For these reasons, the book concludes with a brief epilogue comparing and contrasting the situation in Jackson's day with our own.

ONE

CRISIS AND PROMISE: DECEMBER 1824–MARCH 1825

ALTHOUGH UNSEASONABLY MILD TEMPERATURES BLESSED THE mid-Atlantic region of the United States in the autumn of 1824, a discomforting political chill greeted members of the eighteenth Congress as they gathered in Washington in early December.[1] Uncertainty and anxiety gripped the air, and for good reason: The recent presidential election had failed to produce a winner. Four candidates had divided the electoral vote in a way that denied a majority to any one of them. Consequently, according to Amendment XII of the Constitution, selection of the next chief executive devolved upon the House of Representatives, each state delegation casting one vote and choosing from the three candidates with the most electoral votes. Yet even the slate of three remained undefined, because the election result in Louisiana, with five electoral votes, was not yet known.

The situation was this: General Andrew Jackson of Tennessee, the popular hero of the War of 1812 and currently a member of the Senate, qualified for the run-off election in the House. He had won only a plurality of electoral votes, the reason why the election was going to the representatives in the first place. Louisiana's five votes were too few to give him a majority. Secretary of State John Quincy Adams, second behind Jackson, also qualified, but, even with Louisiana's votes, he could not overcome Jackson's lead. The third candidate for House consideration, however, was either the secretary of the treasury, William H. Crawford of Georgia, or the Speaker of the House, Henry Clay of Kentucky. Clay, who was currently fourth in the electoral tally, needed all five of Louisiana's votes to overtake Crawford and eliminate him from the contest.[2]

Speculation, rumor, and just plain old politics dominated conversations among senators and representatives as they gathered at their various lodgings and favorite watering holes.[3] Partisanship probably distorted much of the discourse because, as one contemporary observed many months before anyone knew that the election would go to the House, an "embittered and violent spirit" characterized the "Presidential question" in 1824.[4]—Jackson's violent temperament rendered him unfit for the presidency!—Adams, in his heart of hearts, was still a Federalist!—Crawford's ill health made it impossible for him to serve!—Clay was a drinker and a gambler!—But as surely as many discussions reflected political loyalties, so too must they have focused on important policy issues, since nothing quite like this had happened in a quarter century.—How had the House organized itself when it confronted the electoral tie between Mr. Jefferson and Mr. Burr in 1801?—Would that precedent control how the House proceeded in the current situation?—Should a plurality of the electoral vote automatically translate into a majority?

The election was on everyone's mind, and rightly so. After all, much was at stake. In three months, the administration of the government of the United States would be transferred, but to whom? Where was the nation heading? Apprehension that a crisis was at hand overhung Capitol Hill.

❧

At the White House, meantime, the mood was not as grim as at the other end of Pennsylvania Avenue, for at least two reasons. First, James Monroe, the outgoing president, was looking forward to retirement. He was almost sixty-eight years old and had served two difficult terms, capping a public career that began with military service in the New York and New Jersey campaigns of 1776. Indeed, he was the last president who could boast that he had fought in the War for Independence. After the 1783 peace treaty with England, he represented Virginia in the Continental Congress, opposed the Constitution at that state's ratifying convention in 1788, was elected to the Senate in 1790, became minister to France in 1794, and five years later, governor of Virginia. He returned to the Foreign Service in 1802 as special envoy to France, a role in which he helped secure the purchase of Louisiana in 1803. Subsequently, he became American minister to Great Britain and, still later, secretary of state under James Madison. His election to the presidency in 1816 allegedly ushered in an "era of good feelings," but his tenure was not without controversy. The Panic of 1819 and the crisis over Missouri's admission to the union as a slave state constituted only two of the many difficulties his administration had been forced to overcome. There were, of course, other successes, but none had come easily: the definition and demilitarization of the border with Canada, the acquisition of Florida, the Transcontinental Treaty with Spain, and, of course, that Western-Hemispheric policy which still bears his name. By the end of 1824 Monroe was weary and eager to retire to the quiet of his Virginia plantation, whoever his successor might be.[5] On the latter important matter, he chose to remain above the political fray and maintain neutrality.[6]

The second reason for optimism at the White House concerned Monroe's last major constitutional obligation—his eighth and final message to Congress on the state of the union. This report, Monroe knew, was swollen with good news and would reflect well on his stewardship of the government. His successor, whoever he was, would inherit a healthy federal union. The president began working on the report a month before Congress convened. On Wednesday, November 10, he presided at a cabinet meeting and solicited input from his department heads. Interestingly, this was the first meeting Treasury Secretary Crawford attended in many months. A year earlier, he had suffered a severe stroke, leaving him partially paralyzed and, for a long period, bedridden. Secretary of State Adams, who had not seen his colleague and presidential rival during the latter's illness, noted that Crawford's "articulation is much affected, and his eyesight is impaired. But his understanding remains, except with some deficiencies of memory."[7] At that juncture, neither Adams nor anyone else knew that the House would have to choose the next president, and Crawford's candidacy, despite the stroke, was formidable. Widely respected, he enjoyed the nomination of the Congressional Caucus—to its critics "King Caucus"—now the traditional vehicle to the White House. Could Crawford serve, and did Adams wonder about it? Three days later, on Saturday, November 13, Monroe held another meeting concerning the upcoming annual message, and Crawford again attended. This time Adams asked Crawford, perhaps to test him, "how the revenue turned out." Without hesitation the Georgian replied: ". . . very good—between seventeen and eighteen millions of imposts, and about one million two hundred thousand dollars for lands. Four millions of seven per cents [in government bonds] have been purchased, and there are seven millions in the Treasury."[8] Crawford may have come prepared for a memory-challenging question, but how reassuring his reply was remains questionable. In December, shortly after he had submitted his report to Congress, Monroe confided to Adams his worries about Crawford's health and his "anxiety" that the secretary of treasury's report to Congress, not yet filed, "might contain views of fiscal concerns different from" his own.[9] Such a development, of course, would deeply embarrass the president. Monroe, in other words, entertained doubts about Crawford's competence. Nonetheless, he maintained scrupulous silence concerning the contest over the succession. In any event, at one last meeting on November 30, Monroe read a draft of the message to the cabinet, received final comments from his department heads, and prepared it for submission. The Senate and the House of Representatives received it on December 7.[10]

The state of the union could not have been better. "The view which I . . . present to you of our affairs, foreign and domestic, realizes the most sanguine anticipations which have been entertained of the public prosperity." There was only good news—new states had joined the union, the population had grown, and the nation was at peace. Moreover, all elements of the economy were humming: "Our agriculture, commerce, manufactures, and navigation flourish." But prosperity meant more than improvement in the quality of American life; it meant an overflowing national treasury. "Our revenue . . . ," the president reported, "continues to be adequate to all the purposes of the Government."[11] This observation, however, understated the matter. In fact, so voluminous were federal revenues that the current $79,000,000 in national debt was shrinking, and shrinking rapidly. Then, in a matter-of-fact way, came a stunning and unprecedented announcement. Because of the healthy condition of the nation's treasury, "a well-founded hope may be entertained that, should no unexpected event occur, the whole of the public debt may be discharged in the course of ten years. . . ." This was no estimation, approximation, or educated guess. Monroe meant ten years. "The last portion of the public debt will be redeemable on the 1st of January 1835. . . ." After that date, the nation would be liberated from interest and principal payments to the public creditors, and sizable funds would become available for other purposes. Monroe spelled out this obvious consequence of national debt freedom. The government would be "at liberty . . . to apply such portions of the revenue as may not be necessary for current expenses to such other objects as may be most conducive to the public security and welfare."[12]

Monroe reminded Congress that the sums would be "very considerable," because other savings were in the offing besides those related to the debt. Since the War of 1812, "a large amount of the public revenue has been applied to the construction of the public buildings" in the federal city—to fortifications, to naval building, to purchasing

Indian lands, to acquiring Florida, and to funding pensions for Revolutionary War veterans and "invalids" from the more recent conflict with Great Britain. Yet, despite the magnitude of these costs, most of them "will annually be diminished and cease at no distant period. . . ." In other words, construction projects would be completed, pensioners would die, and funds dedicated to those programs would become available for other purposes. Anticipated surpluses would grow larger and larger, and future Congresses would have to determine how to apply the swollen revenues to "the public security and welfare." Nevertheless, Monroe urged aggressive debt reduction to accelerate the arrival of national debt freedom. He advised Congress "to seize every opportunity . . . to reduce the rate of interest on every part" of the outstanding debt. "The high state of the public credit and the great abundance of money are at this time very favorable" for refinancing, which would make an even better situation out of an already very good one. Monroe fully understood how positive this news was: "It must be very gratifying to our fellow-citizens to witness this flourishing state of the public finances when it is recollected that no burthen whatever has been imposed upon them."[13] This financial miracle—imminent elimination of the national debt—had been accomplished without any new taxes. Monroe was leaving office with the government's accounts in better than superb condition. At the end of December, Treasury Secretary Crawford filed his department's report. It confirmed Monroe's prediction but assigned debt elimination to the end and not the beginning of 1835.[14] Apparently the twelve-month differential raised no question or controversy. It did, of course, reinforce Monroe's private concerns about Crawford's competence.

⁂

Extinction of the national debt in a decade and subsequent surpluses promised a beneficent future. The press, not surprisingly, welcomed this news. New York's *Albany Argus,* for example, observed that the message was "a plain and ample detail of our boundless prosperity" and that a "prosperous" treasury was paying down the national debt.[15] Yet Monroe's declaration regarding the debt did not dominate public conversation, because this was an extraordinary moment in the nation's history: Attention remained riveted on the upcoming election in the House of Representatives.

On Thursday, December 16, at least some of the tension broke. The much-awaited news from Louisiana finally arrived at the capital: That state had split its vote between Jackson and Adams.[16] The meaning, of course, was clear. Crawford remained in the running; Clay was out. For the Kentuckian, the news could not have been more disappointing. His ambition, if not his mission in life, was to achieve the presidency.[17]

Clay's goal was no mere byproduct of an inflated ego. He was easily among the most qualified men in the country to undertake the responsibilities of chief executive. Now forty-seven years old, he had enjoyed a distinguished career at the state and national levels, having served in the Kentucky legislature, the United States Senate, and the House of Representatives, where currently he sat as Speaker. During the crisis preceding the 1812 war against England, Clay had emerged as one of Congress's leading "War Hawks," insisting on the defense of American neutral rights. In 1814 he joined the American delegation at Ghent and helped negotiate the treaty of peace. Six years later he crafted the compromise that resolved the Missouri controversy, a crisis over slavery which threatened to unravel the union.

Clay's stature on the American political stage transcended his legislative and diplomatic experiences. He was one of very few to hold and promote a true vision of the American future. A staunch unionist, he advocated binding the various sections of the country more and more tightly together. To accomplish this, he espoused a program he called "the American System" by which the economic interests of the North, the South, and the West would become so intertwined that countervailing disunionist pressures were sure to fail. The core of "the American System" consisted of high tariffs to protect developing American industry from foreign competition; federally financed infrastructure projects—"internal improvements," as highways and canals were then called—to foster a national market; and a healthy central, national bank to assure stability to American currency and finance. Accordingly, Clay supported the tariffs of 1816 and 1824, the chartering of the Second Bank of the United States in 1816, and various improvement projects like the Cumberland Road. Clay wanted nothing more than to lead the nation into a prosperous future based on greater industry, commerce, and urbanization.[18]

In the House of Representatives, Clay was extraordinarily popular, even among those who did not share his vision. He was unpretentious and accessible; intelligent and more than just competent in parliamentary procedure; friendly and gregarious. He was, in short, enjoyable company, and friends and colleagues relished the late night drinks and card games in which Clay indulged at the end of the workday. While some found fault with his Washington lifestyle, others found it proof of his down-to-earth humanity. Foreigners visiting the nation's capital invariably found him charming.[19] If anyone had a chance at moving from third to first place in the House election, it was Henry Clay, and he, of course, knew it. The House was his arena. But Clay, always the optimist, was also a realist, and, although the news from Louisiana was disappointing, it did not immobilize him. If the House of Representatives could not make him president, he could, perhaps, still find an important role to play.

Clay had anticipated the scenario that had developed and knew to whom he would throw his support. Crawford, he believed, was simply incapable of serving as president. For Clay, only Jackson and Adams were serious contenders. But Clay objected to Jackson on the ground that the latter had nothing other than an outstanding war record to qualify him for the presidency, and he was frank about this concern. "I can not," he wrote, "consistently with my own principles, support a military man." This judgment, of course, left only one option. "I have long since decided in favor of Mr. Adams, in case the contest should be between him and General Jackson."[20] Clay was comfortable with this decision. He had known the secretary of state for years and respected his intelligence, honesty, and long history of service to the republic. Equally as important, Adams was a nationalist who favored internal improvements at federal expense, the Bank of the United States, and protectionism. In short, Adams was no enemy of the American System. For this reason, elevating Adams to the presidential chair made clear sense, and there was always the chance that Clay might advance his own career in the process.

Clay acted quickly. On Friday, December 17, the day after the news from Louisiana reached Washington, he made the opening move in the endgame that would decide the presidency. Robert P. Letcher, a Kentucky representative and Clay's close friend, visited Adams at the State Department. The two had a long conversation. "The drift of all Letcher's discourse," Adams recorded shortly afterward, "was . . . that Clay would willingly support me if he could thereby serve himself, and the substance of his meaning was, that if Clay's friends could know that he would have a prominent share in the Administration, that might induce them to vote for me, even in face of instructions" to the contrary from state legislatures. This remarkable suggestion came with a disclaimer: "But Letcher," noted Adams, "did not profess to have any authority from Clay for what he said, and he made no definite propositions."[21] Yet the overture was encouraging. Two nights later Adams, who frowned on vote-solicitation as unbecoming a true republican, was nevertheless out making the rounds of boarding houses and hotels where congressional messmates lodged, introducing himself and exchanging good wishes.[22]

The political game grew more intense as the capital prepared for Christmas. On December 23, Congressman Letcher met Adams again. He explained to the secretary of state that in order to secure the presidency Adams would have to win on the first ballot and that, to do so, he needed to carry Kentucky and some other western states. Adams responded that he had "no expectation" of winning Kentucky. Yet Letcher "seemed anxious to convince" him that he "might receive" the vote of the Kentucky delegation. This time Letcher did not mention anything about a post in the administration for Clay, but he probably did not have to. Adams knew the conversation was as delicate as it was serious. "I consider Letcher as moving for Mr. Clay," he confided to his diary.[23] Letcher moved again, and quickly. He returned to Adams on the 29th, assuring him "with the utmost confidence" that Kentucky would vote for him even though the state legislature was likely, formally or informally, to instruct the congressional delegation to vote for Jackson.[24]

New Year's Day brought these sensitive discussions to a head. Official Washington turned out in large numbers for the traditional party at the White House. The president's "drawing room" was "much crowded" with celebrants. Adams was there. So was Robert Letcher. Amidst the hoopla, the Kentuckian drew the secretary of state aside and quietly asked to meet him at the State Department after the party. Adams agreed. Later in the afternoon the secretary went to his office, and shortly afterward Letcher arrived. The congressman had several things to say, too sensitive to share at the crowded White House celebration. First, Kentucky's state legislators had recommended "in their private capacities" but not by enactment that their congressional delegation vote for Jackson. Nevertheless, Letcher said that Adams "might rely upon it" that the recommendation "would have no effect." Letcher seemed certain. "The vote of Kentucky in the House," he told Adams, "was fixed and unalterable" and that vote was for Adams. He suggested that Adams and Clay meet, both to smooth over some differences and to let the entire Kentucky delegation see unity between the two. Adams did not hesitate. "I told him I would very readily, and whenever it might suit the convenience of Mr. Clay."[25]

That same night a dinner honoring the Marquis de Lafayette, the French general who had helped win American independence and who was on a long and well publicized visit to the United States, was held at Williamson's hotel. Many of those who had attended the White House party that afternoon turned out for this event too. Adams, of course, was there, and so too was Henry Clay. Letcher's mediation was about to bear fruit. Clay spoke very briefly to Adams, saying that he wanted to have a "confidential conversation" with him "upon public affairs." Adams replied that he would "be happy to have it" whenever it might suit Clay. After the dinner at Williamson's, Adams returned home and recorded his emotions in his diary: "At the beginning of this year there is in my prospects and anticipations a solemnity and moment never before experienced, and to which unaided nature is inadequate."[26]

At 6:00 p.m., Sunday, January 9, Henry Clay arrived at the home of the secretary of state. Probably over dinner and a bottle of wine or two, Adams and his guest "spent the evening . . . in a long conversation explanatory of the past and prospective of the future." Their review of old times—former agreements and disagreements, disappointments and achievements—led ultimately to a discussion of the current crisis. Clay complained how the friends of other candidates were badgering him for support, specifically mentioning one of Crawford's partisans who had approached him "in a manner so gross that it had disgusted him." Even some of Adams's friends, disclaiming any authority from the secretary, had lobbied him. Clay explained that despite the pressures from all sides, since the news from Louisiana had arrived, he had espoused a neutral posture and had encouraged his friends to do the same, in order to allow "a decent time for his own funeral solemnities as a candidate." Neutrality, he added, would promote the freedom of the House of Representatives "to take that course which might be most conducive to the public interest."[27] In view of his several conversations with Letcher, Adams may have rolled his eyes at these latter remarks, but Clay finally came to the point. "The time had now come" for him to be frank, "and [he] had for that purpose asked this confidential interview." According to Adams, Clay "wished me, as far as I might think proper, to satisfy him with regard to some principles of great public importance," adding that this request entailed no "personal considerations for himself."[28] In other words, Clay sought no *quid pro quo* for his support, but surely Adams remembered that Letcher had hinted at such on December 17. Clay, knowing Adams as well as he did, could not straightforwardly solicit an agreement that would trouble the secretary's sense of propriety and his devotion to republican ethics. How Adams replied remains unknown. Presumably he described his position on matters like the tariff, internal improvements, the new independent states in Latin America, and maybe even the anticipated extinction of the national debt and what it would mean. Whatever Adams said, it reassured the Speaker. "In the question to come before the House between General Jackson, Mr. Crawford, and myself," Adams recorded, Clay "had no hesitation in saying that his preference would be for me."[29]

Adams and Clay reached an understanding on January 9, and they likely shook hands on it before the Speaker went home. But did the understanding include a tacit agreement that Clay would support Adams in exchange for, in Letcher's words, "a prominent share in the Administration?"

The wider Washington community knew nothing of the January 9 Clay-Adams meeting, or so Clay and Adams thought. But the nation's capital has always been a sieve, and before the end of the month a Pennsylvania representative, George Kremer, publicly charged that the secretary and the Speaker had cut a deal—that Clay was throwing his support in the House to Adams in exchange for the secretaryship of state. In effect, Kremer accused both men of bargaining corruptly for the highest trusts the nation had to offer. For Clay the allegation was malicious, outrageous, and dangerous to his career. "A crisis appeared to me to have arisen in my public life," he wrote.[30] He offered a thinly veiled threat to challenge Kremer to a duel and demanded that the House investigate the accusation in order that his "character and conduct may be vindicated."[31] Adams too felt the political heat. When the Kremer story broke, he remarked: "The intenseness of interest in . . . the presidential election increases as the day approaches. . . . The intriguing for votes is excessive, and the means adopted to obtain them desperate."[32] Wednesday, February 9, was Election Day, or, perhaps more correctly, Judgment Day. All attention, it seemed, was focused on it. Henry Clay moaned: "As we have to make a president this session, we shall do but little else."[33]

❧

The House Speaker, of course, overstated the matter. Congress had a great deal of work to do and was doing it. It appropriated funds for the operation of the legislative and executive branches of the government, to support the army and the navy, and for other purposes—and it enacted laws to further organize Michigan Territory, establish new post roads, reimburse the travel expenses of those delivering the official electoral votes to Washington, and to address a host of other matters of national concern, including the awarding of $200,000 and sizable real estate to General Lafayette as an expression of American gratitude to him.[34]

Congress's business included the national debt. When the House finally received Crawford's Report on the State of the Finances, it promptly referred it to the Ways and Means Committee.[35] On January 12, 1825, that committee, after studying the document, reported to the whole House that $19,000,000 of six-percent bonds, contracted in 1813, were redeemable on January 1, 1826. However, a problem existed: Only $7,000,000 from revenues would be available at that time. Accordingly, to assure timely redemption, the committee offered a bill to borrow the other $12,000,000 at 4.5 percent on bonds redeemable in 1829 and 1830, years when no other debt maturities were scheduled. In effect, the proposed bill kept debt elimination on schedule and, at the same time, reduced debt service.[36] The measure passed both chambers and was signed into law on March 3, President Monroe's last full day in office.[37] In this instance, Congress dealt straightforwardly with the debt question.

The status of the national debt, however, affected other congressional business, but less directly. Representative Andrew Stewart of Pennsylvania raised an issue on December 28, 1824, which serves as an example. He reminded colleagues that during the preceding session he had recommended "the creation of a permanent fund for the purpose of internal improvements."[38] Due to the "press of other important business," however, his proposal "was not then disposed of." Now he wanted to revive it, and with reason. "When we advert," he said, "to the flourishing condition of our national finances, as exhibited by the president, in his late message" and "[w]hen we look to the rapid increase of our wealth and resources . . . ," then "it must be admitted . . . that the period had arrived when it would be proper to appropriate, at least, a part of the ample revenues of the country to its *internal improvement.*" From any point of view—"commercial, political, or military"—a system of roads and canals made sense, he argued. He even invoked the authority of George Washington, quoting the first president on the wisdom of infrastructure development. He then offered a resolution to instruct the Committee on Roads and Canals to prepare a bill "pledging the proceeds of the sales of the Public Lands and the dividends of the United States' Bank Stock" to a "permanent fund" for internal improvements. Congress would appropriate the money to the states according to the "ratio" of their House representation and would designate development projects in which the states were to invest. Lastly, unappropriated money would be invested "in United States' or other productive Stocks" to enhance the fund's growth.[39]

More than five weeks passed, and what came out of the Committee on Roads and Canals bore little resemblance to Stewart's proposal, and for good reasons. First, the Pennsylvania representative's recommendation seemed to ignore the fact that many congressmen questioned whether the federal government had the constitutional authority to appropriate money for internal improvement projects that were not clearly national in scope. Second, ever since 1790 the revenue raised from the sale of public lands had been assigned by law to national debt reduction.[40] Congress was hardly going to repeal that legislation in order to spend the money on roads and canals. Representative Stewart should have known that. The committee, accordingly, reported a very different bill, a complicated measure which sought to avoid the constitutional question and which left in place the assignment of land sale revenues to debt reduction. At bottom, the committee proposed borrowing $10,000,000 "on the best terms" possible in order to buy stock in companies involved in internal improvement projects.[41]

The bill was surely controversial, and the committee knew it. The proposed ten-million-dollar loan added new debt to the old. Yet the committee reminded House members what President Monroe had pointed out in his message—that as fortifications were completed, as

Revolutionary War veterans died, and as the population grew, the treasury's resources would increase. In other words, affordability was not an issue. "As to means, on questions of improvements, ability is the only requisite, if the works, when they are completed, will be worth what they cost; the want of money in the Treasury should never form an objection to their execution."[42]

The assertion was provocative—"the want of money in the Treasury should never form an objection" to internal improvement projects. The committee knew it was wading into turbulent waters and stated very frankly that it would not press for passage of the bill during the current session. Its present purpose, it maintained, was simply "to lay the subject generally before the public" and await the next Congress (and, of course, a new president) to debate and vote on the measure.[43]

This was probably wise. While Congress legislated quickly to borrow $12,000,000 to keep debt elimination on schedule and at less cost, it was not going to authorize a loan of $10,000,000 for internal improvements. Refinancing and borrowing were different things. The latter contradicted the policy of debt extinction. This reality represented the financial dimension, as opposed to the constitutional issue, standing in the way of a federal internal improvements program. It was obvious. As matters stood in 1825, an internal improvements policy was going to have to wait for the steady stream of fiscal surpluses Monroe had predicted or for a presidential administration supportive of and able to get such a program through Congress. Selection of the next chief executive was, of course, at hand.

A heavy snowstorm blew into Washington on Wednesday, February 9, 1825, presidential election day in the House of Representatives.[44] Some welcomed the bad weather. Rumor had it that whites of modest incomes in one of the city's wards had prepared an effigy of Adams if he won and that the capital's black community, overwhelmingly sympathetic to the secretary of state, was ill-disposed to tolerate such a demonstration. Racial violence loomed, but as it turned out, nothing happened. Neither white nor black partisans braved the storm. Order prevailed. Indeed, no military presence was "visible," and "even the civil magistrates had nothing to do."[45] Drama remained confined to the Hall of the House of Representatives.

The House was well prepared to play its role. On January 13, Representative John C. Wright of Ohio had proposed creating a special committee to prepare "rules" for election procedures "if," as everyone knew would be the case, "on counting" the electoral votes "in the manner prescribed in the Constitution . . . it shall appear that no person has received a majority."[46]

Five days later, the House created a committee of seven for that purpose, with Wright as chair.[47] On January 26, the select committee reported its proposals—substantially the rules that governed the 1801 election between Jefferson and Burr—to the whole House, and on February 2 debate on them began.[48] At the end of the workday on Monday, February 7, after wide-ranging discussion, the House reached agreement and was ready for the event two days later.[49]

Behind the scenes, rumors of all kinds floated, and politics simmered. The New York delegation, reputedly divided evenly between Crawford and Adams, became the focus of attention. Friends of Clay even approached Martin Van Buren, a staunch Crawford man, in an attempt to push New York into the Adams camp. This effort had no hope of success. Van Buren was not only committed to Crawford but had his own plan for the New York delegation. His head-counting revealed that as long as New York remained tied, no candidate would secure the necessary thirteen state votes to win. Accordingly, he wanted the New York tie to persist through several ballots in the hope that Adams's support in other states would melt away, giving his candidate a shot at winning. The Crawford men in the New York delegation had, meanwhile, all promised Van Buren that they would remain firm for the Georgian.[50]

On the morning of Election Day, however, Stephen Van Rennselaer, a New York representative who hated Adams and was sworn to Crawford, began to waffle. He told Van Buren that he was thinking of voting for Jackson. The former dissuaded him, and Van Rennselaer, reaffirming his support for Crawford, then walked in the snow to the capitol. There Speaker Clay quickly ushered him into his office, where Massachusetts representative Daniel Webster was waiting. The Kentuckian and the New Englander then forcefully pressured Van Rennselaer to vote for Adams on the ground that any other winner would cause the "disorganization" of the government and threaten property rights. Van Rennselaer, they said, owner of a large and original Dutch patroonship, stood to lose everything unless Adams was elected. According to one observer, Van Rennselaer looked "staggered" when he finally emerged from Clay's office.[51] Betrayal was in the works.

The House played to a gallery, noted one spectator, "crowded nearly to suffocation . . . every one was there who could gain admission by art or influence."[52] Foreign ministers and other dignitaries, including the sojourning Marquis de Lafayette, attended.[53] Even Fanny Wright, the radical social reformer, was present.[54] On the chamber floor itself all representatives were in their places except Robert S. Garnett of Virginia, "who was known to be indisposed at his lodgings" in the city.[55]

The proceedings began precisely at noon. The Senate's sergeant-at-arms, followed by John Gaillard of South Carolina, president *pro tem* of the Senate, led members of the upper chamber onto the House floor. Henry Clay invited Gaillard to sit with him at the Speaker's table. The other senators took assigned seats facing Clay and Gaillard. Behind them sat the representatives in their customary places. Gaillard began the ritual, standing and announcing that "the certificates, forwarded by the Electors from each State, would" now "be delivered to the Tellers"–Senator Littleton Tazewell of Virginia, and Representatives John W. Taylor of New York and Philip Barbour of Virginia—who had been appointed to report and affirm the votes. Each teller took a seat at the House Clerk's table, and the electoral tally began.[56]

Senator Gaillard opened two packages from New Hampshire, one sent by special messenger and the other by ordinary mail. Senator

Tazewell read the result from one packet and, for verification of the vote, Representatives Taylor and Barbour from the other. New Hampshire's vote was then announced: all eight of its votes to John Quincy Adams for president and seven votes for John C. Calhoun and one vote for Andrew Jackson for vice president. In this fashion, the results from all twenty-four states were reported. At the conclusion, the tellers approached the Speaker's table, reported the results, and handed the tally to Senator Gaillard, who then announced officially what everyone already knew: Of 261 votes Andrew Jackson had ninety-nine, John Quincy Adams eighty-four, William H. Crawford forty-one, and Henry Clay thirty-seven. Gaillard then declared that since "no person had received a majority of the votes given for president" and that since Jackson, Adams, and Crawford were the three with "the highest number of votes," they constituted the list from which the House would select the next president. Gaillard also announced that John C. Calhoun of South Carolina, with 182 votes had been "duly elected Vice President of the United States." Senators, having discharged their constitutional obligation, then "retired" from the House chamber.[57] So too did foreign dignitaries and official guests like Lafayette, who considered it inappropriate to remain for the House proceeding.[58]

All this, of course, had been a constitutional formality, and when the senators had departed, the House got down to the real business of the day. Speaker Clay took charge. The rules adopted on February 7 were now implemented. The sergeant-at-arms distributed ballot boxes to each state delegation. Clay then "directed that the balloting should proceed."[59] Representatives deposited their ballots in their respective state boxes and then counted the votes. How each delegation divided determined that state's vote. The sergeant-at-arms then returned to each delegation with two additional boxes. Each state recorded its vote on two ballots and deposited them separately in the two boxes.[60] Next, each delegation selected a teller, all twenty-four of whom gathered in two groups of twelve around separate tables. One at each table was chosen to announce the results from the box on that table. One table selected Daniel Webster, the other John Randolph of

Virginia. The votes from each table, of course, had to match. The counting began. Webster's table finished first. "Mr. Speaker," the Massachusetts representative declared, "The Tellers of the votes at this table have proceeded to count the ballots contained in the box set before them. The result they find to be, that there are—For John Quincy Adams . . . 13 votes; For Andrew Jackson . . . 7 votes; For William H. Crawford . . . 4 votes."[61] Randolph thereupon reported the same numbers from his table. Clay, in a "sweet, clear, voice," then announced that "John Quincy Adams, having a majority of the votes of these United States, was duly elected President."[62]

An "intense silence" filled the chamber "for a moment," but the "stillness" quickly yielded to "a low hum of whispers" and then to some "feeble clapping," followed by "hissing." The House suspended its proceeding, and Clay ordered the sergeant-at-arms to clear the gallery.[63] Once the audience left, the representatives quickly appointed an *ad hoc* committee of three—Daniel Webster, Joseph Vance of Ohio, and William S. Archer of Virginia—to inform President Monroe and the President-elect of the House's selection.[64] All was not well, however. Many lawmakers shared the disappointment, if not the outrage, of the public. New York had voted for Adams; Van Rennselaer had, indeed, defected.[65] John Randolph reportedly quipped that "it was impossible to win the game . . . the cards were stacked."[66]

Adams received the news with an uncharacteristic display of emotion. He broke into a cold sweat and began to tremble. He became "so agitated that he could scarcely stand or speak." He finally told the *ad hoc* committee that he would follow Jefferson's "precedent" and reply in writing to the notification.[67] When the committee of three left, he wrote to his father, "asking for his blessing and prayers on the event of this day, the most important day of my life."[68]

A celebration at the White House that night drew a large gathering. Anyone who was anyone was there: Lafayette, General Jackson, Henry Clay, cabinet members, various congressmen and senators, and, of course, President-elect Adams and his wife Louisa. Various lowlifes who crashed the party also mingled among the crowd. A thief picked General Winfield Scott's pocket and made off with $800.00. The mood, however, remained subdued. Adams's friends made "no open" display of "exultation" out of respect for the defeated candidates, and the losers comported themselves with dignity. Jackson congratulated Adams and shook his hand. But beneath the appearances festered anguish and outrage. One party-goer reported what was being whispered about Adams: There "is our *Clay President* . . . who will be moulded at that man's will and pleasure as easily as clay in a potter's hands."[69] Unaware of the gossip buzzing around them, Mr. and Mrs. Adams left the gala relatively early, arriving home shortly before midnight. To the President-elect's delight, "a band of musicians came and serenaded me at my house."[70]

❧

"Gentlemen," Adams wrote to the committee of three the next day, "I pray you to make acceptable to the House, the assurance of my profound gratitude for their confidence. . . ."[71] For Adams, the year 1825 represented triumph. His elevation to the nation's highest office would make his aged father proud. The son had achieved what the elder Adams had achieved. He had fulfilled the expectations of the preceding generation. Moreover, he would assume the presidency under unprecedented financial conditions. Debt extinction was in sight. Indeed, the Saturday before the House vote Adams had visited the capitol to hear the annual report of the Sinking Fund Commission, and afterward he gushed that the "finances of the country are in a very flourishing condition."[72] No president had ever stepped into office under such promising circumstances.

Yet Adams worried that where there was good news there was bound to be bad news too. Perhaps he entertained this pessimism simply because he was an Adams, a bearer of the Calvinist tradition which rejected the notion that God dispensed blessings and good fortune without balancing them with trials and tribulations. Before the election, Adams confided his concerns to his diary more than once. On January 27, for example, Senator Rufus King of New York had told the secretary of state that his prospects in the upcoming House election looked good. Adams wrote privately, "[King's remarks] are flattering for the immediate issue, but the fearful condition of them is, that success would open to a far severer trial than defeat."[73] Or, again, just eight days before the balloting, he wrote: "To me the alternatives are both distressing in prospect, and the most formidable is that of success. All the danger is on the pinnacle. The humiliation of failure will be so much more than compensated by the safety in which it will leave me, that I ought to regard it as a consummation devoutly to be wished, and hope to find consolation in it."[74] The President-elect seemed to sense that a great test lay ahead of him, but did he know that a large part of it would be of his own making?

On Friday, February 11, Henry Clay sent Adams a brief note. "I should be glad to have the opportunity of an early interview with you, this evening, if you are not engaged, or on sunday evening, at such hour as may be most convenient."[75] The President-elect replied promptly, agreeing to meet Clay that very night at 6:30.[76] Clay arrived at Adams's house on time, and the two conversed for "about an hour." Adams then "offered" Clay "the nomination to the Department of State."[77] Clay asked for time to consider the proposal and to consult with friends. Adams advised him "to take his own time."[78] The Speaker of the House did just that, commiserating over the next several days with political associates whose judgment he valued. There were arguments both for and against, but, in the end, Clay wrote, "as their advice to me is to accept, I have resolved accordingly . . . ."[79] On Thursday, February 17, Clay met Adams at 9:00 p.m. and agreed to become secretary of state.[80] Here was a political bombshell of enormous explosiveness, and the new president had not even been sworn in yet.

❧

Adams went sleepless the night before Inauguration Day, March 4, 1825. In fact, he had been unable to sleep the night before either. Anxiety gripped him as he prepared to assume the responsibilities of the presidency. He began the day, as he ordinarily did, with a prayer, making "supplication to Heaven . . . for my country . . . for myself . . . that the last results . . . may be auspicious and blessed."[81] Late in the morning, companies of militia arrived to escort his carriage to the capitol. Riding with him were Samuel Southard, the new secretary of the navy, and William Wirt, the attorney general. In a carriage behind rode James Monroe, now in the very final moments of his presidency. A crowd of ordinary citizens looked on as the procession advanced eastward along Pennsylvania Avenue.[82]

On arriving at the capitol, the President-elect and his party and the retiring chief executive went directly to the Senate Chamber where John C. Calhoun, having already been sworn in as vice president, was presiding, and where the justices of the Supreme Court had assembled. All then proceeded to the other wing of the building and took their designated places in the House chamber. *The National Intelligencer* reported that the "galleries, though filled to overflowing, were remarkable for the stillness and decorum which . . . prevailed."[83] Everyone knew the occasion was solemn, and, when they were finally seated, John Quincy Adams stepped to the podium to deliver his inaugural address.[84]

Adams intended to be conciliatory and reassuring. First and foremost, he explained, as president he would be guided by the Constitution. That "precious inheritance" from the preceding generation had succeeded beyond anyone's expectation: "it has . . . secured the freedom and happiness" of the American people. Progress under the Constitution had been astonishing: a tripling of the population; extension of the western boundary to the Pacific; the creation of new states; peace and amity with the world's powers; land clearance and increase in agricultural production; and expanding commerce.[85]

This "unexaggerated picture of our condition," Adams admitted, tended to conceal "its shades." The road to success had been rocky, but that was "the condition of men upon earth." "From evil—physical, moral, and political—it is not our claim to be exempt." Disagreements over political theory, foreign policy, and sectional interest had on several occasions "threaten[ed] the dissolution of the

Union, and . . . the overthrow of all the enjoyments of our present lot and all our earthly hopes of the future." Yet these "dissensions" had not broken the union. That fact provided "gratification and . . . encouragement" to him and to all Americans. Indeed, prospects for the future of the American republic seemed extraordinarily promising. Discord and "party strife" appeared to have been "uprooted" following the War of 1812. "From that time no difference of principle, connected either with the theory of government or with our intercourse with foreign nations, has existed . . . to sustain a . . . combination of parties." Adams seemed to be saying, without using the phrase itself, that the country had been enjoying an "era of good feelings" for the last decade and that the people, "without a dissenting voice," were solidly unified around "our political creed" of popular sovereignty, frequent elections, economy in government, light taxes, limited state and federal authority, and all other attributes of American republicanism. Unity, in other words, had supplanted division.[86]

For this happy state of affairs, Adams acknowledged the policies and accomplishments of his predecessor. President Monroe had assured peace by keeping the nation strong; had honored "the principles of freedom and equal rights wherever they were proclaimed"; had "discharge[d]" the national debt "with all possible promptitude"; had promoted the welfare of the nation and each of its distinctive sections; and had moved forward on "the great system of internal improvements within the limits" of the Constitution. Monroe had been successful, and Adams declared that Congress and the American people should expect him to follow the same policies pursued by the retiring president. Fulfilling all that Monroe had begun, Adams said, "will embrace the whole sphere of my obligations." Of all Monroe's initiatives, however, Adams emphasized internal improvements: road construction, canal development, harbor clearance—all at federal expense. He expressed the hope that those who questioned the constitutionality of such federal undertakings would ultimately recognize Congress's authority to fund infrastructure projects.[87] Interestingly, he did not at the same time mention the anticipated elimination of the national debt in 1835. If attentive listeners noticed the omission, none, it appears, commented on it. Rather, they probably presumed that Adams's praise of debt reduction under Monroe implied adherence to the latter's schedule for debt freedom. If so, they would shortly be disabused of such confidence.

At the conclusion of his remarks, Adams made brief reference to a matter on the minds of many. "Fellow-citizens," he said, "you are acquainted with the peculiar circumstances of the recent election" and [you] have heard the exposition of the principles which will direct me in the fulfillment of the high and solemn trust imposed upon me in this situation. Less possessed of your confidence in advance than any of my predecessors, I am deeply conscious of the prospect that I shall stand more and oftener in need of your indulgence." He asked for Congress's support, and for God's.[88] Chief Justice John Marshall then administered the oath of office, and the formal inaugural event ended.[89]

Upon leaving the building, the new president reviewed the militia companies that were on hand, and the same procession that had taken him to the capitol earlier reassembled and drove him home. There a large throng waited to greet and congratulate him, and for almost two hours he mingled with his well-wishing guests. At about mid-afternoon, he went to the White House to join numerous other visitors who had gathered there to bid ex-President Monroe farewell. Late in the afternoon, he returned home for dinner and afterward attended an inaugural celebration at Carusi's, one of Washington's finer hotels and banquet centers. After supper was served, he went home, probably anticipating a good night's sleep. "I closed the day," he wrote, "as it had begun, with thanksgiving to God for all His mercies and favors past, and with prayers for the continuance of them to my country, and to myself and mine."[90]

Adams was going to need all God's mercies and favors. Close observers of American politics might have noted that neither the crisis nor the promise that confronted Congress when it convened in

December had been satisfactorily addressed. The crisis over the presidential election, for example, had been transformed but not resolved. The House of Representatives had selected the president as the Constitution required, but its choice was the runner-up in both the electoral and popular votes. Adams was a minority president. But why? Kentucky's vote in the House for Adams, the circumstance resulting in New York's vote for him, followed by Clay's appointment to the State Department, meant to many that George Kremer had been right when he accused both of having cut a deal—a "corrupt bargain"—by which a majority of Americans (not to mention General Jackson himself) were cheated out of the presidency. Henry Clay aspired to the White House, and for the preceding quarter-century the State Department had served as the door to the executive mansion.[91] Clay, it seemed, made Adams president, and in exchange Adams made Clay the heir-apparent. The outcome of the presidential contest therefore raised questions about the legitimacy of the Adams administration. The presidential campaign of 1828 began before John Quincy Adams had time to settle into the White House. The unity that had characterized the Monroe years and which the new president hoped would endure was already a thing of the past, if it had ever truly existed in the first place. In any event, the crisis over the presidential succession had shifted from the question "who would become president?" to "who should have become president?"

In December 1824, of course, there had been promising news—that, barring an emergency, the national debt would be extinguished within a decade. Yet those who heard or read the new president's inaugural address may have wondered whether this promise would be kept. Although Adams praised debt reduction under Monroe and swore to adhere to his predecessor's policies, the fact remained that Adams made no reference to the 1835 extinction of the debt, much less commit himself to that schedule. Rather, he went out of his way to emphasize internal improvements at federal expense. Was the new administration going to abandon fiscal retrenchment and pursue a costly development program? And, if so, would such a program postpone debt freedom and generate new debt?

The crisis over the presidential election and the promise of a debt-free government conjoined with Clay's appointment as secretary of state. Standard republican wisdom held that public debt led to the extension of executive power through corruption, and a principal weapon against the system of checks and balances was the power of patronage. The "corrupt bargain" of 1825, it seemed, constituted a demonstration of executive patronage deployed for the sake of power, and if the new president was not committed to debt freedom, or was perceived not to be, then he would compound the suspicion that constitutional government was in danger.

TWO

THE CRISIS AND PROMISE OF 1824–1825 IN HISTORICAL CONTEXT

John Quincy Adams assumed the presidency with "favors and mercies" enjoyed by few other White House occupants before or since. His entire life had seemed a training experience for the office of chief executive. Born in 1767, he was the oldest son of one of the great American revolutionaries and the second president of the United States. This lineage gave him much more than a recognizable name: It also introduced him at an early age to public service and its importance. When he was only eleven years old, he accompanied his father on diplomatic assignments to Europe. There he attended schools in France and Holland, worked at the American mission in St. Petersburg, and became his father's secretary when the latter represented the United States in London during the 1780s. Upon return to Massachusetts he attended Harvard, subsequently studied the law, and still later was appointed American minister to the Netherlands by George Washington and then to Prussia by his own father.

Early the next century Adams changed his career from international diplomacy to domestic politics. After a brief stint in the Massachusetts state legislature, he was elected to the United States Senate in 1803. He did not, however, serve a full term. He resigned his seat after supporting Jefferson's 1807 Embargo Act, a measure distinctly unpopular in New England. By then Adams had shed his Federalist Party affiliation and began identifying himself as a Jeffersonian Republican. He returned to the Foreign Service under President Madison, serving as American minister to Russia from 1809 to 1814. As a result of his long overseas experience, Adams became fluent in French, Dutch, Swedish, German, and Russian. In 1814 he led the American delegation at Ghent in Belgium, the team that secured the treaty with England, ending the War of 1812. His last foreign assignment was to the post his father had held some thirty years earlier—American minister to Great Britain. In 1817 President Monroe nominated him for secretary of state, a position which, by then, had become the stepping-stone to the White House. Adams's career at the State Department witnessed major diplomatic successes: agreements with Great Britain which defined and demilitarized the United States-Canadian border, a treaty with Spain selling Florida to the United States and extending American territorial claims to the Pacific, and assertion of the principles that later became known as the Monroe Doctrine.[1]

If life itself had guided Adams to the presidency, there was at least one other distinct "favor" he enjoyed as he embarked upon administering the government—the prospect of national debt freedom in a decade. No president before him had stood in the shade of such a financial umbrella. Anticipating debt freedom, of course, was not only a new experience for John Quincy Adams, but for the American people as well. For some, it suggested what the highest priority on the national agenda should be. In January 1825, for example, a month before anyone knew that the House would elevate Adams to the

White House, Representative George McDuffie of South Carolina, during a debate over internal improvements (a subject directly related to federal spending), observed: "It appeared very clear that, for at least ten years to come, all the surplus revenue of this country would be exhausted in paying the public debt—and, from the character and well known wishes of the nation . . . it must be the great object of the next administration to pay that debt."[2]

Indeed, the public debt constituted an issue of extraordinary importance because it went straight to the heart of the American Revolutionary experience and the values that had fostered it.

Adams's father's generation had declared independence in 1776 and waged war to achieve it for reasons directly related to liberty and public indebtedness. A long history connected the two. England's "Glorious Revolution" of 1688—the overthrow of King James II—had resulted in a constitutional arrangement that was uniquely protective of liberty. It established an equality of power among the social estates in English life—royalty, nobility, and commoners—and the institutions which represented them in government—monarchy, the House of Lords, and the House of Commons. Theoretically, after 1688, these three elements checked and balanced each other. Power was pitted against power, which was pitted against power, a three-way contest that rendered liberty, power's traditional victim, safe and secure for the first time in human history. This was a glorious achievement—hence the "Glorious Revolution."[3]

The events of 1688, however, also triggered a long series of wars between England and France and their respective allies. These conflicts were extraordinarily expensive, and ordinary tax revenues were inadequate to pay for them. In dealing with this problem, governments in England and elsewhere not only learned that they could borrow to cover the difference between revenue and expenditure but also that they could keep on borrowing as long as they made the interest payments that the debt contracts required. In short, the perpetual public debt was discovered (or invented) to solve the financial problems of the modern state in a hostile world.[4] For Great Britain, the Bank of England provided the needed credit.

But it seemed, to some at least, that the glories of the constitutional settlement and an ever-growing national debt were incompatible. Self-styled "Real Whigs" argued that the perpetuated debt allowed government ministries, especially Robert Walpole's administration (1721-1742), not only to purchase seats in the House of Commons but also to distribute places and pensions to members of both houses of Parliament, rendering them pliant to the will of the monarch. This "Robinocracy," because of available funds, successfully subverted the checks and balances of the glorious constitution, thereby threatening English liberty. The writers who exposed this corruption of the system—Benjamin Hoadly, John Trenchard, Viscount Bolingbroke, and others—were widely read in the colonies, and their critique of government and politics in eighteenth-century England became the interpretive lens through which Americans saw and understood the world around them.[5] Americans, as a consequence, held an ideological bias against public debt because it corrupted those who were entrusted to exercise power responsibly. It corrupted not by encouraging theft from the public till but by undermining proper constitutional arrangements. As the historian Lance Banning has written: "Constitutional degeneration was the technical definition of 'corruption,' a word which conveyed an image of progressive, organic decay."[6] For Americans, public indebtedness threatened liberty—and, as Walpole's career demonstrated, patronage was one of its principal weapons. By the late eighteenth century, public indebtedness had fallen into disrepute for many reasons. Adam Smith, the intellectual godfather of modern economics, denounced it in his classic, *The Wealth of Nations.*[7]

All these perceptions bore serious consequences. The Anglo-French wars for empire ended in British victory in 1763 but left the imperial government saddled with an enormous debt. As a result, the following year George Grenville's ministry launched a program to raise revenue in America. Besides the unprecedented and, from the colonial perspective, unconstitutional tax measures, the legislation from London over the next several years curtailed the right to trial by jury, violated the traditional rights of elected provincial assemblies, and committed a host of other outrages. By 1776 Americans became convinced that in England a conspiracy against American liberty existed, and that the plotters were bent on extending the evils of Robinocracy to American shores. This perception—this conviction—provided, as Bernard Bailyn has pointed out, the American rebellion its "logic."[8] Only national independence, it seemed, could save American liberty from the corrupt power-establishment in London.

Only war could secure independence from Great Britain. However, the Continental Congress, which had asserted American independence, had no power to tax. To wage war without a revenue stream, the Congress was left with two choices, and it took both. It could and did print fiat money, the notorious "continentals," which depreciated with each issue; and it could and did borrow in various ways from American citizens as well as, it turned out, from foreign powers. As a consequence, the United States was, as Robert E. Wright has written, "born in debt."[9]

Some irony exists here. The British national debt was the parent of all those evils against which Americans rebelled, yet, to resist those evils, Americans themselves were forced to contract debt. Unlike the English, however, the Americans could not service their debts by making timely interest payments. Under the Articles of Confederation, ratified in 1781, the government of the United States remained without the power to tax. The consequences were profound. American certificates of indebtedness depreciated sharply, and American government credit evaporated. Throughout the Confederation era the United States government was broke and therefore powerless. When rebellion erupted in Massachusetts in 1786, the government at Philadelphia was unable to intercede. The American experiment in republicanism seemed destined to fail. This danger resulted in the 1787 Philadelphia convention, which discarded the Articles of Confederation and proposed a new Constitution, giving the United States the power "to lay and collect taxes" and transferring the existing debt burden to the new regime. Ratification of the Constitution in 1788, with its own unique system of checks and balances, gave the American experiment another chance at success.[10] At the same time, the belief that public indebtedness constituted a source of corruption endured as a cardinal feature of the now-republicanized American worldview.

❦

The Washington administration addressed the financial problem promptly. Congress enacted a revenue tariff in 1789, providing the United States government with a steady income for the first time. Revenue, of course, was the *sine qua non* for dealing with the debt and credit issues. In 1790, it will be recalled, Congress allocated revenues from the sale of public lands to debt reduction.[11] More important, that same year Secretary of the Treasury Alexander Hamilton proposed a plan to fund the domestic and foreign debts at face value to current holders of government securities. In addition, he recommended the federal assumption of existing state debts (individual states had also borrowed during the revolution), which meant increasing the size of the national debt. At the same time, his plan provided for the establishment of a Sinking Fund Commission to pare down principal. Both funding and assumption were controversial, but in the end Congress enacted both. The total United States debt at the end of 1790 amounted to $75,468,000, but the means to service it were established, and the nation's credit acquired a sound footing.[12] In short, the nation could borrow again. This is what Hamilton meant when he asserted that a national debt could become "a national blessing."[13] Yet funding meant discharging interest, not principal. Under Hamilton's program, when would the national debt be eliminated? The answer to this question remained unclear, raising another question: Was the Hamiltonian approach going to perpetuate the national debt and resurrect the ghost of Walpolean England?

A year later these concerns deepened. In 1791 Hamilton proposed the establishment of a Bank of the United States—which would serve as repository of federal funds, provide a national currency, implement financial transactions for the government, and offer other services. In effect, the institution would serve as a central bank. Hamilton recommended capitalization at $20,000,000, the government buying twenty percent of the stock, with the remainder marketed to private investors who could buy using government securities to cover as much as seventy-five percent of the purchase price. Under this circumstance government bonds would become the equivalent of cash.[14]

The Bank proposal raised concerns about the Hamiltonian program to a new level. When President Washington polled his other cabinet members regarding the Bank, Secretary of State Thomas Jefferson objected that the federal government had no authority to charter a bank because the Constitution did not grant such a power. The word "bank" did not even appear in the fundamental law. Jefferson's argument against the Bank of the United States represents the first invocation of "strict constructionism" in American history—the view that the powers of the federal government must be understood by the literal meaning of the words in Article I, Section 8 of the Constitution. Interpreting the Constitution in that fashion delimits the power of the federal government and enhances the power of the states. There was, however, (and still is) a financial flipside to strict construction. The less that government may legitimately do, the less it spends; the less it spends, the less it needs to tax or borrow, and the more possible it becomes to shed existing debt and to protect traditional liberty. The famous aphorism, often but incorrectly attributed to Jefferson—"that government is best which governs least"—translates, financially, into "that government governs best which spends the least."[15] In other words, Jefferson's attack on the Bank was more than a defense of states' rights. On another level it was a defense of federal retrenchment and debt reduction. Hamilton, however, won the day. His defense of the Bank's constitutionality on the implied powers of the "necessary and proper" clause of Article I, Section 8 persuaded President Washington to sign the Bank bill into law.[16]

Fearing that funding perpetuated the national debt and that the Bank of the United States was modeled on the Bank of England, the opponents of Hamiltonian finance coalesced quickly into an organized party—the Republican Party. They believed that the emerging system was fostering an aristocracy based on money which, once established, would dismantle republican institutions and create an American monarchy to protect its wealth and privilege. Only a fortunate few would enjoy wealth and power. Liberty in the United States would die. These fears acquired additional credibility when the United States found itself caught in the international crisis of the 1790s. England and its coalition allies waged war against revolutionary France. The Washington administration, guided by Hamilton, pursued a policy of neutrality despite depredations against our commercial shipping by the British navy. Ultimately, the United States signed a treaty with the former mother country which, to the opposition, seemed a selling out of American rights and principles. Administration supporters, styling themselves Federalists, seemed embarrassingly pro-English. Meantime, France, outraged by President Washington's policy, began to attack American shipping. When war with France seemed inevitable, the Federalist Party, now under the leadership of President John Adams, passed laws that transparently violated freedom of speech and press and other constitutional rights. Republican fears concerning the future of American liberty were, it seemed, being realized. Jefferson and his friend James Madison responded with the Kentucky and Virginia Resolutions of 1798, spelling out the right of the states to interpose themselves between their citizens and the national government in order to protect individual liberty against federal attack. The presidential election of 1800 was, in effect, underway.[17]

The Republicans defeated the Federalists in 1800, and early in 1801 the House of Representatives, breaking the electoral tie between Jefferson and his running mate, Aaron Burr, elected the Virginia strict-constructionist president. In foreign policy, the new administration committed itself to keeping the United States at peace. In its domestic policy it committed itself to retrenchment in order to shrink the national debt. Both policies were related. War would necessitate borrowing and increase, rather than decrease, the debt. In this sense Jefferson's domestic priority dictated his foreign policy, and his effort proved successful. Despite repeated violations of American neutrality by Great Britain and Napoleonic France, Jefferson, relying on economic sanctions rather than armed retaliation, avoided war and pared down the public debt. When he took office in 1801, the debt stood at more than $83,000,000.[18] Even though his administration felt compelled to borrow $15,000,000 in order to purchase Louisiana, by the time Jefferson retired in 1809, the national debt had shrunk to slightly more than $57,000,000.[19] In other words, during Jefferson's two terms both peace and retrenchment succeeded in reducing the debt by thirty-one percent.

Jefferson's successor, James Madison, also pursued the twin policies of peace and retrenchment. During his first term another twelve million dollars were shaved from the debt, and, as a result, at the beginning of 1812 the debt amounted to $45,210,000.[20] But 1812 brought crisis. The effort to keep the nation at peace by employing economic weapons finally failed, and in June the Congress declared war against Great Britain. The United States, however, was utterly unprepared, militarily and financially, for conflict. Retrenchment had required keeping the army and navy small, and a year earlier the Republican-dominated Congress allowed the Bank of the United States charter to expire. The one institution that could have effectively and efficiently helped to underwrite the war no longer existed. Borrowing without the Bank of the United States proved difficult, but borrow the government did because it had to. The war was expensive. By the time the Treaty of Ghent was signed at the end of 1814, the national debt had swollen to approximately $100,000,000, and by the end of 1816 it peaked at more than $127,000,000.[21]

The war experience resulted in enormous changes. For one, the Federalist Party, which had opposed the war, tainted itself with treason at the notorious 1814 Hartford Convention and, severely discredited, rapidly disappeared as an institution in American politics. It ran its last candidate for President in 1816. The demise of the Federalists left only one party—the Republicans—in the political arena—hence the "era of good feelings." Yet many Republicans, chastened by the war, began to drift away from the strict constructionism of their founder and leader and to espouse a more nationalist approach to American affairs. Henry Clay, for example, who had favored letting the Bank of the United States die in 1811, now urged the establishment of another bank. Even President Madison, who in 1791 had opposed Hamilton's bank, now agreed that a new Bank of the United States was vital to the national interest. Congress, in fact, chartered a second Bank of the United States in 1816. Moreover, since the war had demonstrated, among other matters, that the United States was deficient in manufactures and therefore vulnerable in case of conflict, the Madison administration embarked on a protectionist program that Alexander Hamilton would have applauded. The tariff of 1816 raised import duties on foreign manufactures to give American startups a competitive edge in the domestic market. The identity of the Republican Party, in other words, began to blur as a neo-Hamiltonian element emerged within its ranks. James Monroe, Madison's successor, pursuing conciliation to keep party factions united, even welcomed former Federalists into the Republican tent—a policy which Martin Van Buren of New York disapprovingly called "fusion."[22] Nevertheless, dealing with the national debt remained a high, if not the highest, priority on the national agenda for all the conventional republican reasons. Years later, Thomas Hart Benton of Missouri succinctly described the challenge confronting the United States after the Treaty of Ghent: "The war had created a debt, which, added to the balance of that of the Revolution, the purchase of Louisiana, and some other items," exceeded $100,000,000—"and the problem was to be solved, whether a national debt could be paid and extinguished in a season of peace, leaving a nation wholly free from that encumbrance; or whether it was to go on increasing, a burthen in itself, and absorbing with its interest and charges an annual portion of the public revenues."[23]

Fortunately, peace brought prosperity. American commerce revived, and the new tariff law poured revenue into the federal treasury, providing the government a surplus. In his last annual message (December, 1816) to Congress, President Madison commented on this surprising development. "[I]t is a subject of great gratification to find, that, even within the short period which has elapsed since the return of peace, the revenue has far exceeded all current demands upon the Treasury" and that, if commerce did not for some reason slip into recession, then each year's surplus "will afford an ample fund for the effectual and early extinguishment of the public debt."[24] Madison, always cautious, avoided predicting or specifying a terminal date for the debt.

Congress responded to this encouraging assessment by enacting in February 1817, a law "to provide for the redemption of the public debt," legislation which governed debt reduction for the next eighteen years.[25] It enjoyed broad support, passing both the House and the Senate without a roll call vote.[26] This statute swept away earlier legislation concerning interest and principal payments on the national debt except for the Sinking Fund Commission and the designation of land sale revenues to debt reduction. It provided an annual appropriation of ten million dollars to the commission to meet interest payments and to purchase as much principal as possible. The law also provided another nine millon "to be paid out of any moneys in the treasury not otherwise appropriated." This provision, however, applied to the year 1817 only, as did another, which allowed an additional four million dollars that year, if deemed "expedient" to redeem more debt, but if any or all of that amount was used, it was to count as an advance on the ten million due to the sinking fund in 1818. The measure also provided that after 1817, whenever the treasury held a surplus of more than $2,000,000, the excess beyond two million was appropriated to the Sinking Fund Commission for debt redemption. Lastly, the act said that if ever, after all due interest and principal payments had been made, a surplus existed in the sinking fund itself, then the commissioners were authorized to repurchase debt "at its market price," as long as the market price did not exceed certain specifications.[27] The Redemption Act of 1817, in short, aggressively attacked the national debt.

Few were unhappy with this legislation. It reaffirmed the nation's commitment to a fundamental Jeffersonian goal—national debt freedom. Nonetheless, in the years following the Treaty of Ghent, the discernible shift among some Republicans toward Hamiltonian views troubled traditionalists, especially the most orthodox. Among this group were John Randolph of Roanoke and John Taylor of Caroline, Virginia, and Nathaniel Macon of North Carolina—widely revered men whom Arthur Schlesinger, Jr. called "the keepers of the Jeffersonian conscience."[28] Each, true to the founder, insisted on inexpensive government. Randolph, who served multiple terms in the House, relentlessly attacked growing government expenditures and the consolidationism he believed motivated them. His prolonged speeches, often fueled by the alcohol he brought with him to the House chamber, often amounted to sarcastic, invective-filled harangues, but his point was always clear: Extravagance in government threatened liberty. His 1828 address on the importance of retrenchment was fairly typical. "[E]xpense and pageantry" were inconsistent with republicanism. "[A]dapting the style of our living to the means we have" meant frugality in government, debt avoidance, and liberty.[29]

Like Randolph, John Taylor also worried about expensive and expansive government and wrote several treatises on political economy to articulate his concerns. In *Tyranny Unmasked*, for example, which attacked national tariff policy, Taylor emphasized the importance of economy in government. "All reflecting individuals," he wrote, "except those bribed by self-interest, believe that liberty can only be preserved by a frugal government. . . ."[30] All taxation or borrowing for purposes beyond the necessities of government was, in Taylor's judgment, oppression.

Nathaniel Macon enjoyed a long and distinguished career as a representative and then as a senator. He was one of the most respected men in Congress, and, like Randolph and Taylor, found the post-

Ghent embrace of Hamiltonian nationalism by some Republicans deeply disturbing. Like his Virginia colleagues, he opposed unnecessary expenditures, public debt, and consolidation.[31]

These men, in fact, were not "keepers of the Jeffersonian conscience" regarding liberty but regarding slavery. They feared that an expensive and energetic federal government could threaten the "peculiar institution," and they wanted none of it. Retrenchment and strict constructionism would protect the labor system on which the South was built.[32] But whatever motivated men like Randolph, Taylor, and Macon, apparently many Americans agreed that republican government should be frugal. When Congress voted itself a raise in 1816, voters retaliated. An overwhelming majority of incumbents went down to defeat at the next election. At its next session, Congress, which got the voters' message, repealed the pay increase.[33] Randolph, Taylor, and Macon, in other words, represented views that were widely shared.

By the time John Quincy Adams became president, these veteran Jeffersonians were advancing in years, but there were other, younger men who had inherited the orthodox Jeffersonian faith and who were determined to hold firm to the principles of their revered leader—strict construction, states' rights, retrenchment, and the elimination of national indebtedness. The new generation of true believers included, among others, William Rives of Virginia, George McDuffie of South Carolina, and Martin Van Buren of New York, all up-and-coming politicians who would play important roles in the post-Ghent era. All were concerned with the direction the nation seemed to be pursuing in the 1820s. As Rives complained late in the decade, "the aggregate expenditures of the Government have notoriously increased."[34]

❧

What was becoming of Republican economy? The neo-Hamiltonians in the party were promoting—with some success—expensive programs, particularly internal improvements. Proponents of federal expenditures on roads and canals justified them on several grounds—

that the recent war had demonstrated the need for more effective transportation and communication; that they brought unsettled areas into production and generated wealth; that they widened markets; and that they facilitated delivery of the mail. The Constitution, they said, justified each of these objectives. After all, the Constitution had been written and adopted "to form a more perfect Union, . . . provide for the common defence," and to "promote the general welfare." Indeed, with respect to the movement of the mail, Congress enjoyed a delegated power to establish and operate a postal system. Moreover, important segments of the population, especially residents of the new western states, wanted infrastructure projects. Supporters of internal improvements could point to the National or Cumberland Road, undertaken, they were pleased to remind everyone, by President Jefferson himself, as a model.

The first significant effort at federal internal improvements was sponsored by John C. Calhoun in 1817, a decade or so before he moved to the states' rights camp. His so-called Bonus bill, passed by Congress, appropriated the 1.5 million-dollar bonus the new second Bank of the United States paid to the government—as well as the dividends earned by the government's shares in the institution—to a special fund for the purpose of underwriting future projects. To Calhoun's dismay, President Madison, who had recommended internal improvements in his 1815 and 1816 annual messages, vetoed the measure.[35] Why? According to the president, the bill exceeded Congress's constitutional authority.[36] In effect, he reaffirmed Jeffersonian strict constructionism. Five years later, advocates of internal improvements suffered another and similar setback when James Monroe, ostensibly a friend of infrastructure development, vetoed a bill to establish tolls on the Cumberland Road, the revenue from which was to keep the road in repair. Again, strict constitutional interpretation justified the veto.[37] In each instance Madison and Monroe reverted to orthodox Jeffersonianism because of the spending implications a federal internal improvements program entailed. Economy in government would vanish; the vaults of the federal treasury would be thrown open; and tax increases or renewed government borrowing (or both) would ensue. As Virginia presidents, as the supposed guardians of the Jeffersonian tradition, neither wanted to endure blame for such possible outcomes.

Yet advocates of internal improvements persisted. In 1824 they forced the treasury door ajar by passing a General Survey Act. This measure authorized the president of the United States to "cause the necessary surveys, plans, and estimates, to be made of the routes of such roads and canals as he may deem of national importance" for commercial, military, or postal reasons. The law appropriated $30,000 so that the president could employ the Army's Corps of Engineers to prepare surveys he considered to be of national significance.[38] The measure funded no particular project, nor was the allocation particularly large. Perhaps for these reasons President Monroe signed it into law. But the legislation, designed as it was, pointed clearly to where the nationalists in the Republican Party were hoping to lead the country. A costly internal improvements program seemed increasingly likely, if not inevitable. Yet President Monroe's annual message at the end of 1824 held the promise, barring an emergency, of national debt freedom on January 1, 1835. Internal improvements and debt extinction, however, were seemingly contradictory ambitions, and each bore different implications. Roads and canals meant material progress, but debt perpetuation meant a threat to American liberty. Complicating this matter was the election of John Quincy Adams to the presidency under circumstances which smacked of "corrupt" executive patronage reminiscent of Robert Walpole. In addition, Adams, it will be recalled, in his inaugural did not commit himself to debt freedom according to the Monroe schedule but had emphasized internal improvements instead. Was John Quincy Adams America's Walpole? If so, or if he were so perceived, he was sure to encounter fierce opposition.

After Adams's inauguration Congress adjourned, and members went home. The new administration settled in and began managing the nation's affairs, but both Adams and Clay were aware of discontent. Clay, always the optimist, dismissed the rumors he heard. The president himself noted that his secretary of state "made light of the threatened opposition" and that he shrugged off the criticism as "mere ebullitions of disappointment" at the election result and "would soon be abandoned."[39] Clay expressed the same sentiment to others. To one associate he wrote: "An opposition is talked of . . . but I regard that as the ebullition of the moment, the natural offspring of chagrin and disappointment."[40] Or, as he wrote to another friend in a somewhat different vein: "An opposition is threatened; but there is no danger of any, unless the course of the Administration shall furnish just occasion for it, which we shall strive to prevent."[41]

Incoming correspondence, however, although encouraging, warned Clay that a storm was brewing and that it would break over the administration.[42] As a consequence, he decided to justify his conduct in a public "Address to the People of the Congressional District" he had represented, a statement which was published not only in Kentucky but in many newspapers throughout the United States.[43] In it he explained why he had ignored the Kentucky legislature's recommendation to support Jackson, why he could not support Crawford, and why Adams was most qualified to serve as president. He reviewed the Kremer affair, arguing that the entire matter had been politically motivated and that he had responded honorably to a vicious lie. "That I have often misconceived your true interests," he told his constituents, "is highly probable. That I have ever sacrificed them to the object of personal aggrandizement I utterly deny."[44]

His published defense preceding him, Clay headed home in May to get some rest, to attend to private matters, and to prepare his family for the move to Washington. Everywhere along the way he was welcomed and feted. "My reception West of the Mountains so far has exceeded my expectations," he reported gleefully.[45] At Wheeling, Virginia, and at Maysville, Lexington, Frankfort, and other places in Kentucky he was wined and dined.[46] "My reception in K.," he wrote to Navy Secretary Samuel Southard in mid-June, "has greatly exceeded in cordiality and enthusiasm any which I ever before obtained. I have been the object of as many public manifestations of regard nearly as La Fayette was. Public dinners, Barbacues and Balls have left me but little leisure. . . . The good feelings towards me are extended to the administration."[47]

To Clay the trip home resembled a triumphal procession. It lifted his spirits and confirmed his optimism that the "corrupt bargain" charge would simply fade away. The new administration, he believed, would be successful. Back in Washington in late summer his confidence held firm. "The Administration gets along very well," he wrote in a letter to James Brown. "The number of unfriendly prints and persons is I think considerably diminished, and the tone of those which remain is somewhat softened."[48] Perhaps, but Congress, of course, was not in session yet, nor did Clay know what President Adams would tell the legislature when it met in December.

Unlike Clay, Adams spent the summer in Washington. He rose each day between four and six, ordinarily reading from his Bible before doing anything else. On cool mornings he took lengthy walks before breakfast. When the weather was hot he went skinny dipping in the Potomac.[49] (On one occasion in June he nearly drowned.)[50] After breakfast he dealt with routine business—meetings and paper work—and in the evenings, after supper, he read, wrote in his diary, played billiards, or did just nothing. But July was hot, and August hotter, and he complained that the heat's "unexampled intensity" made him irritable.[51]

Yet the long hot summer alone may not have accounted fully for the president's unease. Again, unlike Clay, Adams was prone to see the proverbial glass as half empty. He knew that opposition would characterize various factions in Congress, and he knew what the opposition wanted. He also knew that he was going to recommend an expensive programmatic agenda to Congress in December. Accordingly, he may have recalled George McDuffie's observation in January, that eliminating the national debt had to be "the great object of the next administration."[52] Traditional Republicans in Congress would demand retrenchment, because retrenchment was the guarantor of debt freedom. They would be unwilling to spend a dollar on anything except what was plainly necessary. Adams anticipated this disposition. When the United States was invited in the spring of 1825 by newly independent Latin American nations to send delegates to a contemplated conference at Panama, Adams noted in his diary that Congress would probably object to the "expense" of sending two commissioners to the isthmus.[53] Adams, in short, understood better than Clay what the mood of much of Congress would be. Nonetheless, despite his knowledge and experience—a life in preparation for the presidency—Adams determined to walk headlong into the storm.

THREE

THE NATIONAL DEBT AND THE FAILURE OF THE ADAMS ADMINISTRATION

ADAMS NEEDED NO WARNING ABOUT THE DIFFICULTIES HE WAS about to create for himself. He knew and understood. Nonetheless, most of his cabinet officers tried to dissuade him from the path he seemed determined to follow. Their foreboding became clear as the president prepared his first annual message to Congress. He began working on it in the fall, and by the third week of November had a full draft ready. Following the logic of his inaugural address, it advocated, among other matters, a strong federal internal improvements program.

Adams summoned his cabinet to the White House on Wednesday, November 23. All attended except Attorney General William Wirt, who was out of town. At this meeting Adams read his prepared text and solicited comments and suggestions from his department heads. At first, it seems, there was stunned silence, but then Secretary of War James Barbour spoke up. He "objected" to the entire section on internal improvements. Clay spoke next, agreeing with Barbour. Secretary of the Navy Samuel Southard said nothing. Only Richard Rush of Treasury endorsed the entire document.[1] The meeting adjourned with three out of the four cabinet officers present deeply concerned about what the president planned to tell Congress. They had two days to think about it.

On Friday, November 25, Adams met his department heads again, and again William Wirt was absent. The conversation began where it had ended on Wednesday. Barbour insisted that the entire internal improvements portion "be suppressed." Clay, however, seemingly modified his position over the preceding forty-eight hours, now agreeing with Barbour only "partially" but nevertheless recommending that several ideas be dropped. The secretary of state said that he favored the "great part of the . . . things proposed," but added, importantly but tactfully, that he recommended "nothing which . . . would be unlikely to succeed."[2] This *caveat*, it seems, sailed over Adams's head.

The next day the president and his team met again. Barbour, apparently despairing, gave up and "withdrew his objection to the whole topic" of internal improvement. Clay approved the "general principles" of the message, but not its specifics. Southard remained silent. Only Rush heartily affirmed the message.[3]

On Monday, November 28, Attorney General Wirt finally arrived at the White House and had a one-on-one session with the president. Adams gave him a copy of the message, and he read it immediately. Wirt's response probably did not surprise Adams. The attorney general characterized the document as "excessively bold" and argued that it would affront "the party in Virginia," who feared federal consolidation and the abrogation of states' rights and who perceived Adams "as grasping for power." He especially opposed the internal improvements proposal.[4]

In the end, then, only Richard Rush fully supported Adams's upcoming annual message. Barbour opposed it but gave up hope in changing the president's mind. Clay too opposed, but tried tactfully not to alienate the president. Southard's silence hardly counted as approval, and Wirt straightforwardly objected to it. Four of five cabinet officers considered Adams's message a mistake. Nevertheless, Adams determined to go forward. "Thus situated," he wrote, "the perilous experiment must be made. Let me make it with full deliberations, and be prepared for the consequences."[5]

At noon on Tuesday, December 6, Adams sent his message to both houses of Congress. That day Adams experienced "intense anxiety." He knew and understood the storm it would cause. "I await, with whatever composure I can command, the issue."[6]

Adams's first annual message promised neither frugality nor retrenchment but the very opposite. Indeed, it defined an agenda that was unprecedented and visionary—a stunning set of proposals to promote American greatness under federal leadership. What, precisely, did Adams recommend?

The president's remarks began predictably enough, reminding Congress that the nation was prosperous and at peace, and recommending several pieces of legislation. He also informed Congress that the United States had accepted the invitation to attend a conference of newly independent Western Hemisphere states to be held at Panama "to deliberate on objects important to the welfare of all."[7]

Adams did not ignore the nation's finances. "Among the unequivocal indications of our national prosperity," he wrote, "is the flourishing state of our finances. The revenues of the present year . . . will exceed the anticipations of the last."[8] Consequently, "nearly eight millions of the principal of the public debt have been discharged."[9] At the same time, funding of government operations, defense, obligations to Native Americans, and of various internal improvement projects like the Chesapeake and Delaware Canal Company had all been met. Concerning the latter matter, he informed Congress that the Board of Engineers for Internal Improvements, created in 1824, had been working on a number of surveys for new projects and that its reports, nearly completed, were forthcoming.[10]

Then came the president's challenge. "Upon this first occasion of addressing the Legislature of the Union . . . I can not close . . . without recommending to their calm and persevering consideration the general principle" for which government exists. "The great object of the institution of civil government," he declared, "is the improvement of the condition of those who are parties to the social compact, and no government . . . can accomplish the lawful ends of its institution but in proportion as it improves the condition of those over whom it is established."[11] Government, in other words, existed to promote progress, and Adams was not shy about recommending a progressive agenda.

First, "among the most important means of improvement" was infrastructure development—especially roads and canals which facilitated communication, transportation, and commerce "between distant regions and multitudes of men."[12] The salutary effects were obvious. Roads and canals expanded the areas of settlement more quickly than otherwise, brought new regions into production, and broadened the national market. Result? The quality of American life improved.

In addition to federal underwriting of roads and canals, Adams advocated funding a national university because education meant progress. "Among the first, perhaps the very first, instruments for the improvement of the condition of men is knowledge. . . ." Accordingly, he also urged the United States to emulate various European powers by financing "voyages of discovery" to increase human knowledge and benefit humanity. He also urged funding for research on a "uniform standard of weights and measures," the establishment of "an astronomical observatory," employment of an astronomer, and "the periodical publication of his observations."[13]

Adams was not yet done. Despite the nation's territorial expansion and population increase, he asserted, the government had not grown to match the new demands on it. He proposed creating a new executive department of interior, new federal courts, and new federal judgeships. According to Adams, "[t]he exigencies of the public service" rendered these matters urgent. Finally, he recommended that Congress at last make good on one of its resolutions from 1799: to erect "a marble monument" in the federal district to honor George Washington.[14]

By invoking Washington's name, Adams may have aimed at preparing his audience for his bold nationalist conclusion. Just as Washington had been guided by patriotic duty, Adams asserted that his proposals emerged from "an irresistible sense of my own duty." He tried to reassure skeptics that Congress did enjoy constitutional authority to legislate on all his recommendations, reviewing briefly some of the Constitution's enumerated powers and the "necessary and proper" clause of Article I, Section 8. Then he added that if Congress refrained from exercising all its powers "for the benefit of the people," then it would commit "treachery to the most sacred of trusts." Congress, in other words, was obligated—morally—to act affirmatively on his agenda, and the obligation came at an opportune moment in history. "The spirit of improvement is abroad upon the earth," Adams declared. "It stimulates the hearts and sharpens the faculties not of our fellow-citizens alone, but of the nations of Europe and of their rulers." But the United States held an advantage over its European rivals because "[l]iberty is power" and "the nation blessed with the largest portion of liberty must . . . be the most powerful nation upon earth." But power was conditional, requiring responsible exercise. What constituted the responsible exercise of power? According to Adams, the "Creator" entrusted power to humankind in order "to improve" its "condition." Even God, it would seem, favored federally financed roads and canals. Therefore, Adams believed, "were we to slumber in indolence or fold up our arms and proclaim to the world that we are palsied by the will of our constituents, would it not be to cast away the bounties of Providence and doom ourselves to perpetual inferiority?"[15]

President Adams's message constituted an unprecedented summons to employ the power and energy of the federal government to uplift American society and achieve national greatness. His program, of course, would cost money, but the president offered no cost estimates, no timelines, no concrete fiscal information regarding his ambitious agenda. Who could tell how much spending he envisioned? How consistent was his vision with debt freedom? Indeed, the president did not commit himself, as he had not in his inaugural, to Monroe's schedule for eliminating the national debt. Instead, Adams discussed debt reduction in the context of rising federal revenues, particularly from public land sales, remarking that "the entire discharge of the national debt" would permit land sales "to replenish the common Treasury" and to fund "unfailing streams of improvement from the Atlantic to the Pacific Ocean."[16] In other words, to Adams debt elimination meant more, not less, federal spending. Skeptics might have suspected that Adams's program assured future borrowing and the perpetuation of indebtedness and all the dangers to liberty that they entailed.

Concern over Adams's agenda did not end there. His program necessarily entailed creating new government jobs. Most, if not all of these, would increase the number of positions the president had to fill. Adams's patronage, and therefore his power, would grow. His appointment of Clay to the State Department had already revealed, as critics saw it, the cynicism with which he would exercise this power. The corrupting Walpolean combination of perpetuated debt and patronage evoked deep unease, especially among those in the Jeffersonian, strict construction tradition.

Accordingly, anxieties over Adams's agenda (and his perceived "hidden agenda"), already aroused by the circumstances of his election, deepened. Writing to an associate less than two weeks after presentation of the message, Vice President John C. Calhoun observed: "If you had not confidence previously, I take it for granted the Message will not inspire you with it. . . . I know not which is most offended or has greater right to complain, the real friends of the measures of the late administration [including Monroe's scheduled debt elimination] or the State right party. . . . The real supporters of the measures of the late administration are by this injudicious course [i.e., the Adams agenda] alarmed least [sic: lest] a reaction should take place, which may endanger all that has been done; while the

State right party profess to see in it a fulfillment of the evils which they have anticipated. The result has been, that he has gained no support, while he has added greatly to the force of opposition."[17] This observation was hardly surprising. After all, Monroe supporters and states' righters championed debt freedom. To both factions, the Adams agenda seemed inconsistent with retrenchment and the ultimate extinction of the public debt.

❧

If, recalling George McDuffie's observation, eliminating the public debt was not the "great object" of the Adams administration, then Congress could seize the initiative, establish debt freedom as its highest priority, and pursue it through its power over the purse. Although the administration was not without advocates, especially in the House, the opposition agonized over every dollar every appropriation bill proposed to spend. It scrutinized and challenged all expenditures, major and minor, in order to retrench and keep debt extinction on schedule. In fact, Richard Rush's report to Congress, submitted two and a half weeks after the president's message, inadvertently encouraged this disposition. Rush estimated a treasury balance of over $5,284,000 on January 1, 1826, but added so many qualifiers that, in reality, little more than $784,000 of "effective funds" represented the surplus from 1825.[18] Moreover, even though the national debt had shrunk by more than two million dollars in 1825, meeting upcoming payments of $29,000,000 in 1826 and 1827 posed an imminent problem. The act passed in early 1825 to refinance twelve million dollars to facilitate these payments and save on interest had actually raised only a disappointing $1,585,000. That failure threatened timely payments on the debt, and Rush recommended enactment of legislation to borrow fifteen million at 5%, not 4.5% as the 1825 measure required, in the hope of attracting investors.[19]

According to standard procedure, Rush's report was referred to the House Ways and Means Committee, which reviewed it "to ascertain the means of the Treasury" and "the best mode of applying those means to the payment of the public debt."[20] Its report, submitted to the entire House on February 6, 1826, not only clarified and corrected some of Rush's accounting but rejected the proposal to borrow again, recommending instead that the government meet its 1826 and 1827 obligations by partial payments, which the loan contracts specifically allowed.[21] Debt reduction would continue apace without additional government charges. The committee's report, in effect, rebuked Secretary Rush, but the repudiation did not remain confined to the halls of Congress. Rather, the opposition press pummeled him. Critical editorials aroused popular outrage. One unhappy reader, for example, wrote to the *United States' Telegraph* that "The Treasury Report has done much to destroy confidence in the ability of the head of the Treasury."[22] By implication, it also reflected poorly on the entire administration. More than that, it also fostered anxiety over the issue which, more than any other, troubled a growing number of legislators and their constituents: the status of the national debt.

The debt question permeated the proceedings of the nineteenth Congress. In the House of Representatives the opposition made retrenchment the order of the day. Every appropriation bill, whether minor or major, underwent intense scrutiny and debate. The case of Penelope Denny provides an illustrative example. A New York widow, Denny had lost her only son in service to the nation. A gunner in the U.S. Navy, he had been "killed in action with pirates" several years earlier. Since he had been her only source of support, she petitioned Congress for relief—"a half pay pension." The eighteenth Congress had debated but not acted upon the relief bill, but the matter came up again in the nineteenth, triggering heated debate. Opponents of relief for Mrs. Denny argued that the pension law provided benefits to wives and children of servicemen killed in the line of duty but not to parents. Representative Lewis Williams of North Carolina maintained that awarding a pension to Penelope Denny created the danger that others in her predicament might also seek congressional relief, raising the question "to what extent money might be drawn from the Treasury."[23] Yet the relief bill provided only $108.00 *per annum* for five years, hardly a staggering sum.[24] Churchill C.

Cambreling of New York, characterizing the sum as a "pittance," dismissed the notion that Mrs. Denny's precedent would drain future revenues. In the end, the Penelope Denny relief bill passed the House but only by a vote of 98 to 78.[25] Later in the session Edward Everett of Massachusetts, expressing frustration, said, "I do not remember a debate or a question of appropriation, this session, not even on poor Mrs. Denney's pension, in which the payment of the national debt has not been recommended to our anxious consideration."[26]

If Congress argued about a temporary and unsubstantial expenditure of $540 because it threatened the nation's financial health, then it was also going to question more expensive budget items. The nation's fortification system—a crucial element of American defense undertaken after the War of 1812 but not yet completed—was not immune to the kind of challenge Mrs. Denny's relief bill encountered. The House began debate on the Fortifications bill on Thursday, January 26, 1826, a measure that sought a total appropriation of $795,000. This sum included $90,000 to begin construction of a fort in Louisiana and $15,000 for repairs and possible contingencies throughout the existing system. The remaining $690,000 was designated for nine forts already built or nearing completion. One of these was Fort Monroe at Old Point Comfort in Virginia. Representative John Cocke of Tennessee took issue with the projected $115,000 for this site, indicating that in preceding years Fort Monroe had ordinarily been appropriated "75 or 80,000 dollars a year." Recognizing that the fort's "completion must necessarily require an immense sum," Cocke nonetheless wondered why, "in the midst of profound peace," such a huge increase was needed. He considered it "a very strange manner of proceeding." He then added, in a sarcastic swipe at administration supporters, that he "knew very well it was not now a fashionable doctrine to talk any thing about paying the National Debt." He also knew that "it was intended that the money that might remain in the Treasury should find a very different direction." Presumably Cocke was referring to internal improvements and the other proposals contained in the President's message. He recommended cutting the $115,000 requested for Fort Monroe to $80,000.[27]

Cocke's remarks drew a quick response from Louis McLane of Delaware, chair of the Ways and Means Committee. The system of fortifications, the latter pointed out, had been in development for years and was now so far advanced that there could be no question about the "propriety" of completing it. National defense required it. McLane then replied to Cocke's sarcasm: "As to the apprehensions of the member from Tennessee, on the subject of the Public Debt, let me give him a word of comfort. . . . The Committee of Ways and Means have had that subject under their careful attention, and have prepared a report. . . . that, after paying the expense of all the objects provided for in these appropriation bills, the nation will . . . be enabled to pay off" in 1829 all the debt bearing 6% interest as well as the debt due to the Bank of the United States. "Yet," McLane added incredulously, "the gentleman says the Public Debt is never to be paid."[28]

The exchange did not end there. Cocke responded, thanking McLane for the assurance that "there was some prospect of paying a portion of the Public Debt." But, he added testily, "I did not say . . . that the Public Debt never would be paid: but this I will say, that this House . . . last year *exchanged* its stock to the amount of twelve millions. Why did we do this if it was not needed? Would it not have been *better* to save some of the money we are lavishing on this system of fortifications, than to beg our creditors to let us off by paying them four and a half, and five per cent interest, instead of six and seven per cent?"[29] Cocke predicted greater and greater future expenses: the forts had to be manned and maintained; expansion of the system would compel expansion of the army; expansion of the army would compel expansion of the military budget. In other words, the more rapidly the system of fortifications was completed, the sooner new burdens would confront the Treasury. "I have no objections to go on with them [the forts] at a reasonable and proper rate," Cocke said, "but why go on to expend such immense sums to complete them now, and then involve ourselves in the necessity of other vast sums to man and defend them?"[30]

Others chimed into the Cocke-McLane debate. George Kremer of Pennsylvania, who a year earlier had started the "corrupt bargain" rumor, supported Cocke. "This system of extravagance had been now going on for years," he complained. Congress was "squandering the public money to erect a parcel of fortifications that were totally useless, and stood as so many monuments to our folly. . . . No doubt they had afforded good jobs," Kremer observed, "but they were death to the People." Why death? McLane "told us that the Public Debt is soon to be paid off. Sir, the same syren song has been rung in our ears for the last nine years—the same lullaby—lullaby, 'be perfectly secure! your whole debt will soon be paid! ten years more, ten years more, and the day will arrive.'" Kremer's meaning was clear. Just as the enchanting songs of the sirens of Greek mythology sunk the ships of ancient mariners, the song that the public debt would soon be paid, when sung by those spending the public's money, threatened to sink the ship of state. "It is high time we should profit by experience. . . . Let us try to strangle the monster at once." Kremer moved "to strike out the enacting clause" from the fortification bill, but he alone voted for it.[31] This failure did not mean that the fortification bill would pass easily—only that Kremer's position was too extreme for critics as well as friends of the measure.

The debate dragged on. By the end of the day George McDuffie of South Carolina, impatient with the discussion, questioned "whether it was compatible with the interests of this nation that, on every petty question of appropriation, the members of this House shall enter into a debate on the State of the Republic." But "the question is a narrow one," McDuffie said. "[H]ow much money shall we now appropriate for" the fortification system? More precisely, how should the amount be determined? To McDuffie, the answer seemed obvious: by accepting the estimates of the engineers whose expertise no member of Congress could match. Moreover, the "estimates presented to us, correspond with contracts actually made and entered into. If we refuse to appropriate, the gentleman from Tennessee [Cocke] thinks we save the money." McDuffie disagreed. "No, sir, we save not one dollar: the money must be paid: if not to-day, it must be paid some other time, and sooner the better. If the fort can be completed in two years, it is better than to take ten years—it is more economical."[32]

McDuffie then blasted Representative Cocke. "The gentleman from Tennessee moves to reduce the sum for Fort Monroe to $80,000; and on what grounds?" Cocke, McDuffie pointed out, had no cost estimates, had never visited the fortification site, and did not know the price of labor. "Has he made" a "calculation?"—"In a word, . . . does he know any thing about the matter?" McDuffie's sarcasm deepened. "And, without any knowledge whatever of the subject," Cocke proposed $80,000 instead of $115,000. "But why does he fix on $80,000? Why does he not propose seventy thousand? Why not sixty?" Cocke, McDuffie intimated, was simply making numbers up. But, McDuffie said, "the Committee of Ways and Means have made a careful calculation, and they are prepared to tell you that," since the end of the War of 1812, "we have paid one hundred millions of our national debt. . . . Yet the gentleman tells you there is no intention to pay the public debt. . . . can the gentleman be serious?" Could Cocke seriously believe that saving $35,000 would "contribute to pay the national debt?" After all, McDuffie declared, Cocke's "miserable savings . . . would not pay a thousandth part of the interest of that debt." Cocke, McDuffie said, "proposes no important public measure which goes to the payment of this [national] debt." Instead, he simply wasted the House's valuable time.[33]

McDuffie's angry *ad hominem* attack revealed how determination among administration opponents to eliminate the public debt intruded into matters as important as national defense, and the intrusion carried over into the next day's debate. John Forsyth of Georgia moved to table the fortifications bill until the War Department justified its specific appropriation requests. Doing otherwise would simply invite wasting the taxpayers' money. "Let them plan what they please," Forsyth said, but "if you once begin to give them money for it, you must go on giving money as long as they choose to ask it. . . . The principle of this procedure leads directly to the greatest abuses, and to the vilest corruptions."[34] Here, of course, lurked the specter of more government borrowing, patronage, and the unwarranted expansion of executive power. James Buchanan of Pennsylvania expressed the same anxiety, doubting that the fortification bill was consistent with debt elimination.[35] McLane of Delaware, responding after the weekend break, made an important point: "We began this great work" of national defense "when our debt was double as much as it is now. We did not stop then to inquire . . . of what were the means in the Treasury. We began our march with the whole of the war-debt on our backs: and shall we stop now, when we have entirely freed ourselves from that burden?" (McLane meant that the loans contracted specifically for the War of 1812 were on schedule for total discharge in 1829. Other debt, of course, would remain.) "If there is to be any change in our course," he declared, "we ought to go on faster; because we can now go faster with less fatigue."[36] Addressing his remarks to Buchanan, McLane went on to lay out "the data from which I have made the calculation, that the war debt will be paid in 1829." He continued: "The debt amounts to forty million" at six per cent. Therefore, "[i]t is only necessary to pay the interest which remains on this sum, and you extinguish the debt, by the necessary operation of the Sinking Fund [ten million per year by the 1817 Redemption Act]." After all, the secretary of the treasury had reported "an annual surplus of five millions." Therefore, leaving "two millions in the Treasury every year to meet the current expenses" creates "a disposable balance of three millions, which, in four years, will amount to twelve millions, the sum necessary to extinguish this debt."[37]

McLane was determined to reassure opponents that government expenditures were not impeding progress toward debt freedom: "Eleven years ago, we came out of the war without a dollar in our Treasury, and an immense debt on our hands. We have almost got clear of the debt during the interval," and, remarkably, at the same time "we have created a considerable Navy; we have carried on internal improvements; we have purchased Florida; yet the Treasury is full—every man is happy, and the country is prosperous."[38]

Such was the debate over the fortifications system. It dragged on for another month. In the end the measure carried, funded to the full amount of $795,000.[39] Yet it had been difficult. In the wake of the president's message all appropriation bills encountered tough sailing in the House, because many of the people's representatives had their eyes on the distant shore of debt freedom.

The Senate received President Adams's message with much the same dismay as the House. Senator Benjamin Ruggles of Ohio, a state deeply interested in internal improvement projects, proposed creating a standing committee on roads and canals to consider that portion of Adams's message dealing with infrastructure development.[40] John Holmes of Maine, however, argued that the Senate had always dealt with internal improvements on an *ad hoc* basis, and that if a standing committee were created, then the Senate would first have to agree that the government enjoyed the constitutional power to build roads and canals. Otherwise the upper legislative chamber should adhere to precedent and create special committees as needed. The Ruggles resolution was promptly defeated, 19 to 14, offering an early hint of things to come.[41]

Nearly two weeks passed before the matter came up again, but this time from the opposition. On December 20, 1825, Martin Van Buren of New York offered two resolutions: first, that Congress had no power to construct roads and canals within the states and, second, that a select committee be appointed to draft a constitutional amendment "defining the power Congress shall have over the subject of Internal Improvements," making sure at the same time that state sovereignty was protected and that "a just distribution of the benefits" from development appropriations was accorded to all of the states. Van Buren argued that only a constitutional amendment could resolve the differences between proponents and opponents of federally financed internal improvements.[42] While Van Buren's idea never went anywhere, the Senate, like the House of Representatives, dealt with several internal improvement matters: the Florida Canal (January 5), the Indiana Canal (May 11), the Dismal Swamp Canal (May 15), and several others, including the now perennial debate over extending the Cumberland Road.[43] Success greeted only a handful of projects, even though friends of the administration enjoyed a small majority. Imminent debt freedom provided the same context within which Senate debates, like House debates, took place. By the end of the Senate session, Thomas Hart Benton of Missouri was urging, as he had in earlier years, sale of the public lands in graduated fashion, revenue from which would be designated to pay the interest on the public debt, leaving Sinking Fund operations to discharge principal only. Otherwise, he declared, "[t]he public debt will be saddled on us forever." The nation needed to eliminate the debt now, "in this season of peace and prosperity," or "it will be fastened on us to eternity." Failure meant becoming like England in the eighteenth century. "Nothing is easier," he said, "than to pay it within the eight or ten succeeding years, and nothing more honorable than to do so. The Congress which shall accomplish that object will be entitled to the glorious appellation of *blessed*" because " '*the public debt is paid.*' "[44]

Blessed be Congress for redeeming the national debt, because, as many legislators saw it, President Adams was not going to do it. The doubters' suspicions seemed to receive confirmation before the end of the session. In April 1826, Edward Everett of Massachusetts addressed the House on the subject of the debt. Because he was a Massachusetts man, but more especially because he was a close friend of the president, he seemed to speak for the administration, and what he had to say constituted a sharp departure from conventional republican wisdom concerning public indebtedness. A bill providing "for the relief of the surviving officers of the Army of the Revolution," into which the debt question had also intruded, occasioned Everett's remarks.[45] He pointed out what everyone already knew. "This national debt" had become "a standing theme" of the congressional session. It came up again and again, and Everett understood why. "I know . . . it is a sound Republican maxim, to pay off the national debt. I am no believer in the proposition, that a national debt is a national blessing." Government's "relations" with the people, he declared, should be "few and simple" and "there should be as little government as possible." Ideally, "People should do as much as possible for themselves." Public borrowing, Everett admitted, contradicted these venerable Jeffersonian ideals. "It is a violation of these sound doctrines, that Government should stand towards a portion of the citizens in a perpetuated relation of debtorship to a vast amount." This circumstance constituted the "reason" why it was "desirable to pay off the debt."[46]

Having tipped his hat to the time-honored tradition, Everett went on to explain that debt elimination was more complicated than it seemed. His observations began with the unavoidable "but": "But as a financial operation [debt elimination], to relieve or disembarrass the People, it is . . . little better than a farce." Everett then analyzed the debt question from a perspective distinctly ahead of its time. What, he asked, was gained by paying off five million dollars' worth of debt in 1826? The answer, of course, was the saving in interest on that amount. "Granted," said Everett, the interest is saved. "[B]ut where do you get five millions, by which you pay off so much of the debt?" The answer, of course, was taxes, money taken "from the pockets of the People." Government deprived people of their money and the interest on it "forever." "What, then," Everett asked, "have you gained by the operation [of debt reduction]? You have taken a sum of money out of one pocket, and put it into the other."[47]

Everett grew bolder as he argued against rapid debt elimination. "I said this grave procedure was almost a farce. In its direct operation, it is; in its remote results, it is a great loss to the country." He explained why. "The debt is now about eighty millions. Twenty-five years hence, our population will be doubled; our wealth, no doubt, much more than doubled." For the sake of simplifying the arithmetic, however, Everett asked his colleagues to consider the national wealth merely doubling in the coming quarter century. "A nominal debt of eighty millions, twenty-five years hence, will be no more burdensome than one of forty millions now." Everett was simply arguing that economic growth would itself eliminate the debt. "In other words, time, and the happy progress of the country, would of themselves reduce the debt, if you would leave the thing to their silent operation, as fast, perhaps, as the public welfare demands." From this analysis he drew an obvious conclusion: "By hastening to pay the debt, we therefore increase the country's burden." In the end, while avoiding the word "blessing," he characterized the debt positively. "The national debt," declared Everett, "is the evidence of a capital consumed in the public service."[48]

"A capital consumed in the public service?" Here was a characterization that John Quincy Adams or Henry Clay might have uttered. Everett's unorthodox reasoning created no converts. More than likely it antagonized the opposition. Before the session ended Adams came under severe attack as a spendthrift who wasted the public's money on luxuries and who, by implication, cared little about debt redemption. The assault began in May when Everett, chair of the Committee on Public Buildings, reported a bill that included a $25,000 appropriation for finishing a room at and buying new furniture for the White House.[49] The opposition reacted immediately. Philemon Beecher of Ohio wanted "to strike out" the "item." Forsyth of Georgia disagreed, arguing, with sarcasm, that since "the Nation had chosen to erect a palace" for the chief executive, "it was now fit that they should furnish it." All he wanted to know was why "so large a sum" was needed. Everett tried but failed to explain. Daniel Webster sought a compromise, suggesting that only the amount needed to replace furniture "unfit for use" be appropriated.[50] At that point Samuel Carson of North Carolina spoke, pointing out that a year earlier Congress had appropriated $14,000 for the same purpose and that President Adams had assigned his son, John Adams Jr., to oversee the fund. Carson then quoted from the report on how that money was spent: $50.00 for a billiard table, $6.00 for billiard balls, and $23.50 for a chess set.

Carson expressed outrage. "Is it possible . . . to believe that it ever was intended by Congress, that the public money should be applied to the purchase of gaming tables and gambling furniture? And if it is right to purchase billiard tables, and chessmen, why not purchase . . . pharo banks, playing cards, race horses, and every other *necessary* article to complete a system of gambling at the President's palace, and let it at once be understood by the People, that this is a most *splendid gambling* administration."[51]

Carson's comments were an underhanded reference to the "corrupt bargain" inasmuch as Henry Clay was a notorious gambler. But, Carson added, "let it not be said that I charge the President of the United States with being a gambler. I would only be understood as saying that those are articles made use of for that purpose." Clay, of course, as secretary of state frequented the White House and, as secretary of state, he was also the heir-apparent. Presumably, the White House would be ready to serve as a casino when the Kentuckian took his place. "I . . . can never vote for any further sum," Carson said, "until I have an assurance that it will not be expended for the purpose of completing the gambling arrangements of the Palace."[52]

Carson's attack was more than a cheap political shot at the administration. His objection to the billiard table and chess set—an expense of $79.50 from an appropriation of $14,000 (or .0057%)—was as miserly as the objection to Mrs. Denny's relief petition and for the same reason. Both matters shared the same reality for those committed to debt freedom: to achieve it every possible saving seemed necessary. Adams's conduct, however, suggested that he did not share that goal. Carson ridiculed the president on this matter. Quoting John Adams Jr.'s report on the $14,000—"the expenditures have *all* been made with an eye to the strictest economy"—Carson, outraged, shouted: "With an eye to the strictest economy! Item, 'billiard table, $50'—item, 'chessmen, 23.50.' Yet *all* has been expended with an eye to the strictest economy!" Carson's conclusion did not surprise anyone. "But, if this be economy, I, for one, am not disposed to appropriate any more of the public money for *such* economical purposes."[53]

Anti-administration newspapers joined the assault. *The United States' Telegraph* ridiculed Adams for purchasing "baubles" at public expense.[54] The *Steubenville Ledger* asked: "What sign was it, to see the *President of the United States* indulging either his taste for gentility, or for gambling, in expending the money, which is taken from the pockets of the people, in the purchase of *Tables and Balls, which can be used for no purpose but for gambling?*"[55]

✻

Not long after Carson's attack on Adams's carefree spending, the first session of the nineteenth Congress adjourned. Even though friends of the administration had held slender majorities in the House and Senate, particularly the former, they had little about which to boast.

They had, in fact, enacted legislation for government stock subscriptions to several canal companies, a measure for a hodgepodge of local infrastructure projects, even the controversial Panama mission, yet the opposition went home the true winners.[56]

Originally the opposition consisted of at least three disparate factions—southern free traders, New Yorkers allied with the Virginia traditionalists, and vengeful Jackson partisans. Throughout the session these elements coalesced, and the offspring of this union was the Democratic Party. National debt freedom was one of the principal issues by which this new political organization identified itself. It was dedicated to turning Adams out of office and electing to the presidency Andrew Jackson, whose *bona fides* on the debt issue were beyond reproach.[57] Furthermore, this opposition succeeded in framing the debate over the Adams program, insisting that debt freedom, not federally sponsored development, constituted the nation's highest priority. For the opposition, the seeming spend-and-spend policy of the administration guaranteed perpetual debt and all the Walpolean evils that would flow from it. As Martin Van Buren later recalled, the power the administration claimed to underwrite internal improvements "was sure in the end to impoverish the National Treasury by improvident grants to private companies and State works, and to corrupt Federal legislation by the opportunities it would present for favoritism."[58] In addition, the opposition employed effective tactics. It dragged debates out, forcing the session into May, all the while demanding again and again that the national debt be addressed. In this way the opposition kept the debt issue before the public. This stratagem frustrated the administration, especially since—Representative Everett's speech notwithstanding—in 1825 and 1826 it was "politically incorrect" to oppose debt freedom. In short, the first session of the nineteenth Congress prepared the stage for the overthrow of the Adams administration.

The year 1826 was a particularly bad year for the president. Not only did he lose his aged father on July 4, the fiftieth anniversary of the Declaration of Independence, but the midterm congressional elections that fall turned both houses of Congress over to the opposition, creating the first instance of divided executive-legislative government in American history.[59] But even before contending with hostile majorities in the twentieth Congress, which would not convene until December 1827, Adams still had to deal with the nineteenth Congress in its second or "short" session. The outlook was grim. After more than eighteen months in office, Adams knew that his great vision stood little chance of realization. In fact, his second message to Congress was notable not only because it did not renew the call to federal activism but also because it reported that revenues for 1826 fell short of expectation and that 1827's tax receipts were likely to be disappointing as well.[60] This news stunned Congress and emboldened the opposition to intensify its resistance to internal improvements and other administration proposals. The second session of the nineteenth Congress began what its successor, the twentieth Congress, completed—the "spoiling," as John Lauritz Larson has called it, of the internal improvement program.[61]

This is an important matter. Larson, in his excellent study, *Internal Improvement*, attributed the collapse of the federal infrastructure effort, the failure of the Adams administration, and the rise of the "Jackson movement," to two "forces" that had "stalked the American experiment" from its beginning. One was the "fear of monarchy and class rule"; the other, the fear of the "tendency of men in office to abuse their power."[62] Larson was correct on both points, but overlooked the fact that both of these fears derived from the same source—the fear of a perpetuated national debt. In addition, Larson pointed out, again correctly, that the General Survey Act of 1824, intended to create a national plan for internal improvements, in fact promoted the opposite. "Unfortunately," he wrote, "members of Congress—pressed by the desires of their constituents" advanced "pet projects with increasingly dubious claims of national significance" and engaged "in ever more bitter attacks on each other."[63] While they pushed hard for their own local undertakings, they vigorously opposed those of their colleagues. No legislator, wrote Larson, "brought to the table a spirit of accommodation."[64] Larson, in effect, blamed the "spoiling" of the national improvement program on transparent jealousy, narrow-mindedness, and hypocrisy. Yet the national debt issue helps to explain what seems to be irresponsible congressional behavior. Members naturally wanted to gratify their constituents by bringing home "pork," but their constituents also wanted to eliminate the national debt. As a result, individual representatives and senators supported their own but opposed other projects, an effort to have their cake and eat it too. Hence the internal improvement effort was "spoiled" or, perhaps more precisely, "palsied," to borrow President Adams's term, by the will of the voters.

The administration of John Quincy Adams failed not only because of unbridgeable constitutional differences, varying sectional interests, and bitter political partisanship but also on account of money. The most contentious issue was: how should the nation appropriate its revenue? Should it be spent on development and other non-vital federal projects or on eliminating the national debt by January 1, 1835? Adams stood on the wrong side of this question and, as a result, his prospects for reelection in 1828 were dim. More than a year before the upcoming campaign, the *New York Evening Post* bitterly attacked Adams's record, arguing that the reasons to deny him another term were "serious and insuperable." His program was "that of the famous Robert Walpole, that "*every man has his price.*"[65]

Finally, two matters are worth noting. First, several years later, in August 1835, Adams read Volume I of Horace Walpole's correspondence with Sir Horace Mann. He found the letters of 1741 and 1742 "very interesting" because they contained a "detailed account of the breaking up of the Ministry of Sir Robert Walpole." Horace Walpole, the minister's son, provided a "day to day" account of the "fall of a great man from power." The result was "a melancholy but instructive picture of human nature in the high political relations of society." Adams conclusion? "The picture has strong resemblance to others of which I have had more knowledge and experience."[66] Whom did Adams's have in mind? Himself? His father? Both of them?

Second, two years later Adams came close to admitting, in the privacy of his diary, that critics had been right about his determination to spend down the treasury but for reasons, of course, very different from what they had alleged:

"The great effort of my administration was to mature into a permanent and regular system the application of all the superfluous revenue of the Union into internal improvement which at this day would have afforded high wages and constant employment to hundreds of thousands of laborers, and in which every dollar expended would have repaid itself fourfold in the enhanced value of the public lands."[67]

FOUR

THE ACCESSION OF ANDREW JACKSON AND THE END OF INTERNAL IMPROVEMENTS

THE ELECTION OF 1828 WAS AN UGLY AFFAIR. ALTHOUGH important issues like internal improvements confronted the nation, smearing dominated the campaign. Jackson's supporters and their respective newspapers attacked Adams on the grounds that he had stolen the House election in 1825, that he remained a Federalist at heart, that he was a closet monarchist, a consolidationist, a spendthrift, and a threat to republican government. So corrupt was Adams, according to one tale, that while minister to Russia he had pimped for the Czar. The Democratic campaign focused on destroying Adams's reputation rather than addressing the issues and evaluating the president's job performance.

The Adams camp, styling themselves National Republicans, slung the mud back. It denounced Jackson as an ill-tempered, violence-prone murderer. It vilified him as an authoritarian military man who had no respect for traditional republican liberty and constitutional government. It alleged that Jackson's mother had been nothing more than a common prostitute and that Jackson was the offspring of her liaison with a black man. It claimed that Jackson's wife, Rachel, had married him while still married to another man and that she, therefore, was an immoral woman. Little serious discussion of the questions facing the nation elevated the political fight from the gutter.[1]

In the end Jackson, with 56% of the popular vote, won handily: 178 electoral votes to 83. The victory, however, was not merely the product of character assassination. The Democrats were far better organized than the National Republicans. They had launched their effort four years earlier, when the alleged "corrupt bargain" put Adams in the White House and an enraged Andrew Jackson, denouncing the "Judas of the West [Henry Clay]," allowed the Tennessee legislature to nominate him for president three years before the next election.[2] A true opposition party emerged during Adams's first two years and matured into a well-run machine at the state and local levels by the fall of 1826.[3] In a sense, Adams's cause was hopeless.

Nor did Adams use his office to his advantage. Because Clay's appointment to the State Department had provoked opposition and derision, Adams knew that using patronage to enhance his position would merely elicit additional charges that his administration was corrupting the constitutional order. Accordingly, he refused to dismiss civil servants—most especially John McLean at the Post Office Department—who were actively working for Jackson.[4] In effect, Adams helped his enemies win. As a result, by the end of the year he was preparing to move out of the White House.

At the same time General Jackson, at his plantation near Nashville, was preparing to relocate to Washington and to move into the White House. He had been born the same year as Adams, but age was one of very few things that the two had in common. Unlike Adams, the child of a prominent family who was raised in comfortable circumstances, Jackson was born on the South Carolina frontier and raised in hardship. His father had died before he was born, and his mother died when he was barely a teenager. They had owned little, if anything. Unlike Adams, Jackson had little formal education and, again, unlike Adams, whose travels took him to England, France, Russia, Prussia, and other European states, Jackson spent his early life and career in the American backcountry.[5] In western Tennessee in 1791 he married Rachel Robards, whom he deeply loved and whose divorce from her first husband he mistakenly believed (as she did too) had been legally finalized. (Here lay the origin of the 1828 attack on Rachel's morals.) In the meantime, Jackson ingratiated himself with powerful families and advanced politically, serving as Tennessee's first representative in 1796 and, subsequently, as one of its senators. But Jackson was more interested in making his fortune than in pursuing politics, and, after resigning his Senate seat, he devoted his time to buying and selling land and slaves, raising crops, and running a store. Little by little he established himself as a gentleman.

As an *arriviste* Jackson was acutely sensitive about his social status and defended his honor—violently—on several occasions. Two were especially notorious. In 1806 he killed a man in a duel and was himself severely wounded. In 1813, in a scrape with Thomas Hart Benton and his brother, Jackson was again shot and nearly died. (The future president carried bullets in his body for many years after these episodes.) His penchant for combat may have reflected in some unknowable way his interest in military service. He managed to get appointed Major General of Militia and, when war broke out in 1812, he scored a decisive victory over the Creeks at Horseshoe Bend and in January 1815, as Major General in the United States Army, over the British at New Orleans. (The news that a peace agreement had been signed at Ghent a month earlier had not yet reached the United States.) The latter triumph transformed him from a regional into a national hero. He was now as famous as John Quincy Adams. His subsequent adventures in Spanish Florida, which embroiled the Monroe administration in problems with England as well as Spain, perpetuated his reputation as a fearless, decisive, no-nonsense leader. Tennessee rewarded him with a seat in the United States Senate, where he was serving as the 1824 presidential election approached. He did not seek the presidency at that time, but others put his name forward, and his candidacy caught fire. Indeed, it knocked Secretary of War John C. Calhoun out of the contest, the South Carolinian content to settle for the vice presidency. Jackson enjoyed widespread popular support, while candidates Adams, Crawford, and Clay relied upon political insiders to make their way to the White House. With more and more states choosing presidential electors by popular vote, Jackson's esteem among the people conveyed on him a significant advantage. Yet the 1825 House election seemingly stifled the will of the people. Now all that had changed. In December 1828, Andrew Jackson was President-elect of the United States.[6]

Yet where Jackson stood on an important question like internal improvements was far from clear. On the one hand, for a long time he believed that the federal government could lawfully fund only projects that were manifestly national in scope and that states through which such projects ran had to approve.[7] Yet, on the other hand, as a senator Jackson voted for the General Survey bill, a government stock purchase in the Chesapeake and Delaware Canal Company, extension of the Cumberland Road from Canton to Zanesville in Ohio, and an appropriation of $50,000 to remove obstructions in the Mississippi River.[8] Apparently, Jackson's understanding of what was national and what was not lacked clear definition. According to Martin Van Buren, Jackson, before becoming president, had never made a "critical examination" of the constitutional question concerning internal improvements. In addition, he was reluctant to offend Pennsylvania, a state which played a major role in elevating him to the presidency and which strongly supported federally funded infrastructure projects.[9] How the new president addressed this issue remained to be seen.

Jackson's last several weeks at the Hermitage, his plantation, were far from easy. His health was an issue. He was exceedingly thin and frail, and he endured chronic pain from wounds and illnesses suffered long ago. He may have wondered if he would live out his term. Yet there was much to do. He had to arrange for the upkeep and profitable management of the property, the care and oversight of his slaves, the packing and shipment of clothing and various personal belongings to Washington, and, of course, his and Rachel's trip to the nation's capital, always an arduous journey even under the best of conditions. Rachel, meantime, seemed despondent.

Although preoccupied with these matters, Jackson nevertheless made time to consider the challenges that lay ahead and to determine what he hoped to accomplish. On December 9 he wrote a brief memorandum to himself and, possibly, Thomas Ritchie, the Richmond newspaper editor. This list, whether ranked in priority order or not, offers insight into Jackson's thinking as he prepared to assume the reins of government:

> 1rst. a strong constitutional att-genl [attorney general]
> 2nd. a genuine old fashioned Cabinet to act together and form a council consultative
> 3rd. no Edditors [*sic*] to be appointed
> 4th. No Members of Congress, except heads of Departments or Foreign ministers to be appointed
> 5th. no Foreign mission to be originated without the Senate etc. etc.
> 6th. The Public debt paid off, the Tariff modified and no power usurped over internal improvements
> 7th. a high minded enlightened principle in the administration of the Govt. as to appointments and removals. These things will give a brilliant career to the administration
> [Indorsement:] Memorandum of Points to be considered in the administration of the government: to be filed.[10]

While Jackson's "points" generally suggest the high priority he attached to federal appointments, item six specifically reveals the importance he imposed upon eliminating the national debt. It also reveals that Jackson connected the internal improvements issue as well as the tariff to the status of the national debt. For Jackson, it seems, debt freedom would require downward revision of the tariff but not provide the federal government *carte blanche* to spend revenues on infrastructure without respect to states' rights.

As Jackson prepared for the future, his wife's despondency, if not depression, persisted. The campaign had taken a severe toll on Rachel. The allegations of her immorality, spread through the public press as they were, weighed heavily upon her. A few days after the president-elect composed his "Memorandum of Points," she suffered a heart attack. Three days before Christmas she died. Jackson was beside himself with grief. His broken heart blamed the administration's attacks upon her character, and he held Adams and Clay responsible for the tragedy.[11] After Rachel's burial, Jackson observed a period of mourning that lasted several months.

Personal crisis notwithstanding, the duties of the presidency beckoned, and Jackson continued to prepare. Washingtonians expected him to arrive in the city on February 11, 1829, the day the House would officially count the electoral votes. Partisans organized a welcoming celebration for mid-morning, but Jackson, still grieving, "eluded" it by arriving four hours ahead of schedule. He settled into the Gadsby Hotel and conducted business from there.[12] At noon in the House chamber the Speaker, Andrew Stevenson of Virginia, "announced the special order of the day . . . the opening and counting of the votes for President and Vice-president."[13] The ritual affirmed what the nation had known for months: the Hero of New Orleans was elected president and John C. Calhoun reelected as vice president.[14] Neither, of course, attended. When the event ended, celebratory cannon fire, drum rolls, and cheering could be heard from a distance.[15]

The anticipation of change seemed universal. Even before Jackson arrived his supporters were pushing measures that they believed he was likely to champion. In January, Missouri senator Thomas Hart Benton reintroduced a bill that had died in committee the year before—a proposal to amend the Redemption Act of 1817, allowing the Sinking Fund Commission to, among other things, buy back the three percent debt from the Revolutionary era in the open market. That portion of the national debt, more than $13,000,000, Benton said, had acquired "the character of perpetuity" which was "abhorrent to the American notions of public debt. . . ."[16] He also justified his recommendation on the grounds that "a public debt is a public burthen, and that the present debt of the United States is a burthen upon the People of the United States to the amount of more than fifteen millions of dollars per annum; from which they ought to be relieved as soon as possible, and may be relieved in four years, by a 'timely' and 'judicious' application of the means within the power of Congress."[17] Debate took up much of the following week, and Benton's proposals were finally sent to the Finance Committee.[18] Yet there was reason to be hopeful. Was not Andrew Jackson in favor of ridding the nation of debt?

In the House Jackson's supporters also raised the matter of the debt. On February 25, for example, a week before the inauguration, the representatives debated a pension bill for veterans of militia service during the War for Independence. George McDuffie, a Jackson man, moved to recommit the bill because of "the probable effect" of the cost on "the extinguishment of the public debt." He explained that "there was no one point on which public opinion was more completely and definitely settled, than this: that it was a matter of primary importance to pay off the public debt; and he put it to the friends of that policy which had brought into power the coming administration, whether they could consent, by passing such a bill as this, completely to defeat the great and primary measure which gave character to that policy and to that administration." To McDuffie this was hardly the moment for the friends of the incoming administration to abandon retrenchment. "General Jackson," he added. "had been elected to the high station he was soon to occupy, under what may almost be called a pledge to devote the resources of the nation to the extinction of the public debt."[19] Subsequent discussion focused on the need to pay the moral debt owed to surviving militiamen as opposed to the need to pay the public debt. In the end the defenders of the moral debt won; the militia pension bill passed the House by a vote of 111 to 67.[20] Nevertheless, the public debt was clearly on the minds of legislators as the lame duck twentieth Congress prepared to adjourn on the eve of Inauguration Day. It was also clear that many of Jackson's supporters believed that eliminating the debt represented the will of the people and that the administration of government was about to pass into the hands of the man many were already calling "the People's President."[21]

After several days of inclement weather that left the capital slushy and muddy, Inauguration Day, March 4, 1829, dawned brisk but sunny. Thousands had arrived in the preceding days to witness and participate in the elevation of the Old Hero to the presidency. As the People's President, Jackson declined a carriage and honor guard and walked like everyone else to the Capitol. For the first time the inaugural address and swearing-in ceremony were held outdoors, beneath the great portico. Everyone in the great throng could see General Jackson, his long, silver-white hair gleaming in the sun and distinguishing him from the others on the platform. This democratization of the presidential inauguration event went only so far, however. Only those in the rows nearest to him could hear his remarks.[22]

Jackson briefly outlined his duties as president and then explained "the principles of action" that would guide him in fulfilling his responsibilities. He would adhere to "the limitations as well as the extent of the Executive power" defined in the Constitution. Next, he would "preserve peace" and "cultivate friendship" with other countries. Finally, he would demonstrate "proper respect" for the rights of the states.[23] Then he addressed government finance, devoting as much time to it as to the preceding four matters. "The management of the public revenue . . . is among the most delicate and important trusts" in any government and will "demand no inconsiderable share of my official solicitude." He pledged to control spending. "Under every aspect in which it can be considered it would appear that advantage must result from the observance of a strict and faithful economy." Careful and prudent spending was important "because it will facilitate the extinguishment of the national debt, the unnecessary duration of which is incompatible with real independence, and because it will counteract that tendency to public and private profligacy which a profuse expenditure of money by the Government is but too apt to engender."[24] In other words, public indebtedness was inconsistent with the political and moral values of republicanism. He would not be alone, he asserted, in pursuing economy in government. "Powerful auxiliaries to the attainment of this desirable end are to be found in the regulations provided by the wisdom of Congress for the specific appropriation of public money and the prompt accountability of public officers."[25]

Recognizing that the tariff and internal improvements were controversial issues bearing upon the condition of the treasury, Jackson nonetheless devoted only one sentence to each. With respect to the latter his one-liner was innocuous: "Internal improvement and the diffusion of knowledge, so far as they can be promoted by the constitutional acts of the Federal Government, are of high importance."[26] Essentially tautological, the remark suggests that Van Buren was right, that Jackson had not yet taken a clear position on internal improvements. On the other hand, although the comment said nothing, contrasted with what Adams had said about internal improvements in his inaugural and first message to Congress, the statement spoke volumes.

Near the end of the speech Jackson promised to maintain only a small professional military and to develop a "humane" policy toward Native Americans. Lastly, he declared that "public sentiment" imposed upon his "list of Executive duties . . . the task of *reform.*" Jackson meant "the correction of those abuses that have brought the patronage of the Federal Government into conflict with the freedom of elections."[27] Having jabbed at the "corrupt bargain," he swore to appoint to office diligent and talented men who were committed to "the advancement of the public service."[28] At the conclusion, Chief Justice Marshall administered the oath of office, and it was time to celebrate.

The traditionally exclusive White House party became an open-house event. The crowd followed the president, now on horseback, to the other end of Pennsylvania Avenue. It surged into the executive mansion. Rugs were muddied and furniture damaged as a great crush of humanity pushed to get to the refreshments. The Old Hero escaped from the rear of the building to avoid injury.[29] The administration of Andrew Jackson had begun.

The disorder at the White House on Inauguration Day reflected the disorder that characterized the first months of the administration. Despite his inaugural pledge to appoint only men of talent, Jackson's cabinet, with the exception of Martin Van Buren at the State Department, inspired little confidence.[30] Samuel D. Ingham at the Treasury, William T. Barry at the Post Office, and the others seemed in over their heads. Even some diehard Jacksonians worried that the administration set itself up to fail.[31]

The most controversial of the appointments was John H. Eaton as secretary of war. Two months before Jackson's inauguration, Eaton, the president's longtime friend and former Senate colleague from Tennessee, married the young and beautiful Peggy O'Neill Timberlake, daughter of a Washington hotel and tavern keeper and recent widow. Rumor had it that Eaton had been involved with her while her husband, a United States Navy officer, was overseas; that Peggy had become pregnant but aborted the baby; and that Timberlake, who died while on duty abroad, had actually killed himself after learning of his wife's affair with the Tennessean.

The ensuing scandal distracted the president as he tried to put his administration in motion. First of all, it divided Jackson's inner circle because several cabinet wives refused to associate with Peggy Eaton and excluded her and the secretary of war from the dinner parties and other social events that characterized the lifestyle of high Washington society. Moreover, Floride Calhoun, the vice president's wife, allegedly was the ringleader of the collective social snub. Jackson, however, who had known Peggy in his Senate days, believed that her character was under attack for political reasons in much the same way that Rachel's had been a year earlier. He defended Peggy and Secretary Eaton. This situation was the first, albeit not the most serious, of events and circumstances that poisoned the relationship between John C. Calhoun and the president over the next few years. At the same time, the Eaton scandal elevated Martin Van Buren's standing with Jackson because, at least in part, the secretary of state, a widower, was free from spousal pressure to avoid Peggy Eaton. Instead, like Jackson, he defended her, socialized with her, and accorded her the respect that the president believed she deserved. In short, as Calhoun's stock with the president sank, Van Buren's rose. The resulting Calhoun-Van Buren rivalry for the succession became a central element of both national and Democratic Party politics during the Jackson era.[32]

The Eaton scandal distracted the administration for many months but hardly paralyzed it. Work moved forward. The president's inaugural pledge to find qualified appointees proved more successful at the middle management levels of the government departments than at cabinet rank. Jackson began removing executive branch employees who had their hands in the federal till or who were Adams loyalists. Many in the civil service lost their jobs or lived in fear of losing them. Here was the "reform" he had promised, and he subsequently defended his action on the ground that "rotation in office" was more consistent with democratic and republican values than the prevailing system within which office holding had become "a species of property."[33] Careerism in public service promoted individual interest over public interest while broad participation served the common good. Jobs in the departments of the United States government, he believed, were simple enough that anyone with reasonable intelligence could perform them.[34] The reform in patronage proceeded vigorously.

Yet the other reform to which Jackson was deeply committed, as were his supporters in Congress, was the elimination of the national debt. He reported on the progress in debt reduction in his first message to Congress, December 8, 1829. During the preceding year, he said, the debt had been reduced by more than $12,400,000, and that on January 1, 1830, only three weeks hence, the remaining debt would amount to $48,565,406.50. "This state of the finances exhibits the resources of the nation in an aspect highly flattering to its industry and auspicious of the ability of Government in a very short time to extinguish the public debt."[35] Only good things, he believed, would flow from this accomplishment. "When this shall be done our population will be relieved from a considerable portion of its present burthens, and will find not only new motives for patriotic affection, but additional means for the display of individual enterprise. The fiscal power of the States will also be increased, and may be more extensively exerted in favor of education and other public objects, while ample means will remain in the Federal Government to promote the general weal in all the modes permitted to its authority."[36] After debt freedom, Jackson asserted, the treasury would enjoy annual surpluses regardless of any tariff revision, presenting Congress "a subject for . . . serious deliberation."[37] He personally hoped that their distribution to the states, according to their "ratio of representation," would avoid the constitutional and other difficulties associated with federally-funded internal improvements.[38] If, however, the federal government lacked authority to distribute surpluses to the states, then he recommended amending the fundamental law to permit it.[39] In this way, the nation would enjoy the benefits of improved "inland navigation and the construction of highways" without the usual disputes and, implicitly, without forcing the national government to raise taxes or to borrow.[40]

Yet Jackson advocated scratching internal improvements from the national agenda for another important practical reason. The seemingly endless and bitter debates about the propriety of federal funding had been costly; "harmony," Jackson said, had been lost "in the legislative councils."[41] The internal improvements issue remained very much alive, and he was eager to promote conciliation. In both chambers of the new twenty-first Congress strong support for infrastructure development existed. Many Jacksonians from the western states, for example, wanted more, not less, federal internal improvement. Jackson himself did not articulate where he stood on the matter, perhaps because he had not yet taken a clear position. At the very least he simply wanted to remove it from discussion in order to avoid dividing his majorities in the House and Senate against themselves. Unity seemed vital for administration success. At the same time many in Congress remembered Jackson's Senate record on internal improvements. What would President Jackson do if presented with an internal improvement bill? Would he sign or veto it? Jackson's message to Congress left the answer to those questions unclear.

During Jackson's first year in office Congress addressed a number of internal improvement proposals. The most ambitious of these aimed at building a road from Buffalo to New Orleans via the nation's capital. When he introduced the bill in the House in March 1830, Joseph Hemphill of Pennsylvania described the undertaking as "emphatically national" in character and offered as his first defense of the expenditure the assurance that "it is not the design of the friends of national improvements to interfere with the annual extinguishment of the public debt. . . . The regular operation of existing laws will soon clear the nation of debt. The exertions of statesmen towards the accomplishment of this object are no longer required."[42] Forthcoming surpluses, in other words, would soon cover internal improvement expenses. This perspective did not, however, enjoy universal approval. P. P. Barbour of Virginia did not let Hemphill go unchallenged, arguing that if tariff revenues were reduced to match government's operating expenses, then there would be no surplus.[43]

The Buffalo-New Orleans Road bill failed passage in the House, but other infrastructure bills succeeded and passed the Senate also. Of these the most significant, as it turned out, was a measure authorizing the treasury to buy $150,000 worth of stock shares in a company constructing a road from Maysville, Kentucky, located on the Ohio River, to Lexington. The entire highway, in other words, would lie in Henry Clay's home state. For this reason the bill had political as well as other implications. For advice Jackson consulted with Martin Van Buren.

The secretary of state evaluated the Maysville measure politically, as an effort to entrap Jackson. If the president signed the bill into law, approving a project within one state, then the opposition would "saddle" him "with the latitudinarian notions" of the discredited Adams administration. On the other hand, if Jackson vetoed the bill, Jacksonian supporters of internal improvements would join the opposition. Van Buren, however, saw a solution to the dilemma. "I think I see land," he wrote Jackson, "and that it will be in our power to serve the Country and at the same time counteract the machinations" of the opposition.[44] He advised the president to review the secretary of the treasury's most recent financial statement.

Jackson reexamined Samuel D. Ingham's treasury report of December 14, 1829. Section III estimated revenues for 1830 at slightly more than $28,250,000 and expenditures at approximately $23,755,525. Accordingly, the anticipated balance in the treasury on January 1, 1831, amounted to $4,494,545.[45] Yet this amount was inflated. The Redemption Act of 1817 required two million dollars from the estimated surplus to be transferred to the Sinking Fund and applied to the debt. Ingham did not make the subtraction, which actually left an anticipated balance of $2,494,545.[46] Moreover, section II of Ingham's report stated that $2,457,173 of expenses incurred in 1829 were payable in 1830, but the secretary did not subtract that amount from the projected balance either.[47] In fact, the true surplus at the end of 1830 would amount to a mere $37,372. Appropriating $150,000 to purchase Maysville Road stock would create a deficit, and deficit spending, of course, contradicted debt reduction. Here was the "land" that Van Buren saw. The Maysville Road measure and others passed by Congress threatened to realize the financial situation that the Adams program had threatened.

Jackson understood and would have none of it. He complained that "appropriations now exceed the available funds in the Treasury, and the estimates always exceed the real amount available."[48] He wrote Van Buren:

> The people expected reform retrenchment and economy in the administration of this Government. This was the cry from Maine to Louisiana, and instead of these the great object of Congress, *it would seem,* is to make mine one of the most extravagant administrations since the commencement of the Government. This must not be; the Federal Constitution must be obeyed, State-rights preserved, our national debt *must be paid, direct taxes and loans avoided* and the Federal union preserved. These are the objects I have in view, and regardless of all consequences, will carry into effect.[49]

At first congressional supporters of internal improvements did not expect presidential opposition to the Maysville bill, on account of both the popularity of the projects and Jackson's voting record as a senator.[50] But rumors began to circulate that Jackson was going to exercise the veto, causing anxiety among western friends of the administration. Consequently, the latter "induced" the gregarious Richard M. Johnson of Kentucky—Van Buren called him "the friend of the human race"—one of Jackson's old friends, to go to the White House and "sound the President" out on the Maysville Road bill.[51] If Johnson perceived a "danger" of a veto, he was instructed "to remonstrate with him, in their names and his own, against a *veto.*"[52] Johnson, uncomfortable with the assignment he had agreed to undertake, at first procrastinated. But finally he mustered the courage and paid his visit to the executive mansion, arriving while Jackson and Van Buren were alone studying Ingham's treasury report. Johnson explained that he was calling "at the instance of many friends" to "have some conversation . . . upon a very delicate subject" and that he was apprehensive that he might cause offense. The president assured Johnson of his "unqualified confidence" in him and encouraged the Kentuckian to speak freely.[53] Johnson did, and the following scene unfolded:

Johnson: General! If this hand were an anvil on which the sledge hammer of the smith were descending and a fly were to light upon it in time to receive the blow he would not crush it more effectively than you will crush your friends in Kentucky if you veto that Bill!

Jackson quickly rose from his chair and moved toward Johnson. Johnson also got up and moved toward Jackson.

Jackson: Sir, have you looked at the condition of the Treasury—at the amount of money that it contains—at the appropriations already made by Congress—at the amount of other unavoidable claims upon it?

Johnson: No! General, I have not! But there has always been money enough to satisfy appropriations and I do not doubt there will be now!

Jackson: Well, I have, and this is the result. . . .

Jackson then summarized the substance of the Ingham report.

Jackson: . . . and you see there is no money to be expended as my friends desire. Now, I stand committed before the Country to pay off the National Debt, at the earliest practicable moment; this pledge I am determined to redeem, and I cannot do this if I consent to encrease [*sic*] it without necessity. Are you willing—are my friends willing to lay taxes to pay for internal improvements?—for be assured I will not borrow a cent except in cases of absolute necessity!

Johnson: No! . . . [T]hat would be worse than a *veto!*

Johnson picked up a green bag he had carried with him and prepared to depart. Van Buren stopped him, explaining that the Kentuckian should not conclude from the conversation that a veto was inevitable.[54] Jackson added that the matter was still under consideration and that no decision had yet been made.[55] Johnson understood the point of these remarks: not to tell the western supporters of the administration that the Maysville Road bill was doomed. He complied, explaining to his western friends that Jackson was still studying the bill. But Johnson knew that "nothing less than a voice from Heaven would prevent the old man from vetoing the Bill."[56]

❦

God did not call upon Andrew Jackson with regard to the Maysville Road. The veto came down on May 27, 1830. Predictably, the president declared the bill unconstitutional because the proposed road was local and not national in character.[57] The constitutional argument, of course, represented the highest intellectual, moral, and legal ground upon which to stand. But it was not the only ground available to him. He also invoked the state of the public finances—the flip side of the constitutional coin—to justify vetoing the Maysville Road bill. In view of his commitment to discharge the national debt, for Jackson the financial may have been the more compelling reason to veto the measure.

The president reminded Congress that, barring an emergency and any "unusual diversion" from the Sinking Fund, the national debt would be extinguished "in the short period of four years."[58] Yet, "[t]he extent to which this pleasing anticipation [national debt freedom] is dependent upon the policy which may be pursued in relation to measures of the character of the one now under consideration [the Maysville Road bill] must be obvious to all."[59] Developments in the current Congress, he asserted, would inevitably call the public's attention to the status of the national debt. With reference to the treasury's report of 1829, which he appended to his message, "it appears that the bills which have passed into laws, and those which in all probability will pass . . . anticipate appropriations which, with the ordinary expenditures for the support of Government, will exceed considerably the amount in the Treasury for the year 1830."[60] Total appropriations, Jackson claimed, exceeded anticipated treasury receipts by more than ten million dollars.[61] Without restraint on spending, the government could not meet its bills "unless the payment of the national debt be postponed and the means now pledged to that object applied to those enumerated in these bills."[62] Delaying national debt freedom by raiding the Sinking Fund was, to Jackson, unacceptable. So, too, was the imposition of new taxes, but to these unpleasant realities—debt and/or taxes—bills like the Maysville Road led. "Without a well-regulated system of internal improvement this exhausting mode of appropriation is not likely to be avoided, and the plain consequence must be either a continuance of the national debt or a resort to additional taxes."[63] Jackson knew that Americans wanted neither. "Will not the people demand, as they have a right to do, such a prudent system of expenditure as will pay the debts of the Union and authorize the reduction of every tax to as low a point" as possible?[64]

Four days later, Jackson vetoed a stock subscription in the Washington Turnpike Road Company. For his reasons he referred Congress to the Maysville veto.[65] Shortly afterward he pocket-vetoed a bill for lighthouse construction and harbor improvement as well as a stock subscription in the Louisville and Portland Canal Company.[66]

Jackson's policy clearly enjoyed support. More than a week before the Maysville veto, the *Cayuga Patriot* commented: "We should suppose a remedy might be found" for future surpluses "without squandering the money in visionary projects. First pay off every cent of the national debt. . . ."[67] After the veto a reader wrote to the *United States' Telegraph,* praising Jackson for "opposing a system the corrupting influence of which must ere long have sapped the foundation of our Government."[68]

❧

Henry Clay, then enduring a forced but temporary retirement from public life, dismissed the notion that the Maysville Road bill had any bearing at all on the national debt.[69] But Jackson was far more attuned to the mood of the American people than Henry Clay ever was. Jackson's veto message subtly addressed the hopes, fears, and interests of ordinary Americans, including not only their patriotism but their money as well. Everyone wanted, Jackson admitted, internal improvements, "but few . . . are unmindful of the means by which they should be promoted; none certainly are so degenerate as to desire their success at the cost of that sacred instrument with the preservation of which is indissolubly bound our country's hopes."[70] In other words, as desirable as internal improvements were, Americans would not sacrifice the Constitution to secure them. There was also a financial dimension to the president's observation. By adhering strictly to the Constitution, Americans would neither bear the tax burden imposed by the national debt any longer than necessary nor confront any new taxes. Jackson knew that, given the choice, Americans would prefer inexpensive government to expensive government-funded roads and canals. This was clearly the case, as the heated internal improvements debates in Congress during the Adams years demonstrated.

Yet, as those same debates revealed, individual congressional districts, even in the new western states, wanted their own projects enacted but opposed those of their neighbors.[71] Each wanted the benefits of improvement but wanted others to pay for them. This unpleasant and embarrassing reality could not be cloaked in patriotic sentiment. Accordingly, Jackson was less than frank when he addressed this aspect of the internal improvement issue: "If different impressions are entertained in any quarter; if it is expected that the people of this country, reckless of their constitutional obligations, will prefer their local interest to the principles of the Union, such expectations will in the end be disappointed; or if it be not so, then indeed has the world but little to hope from the example of free government."[72] In other words, state and local communities could not reasonably anticipate that the entire nation would pay for their roads and canals. If, however, the federal treasury did pay the bills, then republicanism was doomed—because public indebtedness would be increasingly prolonged, more and more taxes needed to deal with it, and corruption would eat away at the constitutional checks and balances. State and local communities could not have both debt freedom *and* federally funded roads and canals.

The Maysville veto promised national debt freedom and fewer taxes. It appealed to patriotic sentiment and to self-interest. In a short time it defused internal improvements as an explosive political issue.[73] Subsequently, the prime movers behind infrastructure development were the individual states and the private sector. For all practical purposes, the government of the United States was out of the development business. A key element of Henry Clay's American System, for good or for ill, was erased from the national policy agenda.

FIVE

JACKSON, THE BANK WAR, AND THE NATIONAL DEBT

THE BANK OF THE UNITED STATES, OF COURSE, ANOTHER KEY element of the American System, remained in business. But Jackson's accession to the presidency raised anxiety in some quarters concerning the bank's future. The Old Hero's skepticism about banks in general and the Bank of the United States in particular was as widely known as his determination to pay down the national debt. What would Jackson's policy toward the Bank of the United States be, especially since its charter was due to expire in 1836, a year after the anticipated elimination of the debt?

The second Bank of the United States, it will be recalled, chartered by Congress in 1816, was modeled on—but not a clone of—its Hamiltonian predecessor (1791–1811). It was partly government-owned (the United States held 20% of its stock); it was incorporated for twenty years and capitalized at $35,000,000; it provided a national currency; it served as depository for federal funds; it controlled inflation by restraining note issues by state banks; through its numerous branches it extended loans for commercial and industrial enterprises throughout the nation; and it served as the federal government's fiscal agent, which, among other responsibilities, included meeting interest and principal payments on the national debt as they fell due. In short, the Bank of the United States functioned much like a central bank and provided the government special services plus payment of a $1,500,000 bonus in exchange for the privilege of holding, interest free and for profit, federal revenues. After the Panic of 1819, the Bank of the United States created a stable monetary environment for economic growth.[1] Much of the bank's success was attributable to the leadership and administrative skills of its third president, Nicholas Biddle.

Born in 1786 to a prominent Philadelphia family, Biddle had been a precocious youngster. In 1801, for example, at the age of fifteen, he earned a degree from Princeton. He subsequently served in the United States diplomatic corps, and while in Europe became fascinated with ancient Greek history and culture and aspired to scholarship in those subjects. But back in Pennsylvania he practiced law, engaged in state politics, and in 1821 was appointed by President Monroe to the board of directors of the Bank of the United States. Two years later, because of his intelligence, knowledge, and apparent banking expertise, the board elected him president. To some he seemed arrogant and aloof; to others he seemed supremely self-confident. Few, however, doubted his ability to manage effectively the huge financial institution entrusted to his administration. Under his leadership the Bank of the United States enjoyed good relationships with both the Monroe and Adams administrations.[2] The question now was: would harmony characterize the relationship between the bank and the Jackson administration?

In late November 1828, this question worried the outgoing Adams administration. Indeed, for this reason, Treasury Secretary Rush informed Biddle that he intended to "take some notice of your Bank" in his final report to Congress. Such editorializing, he said, was unprecedented in Treasury Department reports—"never yet been done."[3] Naturally, Biddle was grateful. He thanked the secretary, suggesting that the bank "might be appropriately introduced at that part of the report, which will . . . state the amount of debt extinguished during the last four years." Biddle wanted Rush to emphasize the bank's active and efficient role in debt reduction. "It would then be satisfactory to add, that the whole of this amount [total debt reduction during Adams's administration], in addition to the ordinary receipts & disbursements, . . . are transferred to the several points where the public debt is payable, & actually disbursed for that purpose without the delay of amount, or the expense of a dollar—or the slightest risk—the Bank being responsible for the conduct of the agents. . . ." Biddle noted that this arrangement was very different from the one in England where "the Gov[t] pay more than a million of dollars annually for the management of its debt by the Bank of England." Put simply, from the bank the government secured debt reduction free of charges. Biddle also urged Rush to explain how the Bank of the United States paid down the public debt without wild and unpredictable expansions and contractions in the money market. "What is scarcely less important is, that from the arrangements made by the Bank for these payments [to creditors], the inconvenience of a great accumulation of money in the vaults of the Gov[t] followed by an immediate distribution of it is entirely obviated." Biddle wanted to be clear how the Bank of the United States reduced the national debt without provoking financial chaos. "The Bank as the period of payment approaches, anticipates in the form of discounts the disbursement of a considerable portion of the Stock—and the rest becomes absorbed in the mass of its operations so that many millions are paid on a given day, without the slightest previous pressure," or any aftershock in the marketplace.[4] The bank, in other words, raised interest rates and curtailed the volume of its loans to accommodate the payouts. Biddle sought to curry favor with the incoming administration by linking the Bank of the United States to efficient elimination of the national debt.

Secretary Rush, of course, was more than willing to help. That had been his purpose in raising the matter with Biddle in the first place. Accordingly, he accepted Biddle's suggestions. His report to Congress, December 6, 1828, stated that the national debt "will claim the first attention" because "[s]uch is the interest which the nation is known to take in its extinguishment, that what is done at the treasury . . . cannot be too distinctly set forth." Rush provided a lengthy review of the progress made in debt reduction under the Adams administration. The exposition was objective, detailed, and demonstrative of the outgoing administration's commitment to debt elimination. But this portion of the report was as much a political statement as it was financial. The document aligned the outgoing administration with what was, presumably, a primary goal of the incoming Jackson administration, implying that both shared common ground on the debt question. Rush linked the Bank of the United States to successful debt reduction. "The department," he wrote, "feels an obligation of duty to bear its testimony, founded on constant experience" during the preceding four years "to the useful instrumentality of" the Bank of the United States "in all the most important fiscal operations of the nation." He was quite specific regarding debt payments. "In faithful obedience to the conditions of its charter, and aided by its branches, it has afforded the necessary facilities for transferring the public moneys from place to place, concentrating them at the point required. In this manner, all payments on account of the public debt, whether for interest or principal . . . in any part of the Union, have been punctually met."[5]

Would Rush's affirmation of the bank's vital role in debt reduction protect it as the executive office changed hands? Biddle seemed to think so, or at least claimed he did. Shortly before Christmas the Bank of the United States president wrote: "I do not incline to fear anything for the Bank from the change of administration. Mr. Rush's excellent report sets the seal upon that question, & I should think that no administration would venture to set the monied concerns of the country afloat as they once were. When we see who is to be our new Secy of Treasy, we can consider seriously the application for a renewal" of the bank's charter.[6] The new secretary, of course, turned out to be Samuel D. Ingham, a staunch Jacksonian but a fellow Pennsylvanian.

In his inaugural address, it will be recalled, Jackson had pledged his administration to debt extinction. In addition, he had made brief and non-controversial comments about the tariff and internal improvements. Yet he ignored the Bank of the United States altogether, referring to it neither directly nor indirectly.[7] What did the omission mean? Had Rush's endorsement of the bank based on debt reduction had no effect?

The answer to this question began to emerge in the summer of 1829. The Bank of the United States unexpectedly faced allegations by Jackson partisans that during the presidential campaign several of its branch banks had engaged in anti-Jackson politics. Secretary Ingham served as the administration's point man in confronting the bank. Various investigations ensued. The bank repeatedly denied that any of its officers at any of its branches had engaged in party politics in 1828.[8]

In the autumn Biddle, growing nervous, attempted to ingratiate himself and the bank with the administration. His tactic reworked the approach he had made through Richard Rush the year before. He again played to Jackson's determination to extinguish the national debt, but this time with a twist. He informed William B. Lewis, Jackson's close friend and advisor, that he had a plan to eliminate the debt in 1833, two years ahead of schedule. The proposal entailed "sinking or paying off the three per cent Stock" still outstanding from the Revolutionary era.[9] Lewis's response was encouraging. He wrote

Henry Toland, a Pennsylvania representative and friend of the bank president, "If you see Mr. Biddle say to him the President would be glad to see his proposition" regarding the debt. Lewis suggested that Biddle "write to me" about the plan and "I will submit it to the General." Lewis was optimistic, noting: "I think we will find the *old fellow* will do justice to the Bank in his [annual] message [to Congress] for the handsome manner in which it assisted the Gov^{t} in paying the last instalment of the National Debt."[10]

Biddle, of course, complied and sent the plan. What precisely did it provide? Biddle's proposal, as clever as it was simple, required the government to sell all its bank stock to the Bank of the United States itself at a profit of $1,500,000. In addition, the Bank of the United States, presuming recharter, would pay the government a bonus of $1,500,000, as it did in 1816. In return the government would pay the bank half the total of the unfunded three percent debt from the revolution, or $6,648,124. The Bank of the United States would then assume responsibility to pay the entire three percent debt, or $13,296,249.45. According to Biddle's calculation, subsequently confirmed by Secretary Ingham, the government would not only save more than $3,648,000 over the following four years but also witness the total extinction of the national debt by March 4, 1833, which just happened to be inauguration day for whomever was elected president in 1832—possibly, of course, Jackson himself. Nor would the bank suffer a loss by this process. According to Biddle, once the plan was fully implemented the Bank of the United States would earn more than $1,300,000. All interests involved—the general public, the government, its creditors, and the Bank of the United States—gained.[11]

Events unfolded quickly. Lewis presented the Biddle plan to Jackson, who forwarded it to Secretary Ingham for review and evaluation. While the president awaited the treasury secretary's report, Biddle decided to lobby personally in its favor and for recharter, which the bonus feature of the plan implied. He traveled to Washington in late November for a conference with Old Hickory at the White House. Biddle, who wrote a memorandum sometime after the meeting, recalled the conversation this way.[12]

Jackson: "I was very thankful to you for your plan of paying off the debt sent to Major Lewis."

Biddle: "I thought it was my duty to submit it to you."

Jackson: "I would have no difficulty in recommending it to Congress, but I think it right to be perfectly frank with you—I do not think the power of Congress extends to charter a Bank out of the ten mile square [the District of Columbia]. I do not dislike your Bank any more than all Banks."

Here was the rub. Jackson's comment about the debt plan, followed by his "frank" opinion concerning congressional power, was no *non sequitur*. While Jackson might not oppose a plan for early elimination of the national debt, Biddle's proposal entailed recharter of the bank. For Jackson this element posed a problem. Why commit to a fifteen- or twenty-year recharter of the Bank of the United States in exchange for eliminating the debt in 1833? After all, one way or another the debt was going to be eliminated in 1835. Jackson, in effect, told Biddle that the price of his plan was too high, but Biddle, it seems, did not grasp the meaning of the president's indirection.

The interview did not end there.

Jackson: "I feel very sensibly the services rendered by the Bank at the last payment of the national debt & shall take an opportunity of declaring it publicly in my message to Congress."

After a brief digression concerning the alleged partisanship of some bank officers during the presidential race, conversation continued:

Biddle: "Well I am very much gratified at this frank explanation. We shall all be proud of any kind mention in the message."

Jackson: "Sir . . . it would be only an act of justice to mention it."[13]

Biddle left the meeting feeling optimistic. The president had pledged to commend the Bank of the United States for its role in debt reduction. In fact, ground for optimism expanded not long after the conference. In November, Secretary Ingham completed his evaluation of the Biddle plan and reported to Jackson that "I am satisfied of the practicability of the operation."[14] Biddle likely knew the substance of Ingham's assessment. Had his effort to link debt elimination with charter renewal worked? The president's message to Congress revealed the answer.

Jackson's first annual message, December 8, 1829, addressed, like all such reports, a wide variety of matters affecting the state of the union. The portion of the message which dealt with national finance informed Congress that in 1829 the national debt had been reduced by nearly $12,500,000. As a consequence, the remaining debt amounted to $48,565,406.50. Jackson observed: "The payment on account of public debt made on the 1st of July last was $8,715,462.87. It was apprehended that the sudden withdrawal of so large a sum from the banks in which it was deposited, at a time of unusual pressure in the money market, might cause much injury to the interests dependent upon bank accommodations." Then he added: "But this evil was wholly averted by an early anticipation of it at the Treasury, aided by the judicious arrangements of the officers of the Bank of the United States."[15] Here was the president's commendation. Jackson had kept his word. But the praise was lukewarm at best, because Treasury, not the Bank of the United States, was accorded primary credit for avoiding turbulence in the money market when principal and interest payments were made in July. The Bank of the United States, in other words, assisted in securing but did not accomplish this goal. Its role was subsidiary, a mere agent. Jackson's judgment turned Richard Rush's assessment a year earlier upside down.

The president's tepid commendation of the Bank of the United States was consistent with his remarks at the end of the message. "The charter of the Bank of the United States expires in 1836," he pointed out, "and its stockholders will most probably apply for a renewal of their privileges." Renewing the bank, he declared, was a matter "involving such important principles" that the national legislature needed to address the issue "soon." He claimed that "a large portion of" American citizens "well questioned" the constitutionality and expediency of the bank, and he asserted that the institution had "failed" to provide the nation a uniform and stable currency. True or not, these were serious allegations, and Jackson concluded by suggesting that perhaps an entirely new bank could be established—one which avoided constitutional objections and which fulfilled the tasks "expected . . . from the present bank."[16]

Finally, for Biddle at least, what the president did not say must have been as powerful as what he did say. The message contained no reference to Biddle's plan to extinguish the national debt two years ahead of schedule.

The message within the president's annual message could not have been clearer. Jackson had no intention of trading debt extinction advanced by two years for rechartering the bank for a decade and a half or two. Jackson remained hostile to the Bank of the United States, and its future stood in jeopardy. Two days after the message, Alexander Hamilton Jr., son of the distinguished treasury secretary, wrote Biddle and, ridiculing the Bank of the United States president's earlier optimism, bluntly spelled out the problem he faced. "If . . . you had not appeared quite so confident in your conclusions [about the bank's future], I should have endeavoured to prove, that you were under a delusion. The die is now cast; it therefore, only remains for you, to make the best of an unpromising cause." Hamilton asked an obvious question: "Under these circumstances, do you not think it would be very unwise policy to make any application to Congress [for recharter] . . . at the present session?"[17] There could be only one response, and Biddle replied quickly: "We have never had any idea of applying to Congress for a renewal of the Charter at the present session—and of course should abstain from doing so now."[18] Biddle had little choice but to bide his time.

Throughout 1830 Biddle waited and worried. From time to time, however, he acted personally or through intermediaries to influence the administration. In May, for example, he wrote to William B. Lewis that "it would be exceedingly gratifying to know the feelings of the president towards the Bank at the present moment" because of widespread concern that he might veto a recharter bill. Biddle was hoping that in the interval since the annual message Jackson had had "an opportunity of examing [*sic*] more attentively the effects & operations of the Institution" and "of witnessing its utility to the finances of the Government."[19] In August he appealed to Josiah Nichol of the Nashville branch bank, a personal friend of Jackson, to insinuate to the president that his next annual message provided "a fair opportunity" to alleviate national anxiety over the bank's future. He stressed the bank's role in debt reduction. "In his next message he will be able to state that since his last message nearly 10 millions of principal of the public Debt were paid off in January and July. In his last message he was kind enough to speak with approbation of the agency of the Bank in making that payment without the least inconvenience to the Country. Now, . . . he should renew the expression of that approbation. . . . This is a very . . . easy thing to do."[20]

In the meantime, Congress addressed the Bank issue as the president had requested. The Senate Finance Committee filed a report on March 29, 1830, refuting Jackson's comments about the currency, and the House Ways and Means Committee reported on April 13, reaffirming the constitutionality and expediency of the Bank of the United States.[21] In May, the House quickly tabled a resolution by Robert Potter of North Carolina, which criticized the Bank of the United States and asserted that the lower chamber would oppose charter renewal.[22] The bank's friends controlled Congress.

While circumstances in the legislature may have reassured Biddle, the president's second annual message did not. Once again Jackson questioned the propriety of renewing the bank's charter, this time with no commendation for the bank's role in debt reduction. "The importance of the principles involved in the inquiry whether it will be proper to recharter the Bank of the United States requires that I should again call the attention of Congress to the subject." He continued: "Nothing has occurred to lessen . . . the dangers which many of our citizens apprehend from that institution as at present organized." He then outlined various ideas for altering the bank "to obviate constitutional and other objections," such as stripping the bank of incorporated status, making it a branch of the Treasury Department, and several other possibilities. These were not "recommendations,"

Jackson said, but merely a way of "calling the attention of Congress to the possible modifications of a system which can not continue to exist in its present form without occasional collisions with the local authorities and perpetual apprehension and discontent on the part of the States and the people."[23]

"Can not continue to exist"—these were menacing words to the bank's supporters. Biddle's friends in and out of Congress advised him to seek recharter during the current legislative session.[24] Biddle, however, resisted these suggestions, hoping instead that the House Ways and Means Committee would sponsor a recharter bill rather than keep the public in long suspense over the bank question.[25] As it turned out, the chairman of that committee and a strong supporter of the bank, South Carolina's George McDuffie, took no action.

The bank's opponents, however, perhaps emboldened by the president's message, became more assertive. On February 2, 1831, Senator Thomas Hart Benton of Missouri offered a resolution "that the charter of the Bank of the United States ought not to be renewed."[26] He justified his proposal in a withering philippic against the bank, which anticipated and even went beyond the objections Jackson would later lay out in his veto message. At great length Benton denounced the "prodigious" power of the Bank of the United States to "subjugate the Government."[27] Its charter, he claimed, conferred "exclusive privileges" on the bank and legitimized an "anti-republican monopoly."[28] He provided numerous examples to document his allegations. As he neared conclusion, he repeated that "the charter of the Bank of the United States cannot be renewed." Then came the crucial, albeit lengthy, summation: "And, in coming to . . . this peremptory opinion, I . . . joyfully exclaim, it is no longer the year 1816! Fifteen years have gone by; times have changed; and former arguments have lost their application." What precisely did he mean? In 1816, Benton explained, "[w]e were . . . fresh from war, loaded with debt, and with all the embarrassments which follow in the train of war." But fifteen years of "peace and tranquility" had bestowed "blessings" which did not exist in 1816. "There is no longer a single consideration urged in favor of chartering the bank in 1816, which can have the least weight or application, in favor of rechartering it now." For example, "What were the arguments of 1816? Why, first, 'to pay the public creditors.' I answer this is no longer anything: for before 1836 [when the Bank of the United States charter would expire] that function will cease: there will be no more creditors to pay."[29] After all, the national debt will have been paid off. Renewing the bank's charter under that circumstance meant that the Bank of the United States would outlive its "first" reason for existing at all.

Benton had more to say on this score. Another 1816 reason to charter the Bank of the United States, he asserted, was "to transfer the public moneys." But that function "will be nothing" too, because "after the payment of the public debt, we shall have no moneys to transfer."[30] Benton elaborated: "The twelve millions of dollars which are now transferred annually to the northeast, to pay the public creditors, will then remain in the pockets of the people, and the reduced expenditures of the Government will be made where the money is collected. The army and the navy, after extinction of the debt, will be the chief objects of expenditure; and they will require the money, either on the frontiers, convenient to the land office, or on the seaboard, convenient to the custom-houses. Thus will transfers of revenue become unnecessary."[31] In brief, eliminating the national debt also meant eliminating a major reason for the bank's existence.

Benton was not yet finished with this theme. Another reason for chartering the Bank of the United States in 1816 was to "make loans to the Federal Government." After the War of 1812, he admitted, loans were indeed needed. But in 1831 that service also "is nothing," the Missouri senator maintained, "for the Federal Government will want no loans in time of peace, not even out of its own deposits; and the prospect of war is rather too distant at present to make loans on that account."[32] Without a grave foreign crisis the United States government would contract no new debt. Again, debt extinction meant the Bank of the United States was no longer needed.

Lest he had not adequately made his point, Benton pressed on. A fourth 1816 reason for establishing the Bank of the United States was to "pay the pensioners." Obligations to Revolutionary War veterans constituted a species of debt, and in 1816 many entitled veterans were still alive. The bank facilitated payments to them. But, Benton argued, after 1836, when the current bank charter expired, so few survivors would remain that the government itself could pay them without the bank's agency.[33] This argument simply reinforced the earlier ones: Eliminating the national debt eliminated justification for rechartering the Bank of the United States. "The bank is done. The arguments of 1816 will no longer apply. Times have changed; and the policy of the Republic changes with the times. The war made the bank; peace will unmake it." Benton might well have said the War of 1812 created the national debt, necessitating the Bank of the United States, and that elimination of the debt now necessitated elimination of the bank. Benton's point could be framed as a question: Why recharter the Bank of the United States for fifteen or twenty years when the debt would be gone in four? Daniel Webster "demanded" an immediate vote on Benton's resolution. It was defeated, but the margin of victory was narrow: 23 to 20.[34]

❧

Despite the vote, Benton's speech was profoundly important. It was common knowledge that the Missouri senator "spoke for" the administration, and, accordingly, his remarks reflected the thinking in the Jackson White House. They revealed that Biddle's main tactic to win recharter had been a gross mistake. The bank's efficiency in paying down the national debt, far from justifying charter renewal, was, in fact, justifying the reverse. Biddle, without realizing it, had been pursuing a suicidal approach. A change seemed necessary. But to what? Biddle had no clear answer, but at the same time he did not believe that the Bank of the United States was lost. In fact, he drew encouragement from Jackson's shuffle of his cabinet in the spring of 1831, because Louis McLane of Delaware, a well-known supporter of the bank, became the secretary of the treasury. Indeed, as the presidential election year of 1832 approached, the administration, through McLane, reached out to Biddle.

On October 19, 1831, McLane, with Jackson's knowledge, visited Biddle at Bank of the United States headquarters in Philadelphia. The secretary's purpose was to inform the bank president where the Bank of the United States stood vis-a-vis the administration on the eve of an election year. McLane recounted a recent meeting with Jackson at which several matters were agreed: first, that the secretary of the treasury's annual report to Congress would endorse renewal of the Bank of the United States charter and early payment of the national debt through the sale of the government's shares to the bank for $8,000,000; that recharter would include "such modifications" as are "acceptable to the Executive"; and that Jackson in his upcoming message would simply leave the bank question to Congress to address. In return, Biddle would refrain from seeking charter renewal in the election year.[35] When McLane left, Biddle summed up the substance of the meeting in a memorandum for his own files: "The footing then on which the matter stands is this: The President is to say that having previously brought the subject to Congress, he now leaves it with them. The Secretary is to recommend the renewal."[36] A deal had been cut—or so it seemed.

Jackson's third annual message, December 6, 1831, left the bank issue to Congress, as agreed, but couched in language that Biddle had not anticipated. For one thing, Jackson introduced the matter by reaffirming "the opinions heretofore expressed in relation to the Bank of the United States, as at present organized. . . ." Second, Jackson's deferral of the question to the House and Senate was qualified by the phrase "for the present."[37] Close reading of the message revealed the president's unending hostility toward the bank and his option to intervene on the issue in the future. These ingredients had not been part of the handshake agreement at Biddle's office the previous October.

Secretary McLane's report to Congress had also been part of the October understanding. Dated December 7, it indeed recommended recharter with "such modifications . . . calculated to recommend it to the approbation of the Executive." But the recommendation was qualified—renewal should occur "at the proper time." McLane, however, did not identify "the proper time."[38]

McLane also addressed the national debt, documenting reduction in 1831 by more than $16,000,000 in principal and interest. In January 1832, the total remaining debt would amount to little more than $24,300,000. The secretary explained that Treasury "has endeavored to carry into effect the policy indicated by the laws, and the views of the President in regard to the early extinguishment of the public debt." During the three preceding years more than $40,000,000 had been applied to debt reduction. Therefore, McLane said, "The occasion is deemed a propitious one to bring to the view of the Legislature the subject of the debt, with a view to its redemption at a period not only earlier than has been . . . anticipated, but before the termination of the present Congress." Then came the plan. The current and anticipated 1832 revenue surplus would trim the debt to little more than $10,000,000 by the end of the coming year. He suggested, as Biddle expected from the October meeting, that the government sell its Bank of the United States shares to the bank for eight million dollars and apply that amount to the debt. Revenue in early 1833 would generate the remaining two million, and, as a result, the national debt would be totally eliminated by March 3 of that year. An "indispensable part" of achieving that target was the sale of the government shares at the stated price. Redemption of the debt would justify the transaction. "The moral influence," McLane wrote, "which such an example would necessarily produce throughout the world, . . . inspiring new confidence in our free institutions, cannot be questioned." Moreover, "[t]he anxious hope with which the people have looked forward to this period [of debt freedom], not less than the present state of the public mind, and the real interests of the community at large, recommend the prompt application of these means [the government's stock in the Bank of the United States] to that great object"—the elimination of the national debt.[39]

What did all of this mean? For Nicholas Biddle, certain matters seemed clear. First, the president's message delivered less than what he expected as a result of the October 19 meeting. Jackson did not yield future freedom of action against the bank. Once the upcoming election was over, assuming a Jackson victory, what would or could stop the president from reneging on the deal and vetoing a recharter bill? In short, nothing. Yet Biddle's obligation under the October agreement was to avoid making the bank's future an issue in the election. Suddenly the deck seemed stacked against the Bank of the United States. In addition, Biddle knew, of course, that the plan to eliminate the debt by March 1833, simply reworked the plan that he himself had proposed to William B. Lewis three years earlier. The revisions were significant, however. Under the original scheme, the bank would buy the government shares for $1,500,000; under the current plan, the sale price was $8,000,000—a huge markup. More important, under the original plan the Bank of the United States paid a bonus to the government which would have ensured recharter; under the current plan there was no bonus or any guarantee mechanism. All these matters troubled Biddle. After all, recent bitter experience had taught him that the more rapidly the debt was reduced, the less "necessary and proper" the bank became, especially to its opponents. Debt extinction did not serve the best interests of the Bank of the United States, and the sale of the government's shares in the bank to pay off most of the remaining debt implied the complete divorce of government and bank. Was Biddle being manipulated? Would continued adherence to the October agreement ultimately make himself complicit in the demise of the Bank of the United States? By mid-December 1831, Biddle smelled a rat, and for good reasons.[40] When that same month the administration's opponents gathered at Baltimore and nominated Henry Clay for president, Biddle concluded that the moment to seek recharter had arrived.

Biddle made his move early in the new year. On January 9, 1832, memorials from the president and directors of the Bank of the United States seeking recharter were introduced in both the Senate and the House of Representatives.[41] The bank controversy now entered a new phase.

❧

The Senate created "a select committee" of five bank proponents to consider the memorial.[42] This mobilized the opposition. "Seeing the state of parties in Congress," Senator Benton later recalled, "and the tactics of the bank . . . our course of action became obvious, which was—to attack incessantly, assail at all points, display the evil of the institution, rouse the people—and prepare them to sustain the [inevitable] veto."[43] Indeed, the assault on the bank seemed relentless. The opposition challenged the legality of branch bank notes; questioned the duration of the bank's charter; fumed over foreign ownership of bank stock; demanded state approval for establishing new branch banks, and insisted that states be permitted to tax bank stock within their borders.[44] At long last, on March 13, the special committee "reported a bill to renew the charter of the Bank of the United States for the term of fifteen years," becoming effective when the current charter expired in 1836.[45]

The opposition, of course, did not quit. Instead, it became more vehement. Benton now alleged that in 1817 the Bank of the United States had lost at least ten million dollars of public money by failing to buy the three percent bonds when they were selling for sixty-five cents on a dollar.[46] The bank's friends responded. J. S. Johnston of Louisiana labeled Benton's assertion a "very serious" charge and reminded the Senate that responsibility for debt reduction rested with the Sinking Fund Commission, not the Bank of the United States. He explained that in 1817 the commission had purchased as much of the three percent debt as it could, but that the purchase itself had forced the price upward and "they could buy no more." Remaining funds were then applied to the redemption of six percent bonds. Johnston concluded: "Now it is . . . obvious that the bank was the mere depository of the money; that it had nothing to do with the purchasing of stocks [i.e., the government bonds]; that it paid the money as demanded [by the Sinking Fund Commission]; that the commissioners could not purchase the three per cents at sixty-five" and that "they purchased what was most advantageous to the Government."[47]

Benton's line of argument—that the Bank of the United States had failed to reduce the public debt efficiently and had lost the government money—was new, and he refused to drop it, despite Johnston's explanation. On his feet again, the Missouri senator repeated his accusation regarding the three percent bonds, adding that he had not intended to question the integrity of the Sinking Fund Commission.[48] An exasperated Senator Johnston complained in reply that Benton had "entirely forgotten the point" and dismissed the Missourian's claim "not . . . to impugn the conduct" of the commissioners. If Benton were right, no other conclusion could be drawn except that they had served the country poorly. "The money was placed in their hands to pay the public debt; if they have so managed the fund as to lose ten millions to the Government, it would evince the grossest mismanagement."[49] But was this the case? According to Johnston, "the [sinking] fund has been ably administered; and there is no just ground of censure or complaint. . . . [T]hey have regularly applied the money to the purchase of the stocks bearing the highest interest, and which were most advantageous to the Government." Indeed, Johnston explained that the government's bank stock dividends paid the interest on the three-percents and that the government had lost nothing.[50] Samuel Smith of Maryland vigorously supported Johnston against Benton; so too did Benton's Missouri colleague, Alexander Buckner—but it did not matter.[51] Benton challenged the bank's record on and reputation for effective debt payment, and, once injected into the debate, the matter did not easily go away.

In the meantime, the House of Representatives also addressed the recharter issue, and, as in the Senate, the status of the national debt soon intruded into the discussion. It first arose over a procedural question. Ways and Means Chairman George McDuffie, who introduced the bank's petition, moved that it be referred to his committee.[52] This proposal encountered immediate resistance. James M. Wayne of Georgia, objecting that the "presentation of the memorial was . . . a party measure," recommended the appointment of a special committee to deal with the matter because Ways and Means, already on record favoring the bank, could not be objective.[53] Others insisted that the House address the memorial as a Committee of the Whole. Debate focused on the three alternatives. One representative, Jabez W. Huntington of Connecticut, argued that Ways and Means should address the question because that committee had dealt with Jackson's comments about the Bank of the United States in his 1831 annual message and with McLane's Treasury report. In making his case, Huntington specifically linked the procedural question with McLane's endorsement of bank recharter and his plan to eliminate the debt in 1833. McLane's report contained "a proposition" to authorize the sale of the government's shares in the Bank of the United States, an investment "now yielding an interest of seven percent, . . . to enable the Government to pay, among other debts, one bearing an interest of three percent only, and thus to present the great 'moral spectacle' of the reimbursement of the public debt before the 4th of March, 1833!"[54] Huntington made no effort to suppress sarcasm. For him and for other Bank of the United States supporters, it was patently absurd to sell assets earning seven percent to discharge obligations costing three percent. But if the House were to act on such a recommendation, then "it was . . . proper that it should be well considered . . . and as the Committee of Ways and Means had been charged with the duty of examining into the propriety" of McLane's proposal, then "it was obviously proper that to them should be confided the duty" of evaluating the merit of the Bank of the United States recharter petition. The secretary's recommendation for early debt elimination was, after all, "most intimately connected" to the bank question. Huntington put it well. Indeed, from the administration's point of view, charter renewal and debt elimination were "intimately connected." He then posed the procedural question again: "Will the House refer to one committee every matter connected with the renewal of the charter of the bank, . . . and to another committee the application for its renewal?"[55] The bank's friends carried the day. By a vote of 100 to 90, they sent the Bank of the United States memorial to the Committee on Ways and Means.[56]

Precisely a month later, on February 9, the committee filed a divided report. The majority, favoring renewal, defended the bank's constitutionality, its expediency, and its role in creating a stable, uniform national currency. It rejected any notion of establishing a government-operated bank, as Jackson had intimated in his annual message, to take the Bank of the United States's place. It also argued that the national debt issue justified renewal. The majority reminded Congress that the "Government borrowed, during the short period of the war, eighty millions of dollars" and that the Bank of the United States was established in 1816 to deal with that debt. Although the debt was now nearly extinct, it would be unwise to let the bank share the fate of the debt: ". . . neither reason nor experience will permit us to doubt that a state of war would speedily bring about all the evils which so fatally affected the credit of the Government and the national currency during the late war. . . . We should be again driven to the same miserable round of financial expedients, which, in little more than two years, brought a wealthy community almost to the very brink of a declared national bankruptcy."[57] In the majority's opinion, the Bank of the United States had remedied the post-war debt problem: better to keep the bank and avoid, in case of an international emergency, a repetition of the credit crisis.

The minority, of course, held a different view. Its report denied the bank's constitutionality, its alleged expediency, and its success in fostering a national currency.[58] The minority also rejected the bank's utility regarding future debt. After all, the nation was not only at peace but also at the brink of eliminating the national debt. The latter circumstance warranted rejection of charter renewal. "So far as the fiscal operations of the Government are concerned, which now consists chiefly in transferring its funds from one part of the country to the other, a bank, with a capital of thirty-five millions . . . can scarcely be necessary, after the payment of the public debt, when the expenditures of the Government will not require more than eleven millions of dollars. It is believed the Secretary of the Treasury will find no difficulty in managing its concerns through the agency of the State banks, upon nearly as favorable terms as it now does through the

United States' Bank."[59] This assessment simply restated Benton's argument in the Senate a year earlier: no national debt, no need for the Bank of the United States.

The next day, February 10, Ways and Means offered "a bill to renew and modify the charter of the Bank of the United States."[60] At the same time the House adopted two resolutions by which to facilitate enactment. One directed the secretary of the treasury to provide semiannual statements from 1816 through 1831 documenting bill issues by the Bank of the United States and its branches, payments on the national debt, and a large volume of other data; the second required Treasury to report "the rates" at which the Bank of the United States had "purchased foreign and domestic bills of exchange" at each of its offices for every month since 1816.[61] Secretary McLane secured this information from Biddle and transmitted it to the House on March 2.[62] The House was ready to proceed on the recharter bill—or almost.

In the interim between the introduction of the recharter bill and the acquisition of data from the Department of Treasury, the House opposition to the Bank of the United States took the offensive. As in the Senate, antibank representatives were advised, organized, and emboldened by Thomas Hart Benton. "I conceived this movement," he later wrote, "and had charge of its direction." His strategy: to push for a House investigating committee empowered to call persons and papers before any vote on the bank's future took place. An open-ended inquiry into the bank's affairs would delay consideration of a recharter bill, possibly until after the presidential election. According to Benton, if the bank's supporters opposed an investigating committee, it would look like "guilt shrinking from detection." On the other hand, if the bank's supporters agreed to an investigation, then "mischief would be found." To maneuver the friends of the bank into this no-win position, Benton recruited a new Georgia representative, Augustus Clayton, who had recently arrived to take his seat and who had earlier authored an anti-Bank of the United States pamphlet. Benton gave Clayton a list of "seven alleged breaches" of the bank's charter for an investigating committee to probe.[63]

On February 23 Clayton followed Benton's script, proposing a resolution that "a select committee be appointed to examine into the affairs of the Bank of the United States, with power to send for persons and papers, and to report the result of their inquiries to this House." Consideration was promptly postponed until Monday, February 27.[64] Debate began that day when Clayton offered an "indictment" of the Bank of the United States on seven charges supported by fifteen specifications. None of these entailed the national debt.[65] The discussion was long and often heated. It dragged on into March. Each side accused the other of acting from purely partisan motives.[66] Not until March 8 did the imminent extinction of the national debt emerge in the debate. John C. Bell of Tennessee raised the matter first. "If we recharter the bank now," he said, "we shall be willfully rejecting the proffered lights of experience. We are on the eve of a great event—an event most extraordinary in the history of nations. . . . The House must perceive that I allude to the payment of the public debt." According to Bell, the approach of that "great event" required that the Bank of the United States recharter question be postponed to a future Congress. "This event will take place within a period sufficiently in advance of the expiration of the charter of the bank, to afford us some experience of its effects before we shall be compelled" to address charter renewal. "The great amount of capital," Bell explained, "which has always been accumulated, and must continue to accumulate, in the hands of individuals by the rapid discharge of the public debt, and which must find new modes of investment, cannot be without its effects upon the general interests of the country." No one, he said, could predict the "precise nature and character" of debt freedom's impact on "the general currency of the country, upon the local banks, foreign and domestic exchange, and upon the trade and commerce of the country, internal and external. . . ." Yet no one doubted that the effects of debt freedom would be significant and beneficent. "We know they will probably be very great and striking, and it is of no little importance that we should know something more from experience upon this subject than we do now" before taking action on the Bank of the United States—"an institution which is intended to regulate the effects of this new state of things." The approaching era of debt freedom, Bell continued, "must be pregnant with the most important developments in relation to the commerce and currency of the country"; wisdom required waiting to see what the impact of debt extinction would be before taking action on the bank. "Shall we recklessly fling away, or disregard the lights which the next three years must shed upon this subject?"[67] In brief, to John C. Bell, the elimination of the national debt required postponing the recharter issue for a few years.

Bell was not alone in holding this view. A few days later Augustus Clayton agreed, remarking that "an interesting reason" existed "for the postponement" of the bank question "to a distant date." Closely echoing Bell's language, Clayton declared: "We are now upon the eve of a change in our condition, which makes this nation the envy and admiration of all other nations. In one year [if McLane's plan were implemented], and three before the charter of the bank will expire, the public debt will be paid." Like Bell, he believed that the effects of debt freedom could not be precisely predicted. "The prospect," however, "is favorable, cheering, but made up of so many contingencies, that no presumption dares to determine what will be its aspect . . . in a year or two hence." But Clayton went beyond Bell by audaciously quoting Henry Clay, Jackson's presidential rival, to support his own position. "Sir, the connexion which rechartering the bank has with the payment of our national debt, has been happily and forcibly expressed by the Senator from Kentucky." He then referred to a speech made by Clay at Cincinnati two years earlier. According to the Georgia representative, Clay had said: "Whether the [Bank of the United States] charter ought to be renewed or not . . . is a question of expediency, to be decided by the existing state of the country. It will be necessary . . . to look carefully at the condition of both the bank and the nation, to ascertain if the public debt shall, in the meantime, be paid off, what effect that will produce, what will then be our financial condition; what that of the local banks; the state of our commerce, foreign and domestic, as well as the concerns of the currency generally." Clay, at that time, refused to endorse or oppose recharter.[68]

Clayton's speech was clever but inconsequential. Invoking Henry Clay in support of his position had no effect on the course of events. Delay failed. On March 14, an overwhelming majority (164 to 26) defeated the resolution for an open-ended, unrestricted inquiry into the bank's affairs. Instead the House approved creation of an investigating committee "to report whether the provisions" of the Bank of the United States charter "have been violated" and to offer "a final report . . . on or before" April 21. Despite the intense minority opposition, the bank's friends remained in control. They had, in fact, frustrated Senator Benton's strategy. By approving an inquiry they avoided the appearance of "guilt shrinking from detection." At the same time, by imposing a brief time limit on the investigation, they assured an early vote on recharter and made it unlikely that any malfeasance on the part of the bank would be discovered. Representative Clayton now regretted his role in the drama. "I hope I may be permitted to take a parting leave of my resolution," he told his colleagues on March 14, "as I very plainly perceive that it is going the way of all flesh."[69]

But Clayton's role did not end. The next day, March 15, the House appointed a committee of seven—four bank opponents and three proponents—to undertake the investigation. The membership included Clayton, who was designated chair, and former president John Quincy Adams, who now represented a Massachusetts district in the House.[70] The seven left for Philadelphia. There they interviewed Biddle and other bank personnel, examined internal bank documents, and compiled a report (actually three reports—one by the majority, one by the minority, and one by John Quincy Adams), which was presented to the House at the end of April.

The majority report accused the Bank of the United States of usury, issuing branch bank notes as currency, and the several other charges Clayton had laid out in his original "indictment" of the bank on the House floor. But the majority now added a new allegation, that the Bank of the United States had requested and secured a postponement of the payment on the public debt due July 1, 1832.[71] Indeed, the postponement had been made while the committee was in the midst of its investigation, and the representatives had interrogated Biddle about it. "I have made no application to the Government," Biddle explained, "nor have I requested any suspension of the payment of any portion of the public debt." Rather, a letter from the secretary of the treasury, dated March 24, 1832, and marked "confidential," had informed Biddle that the government was to announce on April 1 that it would pay one half the three percent debt on July 1. On that day "each stockholder" would receive "one half of the amount of his certificate." The secretary added: "If any objection occurs to you either as to the amount or mode of payment, I will thank you to suggest it." Biddle accepted the invitation to offer advice. In a letter to McLane, March 29, he wrote that he had "no objection" to the proposed payment because the government's bank revenues were sufficient for the operation. He cautioned, however, that the current depressed condition of commerce and the demand by European holders of three-percents "might endanger the punctual payment" of this portion of the debt. In other words, meeting the July 1 deadline in Europe might not be possible. Moreover, trying to do so by suddenly sending a large volume of cash to the Continent in the midst of a recession could trigger more severe domestic credit pressures. Biddle also questioned the wisdom of paying only half rather than the whole of the three percent debt. He told the investigating committee that he had done his duty. His input had been solicited, he had provided it, and he "left it . . . to the Government to decide." Then he added, "On the part of the bank, I sought nothing, I requested nothing." The Treasury, Biddle maintained, was inclined to accept postponement but worried that the Sinking Fund would bear three months' additional interest as a result. To overcome that difficulty Biddle pledged that the Bank of the United States itself would pay the interest charges on the three-percents from July 1 to October 1, and "so the matter stands."[72] In brief, Biddle encouraged postponement.

The majority report was deeply critical of what had happened. It acknowledged that the Bank of the United States had not technically sought or requested a postponement of the July debt payment, but that "if such postponement had not been made, the bank would not, on the 1st of July, have possessed the ability to have met the demand, without causing a scene of great distress in the commercial community."[73] The Bank of the United States, in short, was mismanaged, and its recklessness had forced a delay in debt extinction. In the end, the majority recommended that Congress not "act upon the question of rechartering" the Bank of the United States "or of chartering any other national bank, until the public debt shall have been paid off, and the public revenue shall have been adjusted to the measure of our federal expenditures."[74]

The minority report dismissed as absurd the usury charge, the branch bank note question, and the other allegations that the Clayton "indictment" of the Bank of the United States had specified. It made its disdain for the majority view clear: "The minority of the committee will barely advert" to the topics raised by the majority.[75] One of those topics was the postponement of the July payment on the national debt. The minority simply ignored it.

Although John Quincy Adams signed the minority report, he felt obliged to offer a report of his own. He too rejected any notion that the Bank of the United States had violated its charter but directly addressed the question raised by the recent postponement. Adams put the matter into a larger context. He pointed out that since October 1831, "severe pressure" had characterized the money market and that the Bank of the United States had been acting prudently in "breaking its force." Moreover, Adams reminded the House that in the preceding autumn the government had announced "a payment of six millions of funded debt" on January 1, 1832. But the Treasury Department's statement "authorized . . . creditors" to receive payment "at any time" during the preceding quarter, allowing, in effect, early redemption. According to Adams, the treasury espoused this policy even though "the Government had in deposite scarcely half the sum" needed to make the payment. What did the Bank of the United States do? "The bank made no complaint, but took its measure of precaution" by curtailing loans. Complicating the bank's situation was the spring overflow of the Ohio River, heavily flooding Cincinnati and Louisville. To facilitate relief and reconstruction in those communities the bank eased credit. These circumstances, Adams asserted, constituted the environment within which the treasury made "a confidential intimation of a wish to pay off six millions of three per cent stocks, on the 1st of July next." Biddle's suggestion to postpone payment until October was designed to "ease the pressure" upon the entire commercial community, especially New York's. The secretary of the treasury agreed, and the bank assumed the burden of the third quarter's interest on the three-percents. Result? According to Adams, "this adjustment" benefited everyone: the government, bondholders, debtors, and the entire commercial sector. Yet the postponement "is seized upon in the majority report as if" the Bank of the United States was "in the very agonies of bankruptcy." But, of course, nothing could have been further from the truth. Indeed, Adams believed that the Bank of the United States provided enormous public services, including paying the national debt without charging any fees, "saving the expense of loan offices," which, otherwise, government would have to maintain. The bank's role in debt elimination justified recharter.[76]

In any event, the postponement of the July 1832 payment on the national debt was unprecedented, and possibly the majority, minority, and Adams reports missed its real significance. Had Biddle been frank with the investigating committee? Or did he encourage postponement from the belated realization that efficient debt elimination undermined justification for recharter? Was he trying an alternative tactic in order to secure his goal? The answers to these questions remain unclear. What is clear is this: The antibank forces used the national debt against the Bank of the United States, whether it paid down the debt efficiently or not. For the bank's opponents, effective debt elimination meant the Bank of the United States was no longer needed; on the other hand, ineffective debt elimination meant the Bank of the United States was mismanaged and in violation of its charter. With respect to the national debt, Biddle and the Bank of the United States were stuck between the proverbial rock and a hard place.

The investigative committee's reports were filed in the House. The recharter bill underwent its first reading on June 12. Debate was long and heated. The opposition tried to recommit the bill and in various ways throw obstacles in the way of quick passage. These efforts failed. On July 3, the bank bill passed the House by a vote of 106 to 84.[77]

The recharter bill came before the Senate on Wednesday, May 23, and consumed much of the upper chamber's time during the next five weeks.[78] The bank's opponents repeated all the usual objections: the bank was unconstitutional; it represented unjustifiable monopoly privilege; it was subject to foreign influence; it threatened republican institutions, including the electoral system; it engaged in usury; it illegally permitted its branch banks to issue notes; and all the other allegations which had been offered in recent months. The national debt, of course, also factored into the debate. Friends and enemies of the bank alluded to it. Daniel Webster, a bank proponent, exclaimed on May 25, "Look to the disbursement of the revenue." Without the Bank of the United States, how would this be accomplished?[79] Thomas Hart Benton, on the other hand, objected to the bonus the bank would pay the government. (The bill required $3 million from the bank, double the 1816 bonus.) With debt extinction imminent, "[t]he struggle now was to keep money out of the treasury; to prevent the accumulation of a surplus; and the reception of this bonus would go to aggravate that difficulty, by increasing that surplus."[80] A treasury surplus in an era of debt freedom was not the only matter that troubled the Missouri senator. He grumbled about the fact that many Americans had fallen into debt to the Bank of the United States—"a frightful debt," he said, amounting to $70,000,000 in all. "We are rejoicing at emancipation from a national debt, at the moment we have fallen" as individuals "into a bank debt. . . ." Benton's complaints against the Bank of the United States meandered from one point to another, winding up at the recent postponement of the July payment on the national debt.[81]

The bank's supporters came to its defense. On June 6, for example, Samuel Smith of Maryland reminded his colleagues of the benefits the Bank of the United States provided the nation. "The present Bank . . . pays the public debt," he said, "by which it is subjected to large drains of specie, which are highly injurious to its other operations. . . ."[82] He asked, "Did the old Bank of the United States pay the public debt? No. Commissioners did this service, and received nearly $20,000 per annum from the treasury."[83] And on and on the debate went. But in the Senate, as in the House of Representatives, the bank's supporters retained control. On June 11, the recharter bill passed the Senate by a vote of 28 to 20.[84]

Early the next month the House/Senate measure went to the president, and on July 10 Andrew Jackson vetoed it. His action surprised few, and his reasons even fewer. Despite the Supreme Court's 1819 ruling in *McCulloch v. Maryland* upholding the bank's constitutionality, Jackson declared that the Bank of the United States violated the Constitution. In addition, he denounced the bank as an institution of privilege inconsistent with American democracy; as a monopoly which stifled free and fair competition; as an enterprise which widened the gap between the rich and the poor; and, since foreigners owned 30% of the bank's stock, as a government-chartered corporation subject to the influence of other countries.[85] These objections did not represent the complete list of Jackson's reasons for rejecting the recharter bill. There was at least one other. His veto message referred twice, once directly and once indirectly, to the imminent elimination of the national debt. He pointed out that the existing bank was capitalized at many millions more than the first Bank of the United States, but that the latter had been able "to perform its public functions" anyway. He continued: "The public debt, which existed during the period of the old bank, and on the establishment of the new, has been nearly paid off, and our revenue will soon be reduced." The increased bank capitalization provided by the recharter bill "is, therefore, not for public, but for private purposes."[86] Accordingly, the bank bill went beyond Congress's legislative authority.

Moreover, Jackson questioned the propriety of the bonus the bank would pay the government upon recharter. The bill, it will be recalled, doubled the 1816 bonus to $3,000,000. But why? These sums (1816 and 1832) "are not exacted," the president asserted, "for the privilege" of transferring funds from "place to place" to satisfy "the public creditors." After all, the "Government does not tax its officers and agents for the privileges of serving it." The bank did not pay the bonus, argued Jackson, for the honor of discharging the public debt but for the advantages gained by its stockholders.[87] Accordingly, the bonus feature of the 1816 charter and the 1832 recharter bill was improper and, with the national debt winding down, also unnecessary. The bonus, in other words, was not protected by the Constitution's so-called elastic clause. In short, the status of the public debt factored into Jackson's reasons for veto. Nor was this surprising. Debt reduction and the future of the Bank of the United States had, in fact, been linked together since the early months of the Jackson presidency. The bottom line was that impending national debt freedom helped doom the Bank of the United States.

The veto transformed the ongoing skirmishing between the bank and the administration into open warfare.[88] The Bank of the United States emerged as the principal issue in the election of 1832, but Jackson easily defeated Henry Clay. Secretary McLane's plan to pay off the national debt in 1833 went nowhere. Congress that session did not even discuss selling the government's shares in the bank. Jackson, it seems, did not care. The debt was going to be eliminated, one way or another, on his watch, and the Bank of the United States too. But before Jackson could reengage in the bank war, he had another and more urgent problem to confront—a problem symbolized by John C. Calhoun's resignation as vice president at the end of 1832.

President James Monroe.

President John Quincy Adams.

Vice President John C. Calhoun.

President Andrew Jackson.

All images are from the Library of Congress.

Senator Henry Clay of Kentucky.

Secretary of State, later Vice President, Martin Van Buren.

Samuel D. Ingham, Secretary of the Treasury

Senator Thomas Hart Benton of Missouri.

Opposite: ".0001 the value of a unit with four cyphers going before it." An 1831 lithograph satirizing the resignations of several members of Jackson's Cabinet. The rats are (left to right) Martin Van Buren, John H. Eaton, John Branch, and Samuel D. Ingham. John C. Calhoun is a terrier menacing Van Buren. Daniel Webster and Henry Clay observe from the window.

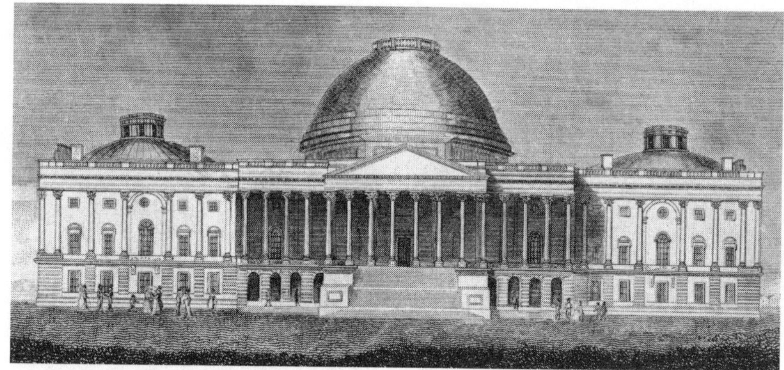

The front or east view of the U.S. Capitol as it appeared in 1829, at the beginning of President Andrew Jackson's administration.

The Second Bank of the United States, Philadelphia.

Philadelphia financier Nicholas Biddle.

"Old Jack, the famous New Orleans mouser, clearing Uncle Sam's barn of bank and Clay rats." A pro-Jackson satire on the president's campaign to destroy the Bank of the United States that appeared soon after his veto of the bill to recharter the bank in July 1832. Uncle Sam and his "active laborers" watch as the Andrew Jackson cat attacks rats, including Henry Clay, Nicholas Biddle, and pro-bank newspaper editors.

An 1834 cartoon supporting President Jackson's decision to withdraw federal funds from the Bank of the United States and distribute them among state banks. Henry Clay and Nicholas Biddle are seen attempting to stop the removal.

An 1836 satire on the Jackson administration's continued battle against the Bank of the United States. Andrew Jackson and Martin Van Buren flee Nicholas Biddle holding the bank's recharter by the Whig-controlled Pennsylvania Legislature in defiance of the administration.

The Nullification Crisis inspired this prescient 1833 print, showing John C. Calhoun and his colleagues climbing the steps of treason and civil war to attain their goal. Jackson, right, threatens them: "By the Eternal, I'll hang you all."

A derisive 1836 cartoon showing Vice President Martin Van Buren, left, Richard M. Johnson, his running-mate for the next election, and President Andrew Jackson, right, discussing how best to distribute surplus federal funds among the states in order to secure Van Buren's election to the presidency.

SIX

THE NULLIFICATION CRISIS AND DEBT FREEDOM

JOHN CALDWELL CALHOUN, SOUTH CAROLINA'S MOST prominent son, was more than disenchanted by the course of events. He became increasingly alienated from the administration in the wake of the Eaton scandal. In 1830 Jackson learned that Calhoun, as Monroe's secretary of war, had wanted to censure the general for exceeding orders during his incursion into Spanish Florida. Jackson, of course, was resentful, even outraged. Moreover, by the spring of 1830 Calhoun had moved straightforwardly into the radical states' rights position that many of his colleagues among South Carolina's ruling oligarchy championed. The vice president's stance became clear at the Jefferson Day Dinner on April 13. Jackson toasted: "Our Union—it must be preserved." Calhoun counter-toasted: "The Union—next to our liberty the most dear. May we all remember that it can only be preserved by respecting the rights of the States and distributing equally the benefit and burden of the Union."[1] Calhoun's personal and political estrangement from the president meant that his own ambition to succeed Jackson was dashed, and that Secretary of State Van Buren was now the heir apparent. Calhoun was not a happy man.

Born in 1782 to modest but comfortable circumstances, he had graduated from Yale in 1804, subsequently studied law in Connecticut, and ultimately returned to South Carolina and married into another but wealthier branch of his own family. In 1810, he was elected to the House of Representatives and ardently supported the 1812 war against England. Indeed, he was a strong nationalist. After the war he supported chartering the second Bank of the United States, tariff protection for American industry, and, of course, federally supported internal improvements. The 1817 Bonus bill, it will be recalled, although vetoed by Madison, had been his special project. That same year President Monroe named him to his cabinet, and for the next eight years Calhoun administered the Department of War with distinction. In 1824 he ran for president, but withdrew after encountering unanticipated Jackson strength in Pennsylvania. He settled for the vice presidency instead.[2]

By then, however, Calhoun's nationalism was melting, and he was moving more and more closely to the states' rights school of the Jeffersonian tradition. His shift from one position to the other paralleled the ongoing reduction of the national debt. The concurrence was not coincidental. Now believing that protectionism imposed economic hardship on South Carolina—hardship endured to pay down the debt—Calhoun also believed that tariff duties had to be slashed as the debt neared extinction. For him, national debt freedom also meant free trade. For this reason, in 1828 Calhoun supported Jackson over Adams. He could not accept Adams's commitment to high tariffs under the American System. Where Jackson stood on the tariff question, however, was unclear—the general often spoke in favor of a "judicious tariff," whatever that meant—but the Old Hero's lack of specificity was more promising than Adams's specificity.[3] Jackson was, in other words, in 1828 the better bet for tariff reduction. By 1832, Calhoun felt as alienated from the president on this matter as on others.

By all accounts Calhoun was a gifted man. Tall and slim, with thick black hair and deep, shining dark eyes, he was a man with "presence" wherever he went. But his most extraordinary gift—friends and foes alike agreed on this—was the quality of his intellect. Calhoun's capacity to theorize, to enter into and engage the world of ideas, to identify and parse esoteric distinctions, and to achieve clarity and consistency in presentation, elevated him above most, if not all, public men of his time.[4] Even the historian Richard Hofstadter, no admirer of Calhoun, admitted that the South Carolinian's "analysis" of American politics "ranks among the most impressive intellectual achievements of American statesmen."[5]

❧

No issue of the Jackson era was more closely tied to the national debt than the tariff. Southern discontent with federal import duties had been brewing for some time, but especially after 1824 when Congress raised imposts and President Monroe announced likely debt freedom in 1835. When Congress increased tariff rates to "abominable" levels in 1828, South Carolina groaned. Calhoun responded by spelling out his state's constitutional and economic objections to protectionism in an essay subsequently edited and published by the South Carolina state legislature. The vice president's *Exposition* maintained that the protective tariff unfairly taxed the agricultural south to the advantage of the commercial and manufacturing north, transferring wealth from one region to another and from one class of citizens to another. The Constitution, of course, gave the federal government authority to levy import duties, but this power was to raise revenue for government operations and to pay down debt, not to protect a particular segment of the economy. Accordingly, protectionism was unconstitutional. Where, then, rested the authority to settle disputes over the precise sphere of legitimate federal activity? As an equal co-partner in the federal government, the Supreme Court of the United States could not serve as ultimate arbiter of federal-state disputes over the locus of power. Rather, according to Calhoun, since the Constitution was a compact among the several states and not an expression of sovereignty by the collective American people, then each state reserved to itself, explicitly under Amendment X, the final authority to determine whether the terms of the compact had been violated. Interposition—a state's power to nullify or veto federal law within its own borders—was the remedy that each state enjoyed. Each state might employ that remedy through a special convention summoned to adjudge the matter, the same institution which had ratified the Constitution in the first place.[6] Despite its apparent radicalism, this states' rights theory of the Constitution had a respectable history. After all, "interposition," now more commonly called "nullification," was reminiscent of the much admired Kentucky and Virginia Resolutions of 1798, authored by Thomas Jefferson and James Madison, the gurus of American republicanism.[7] Yet Calhoun apparently believed that nullification would not be necessary if South Carolina's demands were met. "We want free trade. . . . We want moderate taxes, frugality in the government, economy, accountability, and a rigid application of the public money, to the payment of the public debt, and the objects authorized by the Constitution."[8]

In December 1828, the South Carolina legislature adopted a series of resolutions, the so-called *Protest,* spelling out the state's complaints against the protective tariff and declaring it "unconstitutional, oppressive, and unjust."[9] In 1828, of course, tariff critics like Calhoun hoped that Andrew Jackson would be sympathetic to their point of view. Yet from the outset of his administration the new president's position was unclear and cryptic. In his inaugural address he devoted only one sentence, albeit a long one, to the tariff. "[I]t would seem to me," he said, "that the spirit of equity, caution, and compromise . . . requires that the great interests of agriculture, commerce, and manufactures should be equally favored" except that products "essential to our national independence" merited "peculiar encouragement."[10] What did this mean? How could government bestow equal favor upon all three great economic interests? And if products necessary for national security deserved protection, then how would those products be defined? Jackson's comment was more platitude than policy statement.

In his first annual message, in December 1829, Jackson addressed the tariff at some length. He began by asserting that the 1828 tariff "has not proved so injurious" to agriculture and commerce or "as beneficial" to manufactures "as was anticipated." The tariff, in other words, was not as "abominable" as South Carolina maintained. Instead, all was well. But, he continued, promoting the prosperity of agriculture, commerce, and manufacturing "equally . . . is one of the most difficult tasks of Government."[11] And while free trade might be the ultimate desirable goal, "selfish legislation" by other nations "compelled" us "to adapt our own to their regulations . . . to avoid serious injury" to our economy. Foreign protectionism necessitated domestic protectionism. Nonetheless, with that reality in mind, "I invite your attention to the existing tariff, believing that some of its provisions require modification." But he advised the "utmost caution" regarding tariff revision. Partisan and sectional interests should not dictate policy—only the agreed upon national interest. Accordingly, taxes on items which did not compete with our own productions could most justifiably be considered for reduction, especially since, with national debt freedom on the short horizon, "the sinking fund will" soon "no longer be required." In light of this imminent circumstance, Jackson recommended reducing the taxes on imported tea and coffee.[12] This proposal, of course, fell far short of South Carolina's vision of serious tariff reform.

South Carolina could draw little comfort from Jackson's second message the following year. On that occasion the president referred to "the payment of the public debt" as "the highest of all our obligations," the one that dictated his policy with regard to expenditures.[13] But he also made clear that the same consideration dictated his policy toward revenue. "[T]he condition of our impost revenue deserves special mention, inasmuch as it promises the means of extinguishing the public debt sooner than was anticipated."[14] Jackson, obviously, was still entertaining the hope that debt freedom would be achieved in 1833. But for that to happen tariff revenues were essential. Accordingly, he proceeded to defend the government's constitutional right to levy protective duties. If it lacked such authority, he said, then the Constitution created "the anomaly of a people stripped of the right to foster their own industry, and to counteract" the protectionist policies of other countries. Common sense rejected the validity of such a circumstance. He went even further, defending the 1828 law. "The effects of the present tariff are doubtless overrated, both in its evils and in its advantages."[15] Yet tariff reform was possible. The "difficulties of a more expedient adjustment of the present tariff, although great, are far from being insurmountable."[16] The national interest alone should determine the objects of protection. Making tariff revision a partisan or sectional issue, however, would court disaster. "I cannot, therefore, . . . too earnestly for my own feelings or the common good, warn you against the blighting consequences of such a course."[17]

Yet the tariff issue was clearly on a "blighting" course. The South generally and South Carolina especially grew increasingly vehement about protectionism, and the word "nullification" became increasingly common in discussions of the matter. Throughout 1831 the tariff question acquired deepening urgency. What if South Carolina and other southern states actually invoked nullification theory and tried to prevent revenue collection within their borders? Would civil war ensue? Even advocates of the American System recognized that adjustments had to be made in the tariff law. Henry Clay himself admitted both publicly and privately that, with both national debt reduction and southern protests as advanced as they were, "a considerable modification of the existing tariff" of 1828 was prudent and necessary.[18]

After Congress convened in December, temperatures in the nation's capital plummeted, and a very bitter winter set in. The Potomac froze over. But, despite the harsh weather, administration opponents held secret weekly meetings to address the tariff question. They rotated their private homes as locations for these strategy sessions in order to avoid attracting attention to their activities. The final meeting was held on Wednesday night, December 28, at Edward Everett's house. Surely a fire blazed as various lawmakers gathered there. John Quincy Adams attended. So too did Senator Clay, who, earlier that month, had become the National Republican nominee for president. The Kentuckian brought with him the draft of a bill to lower the tariff and, on this occasion at least, addressed the tariff question in partisan terms. He explained that "the policy of our adversaries was obvious—to break down the American system by accumulation of the revenue" in the Treasury. A federal surplus, in other words, would undermine justification of the protective system. "Ours, therefore," Clay said, "should be specially adapted to counteract it, by reducing immediately the revenue to the amount of seven or eight millions this very coming year."[19]

Adams paid close attention to Clay's remarks. He did not oppose the proposed bill but pointed out that the House Committee on Manufactures, which he chaired, had already gone on record that any tariff reductions "should be prospective," that is, "not to commence until after the extinguishment of the national debt."[20] This, of course, was Jackson's view as well. But Clay was dismissive, saying, "there was no necessity for the payment of the debt on the 4th March, 1833."[21] Adams responded that "without determining whether the President's passion to pay off the whole of the public debt by" that date "was the wisest idea that ever entered into the heart of man," nevertheless, he thought, Jackson "ought to be indulged, and not opposed." After all, Adams said, it was "an idea which would take greatly with the people." Opposing it would be "invidious." Moreover, Adams remarked, "there was justice in it." The holders of the three percent bonds will "be paid off dollar for dollar. . . ." And, needless to say, it will "be a great and glorious day when the United States shall be able to say that they owe not a dollar in the world." Finally and more importantly, according to Adams, paying off the debt promptly "would obviate" the "difficulty suggested by Mr. Clay. There would certainly be no accumulation of revenue" while the debt was being dismantled.[22] Clay, however, was adamant, and Adams had to repeat that the

Committee on Manufactures concurred with the president that tariff reduction should follow debt extinction. Clay's response: "Then the committee have given a very foolish and improvident pledge."[23]

Adams, it is worth noting, doubted Clay's motives, probably because, although he did not say so, nullification threats did not factor into Clay's insistence on immediate tariff reductions. Rather, he confided to his diary, "Clay's motive is obvious." Referring to Clay's presidential bid, Adams wrote: "He sees that next November . . . the great and irresistible Jackson electioneering cry will be the extinction of the debt." Clay's real purpose was to deny Jackson's taking credit for national debt freedom. "By the instant repeal of all these duties he wants to withdraw seven or eight millions from the Treasury and make it impossible to extinguish it by the 3d of March, 1833. It is an electioneering movement, and this was the secret of these meetings, as well as of the desperate effort to take the whole business of the reduction of the tariff into his own hands."[24] If Adams was right, then Clay was engaging in a game that both Nicholas Biddle and South Carolina would play a year later—using the delay of debt extinction as a weapon against Andrew Jackson.

Meanwhile, perhaps ironically, the president was entertaining the same notion, but for a different purpose: using debt freedom as a weapon against his enemies. South Carolina's extremists were his targets. In November, for example, he wrote to James A. Hamilton: "If I judge right of the American people I think . . . the prosperity of the Nation and our capability, with the aid of Congress, to pay the National Debt on the 3d of March, 1833, will destroy the Nullifiers by not leaving a single stone for them to stand on." Moreover, "Congress will find a source of contemplation and action by being called upon to reduce the tariff to the wants of the Government after the debt is paid, to go into effect and operation on the 4th March, 1833."[25] In any event, it appeared that the administration, the National Republican opposition, and the Calhounites were all seeking the same objective—tariff reduction—but for different reasons.

The consensus among these conflicting interests assured that Congress would address the tariff issue in 1832. Long and often heated debates in the House and Senate characterized passage of a measure in July, with reduced rates set to go into effect the following March. This new tariff, however, while it lowered duties on many items, came nowhere near a free trade measure. In fact, it was straightforwardly protectionist. Accordingly, it failed to appease South Carolina's radicals, who determined to take action. They did. On November 24, 1832, a special convention at Charleston declared the federal tariffs of both 1828 and 1832 "null, void, and no law" within South Carolina's borders. Its reason for this extraordinary step surprised no one. The tariffs, the convention asserted, aimed at protecting "domestic manufactures" and not raising revenue to sustain government operations and pay down debt. Therefore, the imposts "violated the true meaning and intent of the Constitution." Any federal effort to enforce the measures, the convention threatened, would result in South Carolina's secession from the union.[26] The United States now faced the specter of civil war.

❧

Severe crisis confronted the twenty-second Congress as it assembled for its second session in December 1832. Indeed, nullification and the threat of disunion made the 1824 controversy over the presidential election that year seem a comparatively minor matter. Here, after all, was a constitutional question of the most profound importance, one that challenged the very survival of the nation. South Carolina, of course, had little choice but to justify its action on the elevated plane of the Constitution. To defend it on any other ground would have exposed South Carolina's nullification for what it really was: not only an assault on the Constitution but also an assault on the federal revenue system. If successful, it threatened the timely arrival of national debt freedom because after February 1, 1833, when nullification was to take effect, federal revenue from South Carolina would no longer be collected, confronting the Treasury with a shortfall. Asserting this threat frankly was unlikely to win much sympathy for South Carolina, because it would seem that South Carolina had taken national debt freedom as a hostage in its demand for free trade. It would transform nullification into extortion. The public finance dimension of the nullification crisis was, in fact, the underside of the constitutional question. How would President Jackson respond? Congress awaited his annual message with grim anticipation.

Jackson, of course, could not ignore the tariff matter. His message, dated December 4, 1832, devoted several paragraphs to it. Not surprisingly, the president raised the issue in the context of imminent national debt freedom. He reported that the "national finances" were "in a highly prosperous state." Customs receipts had exceeded earlier estimates, allowing the government not only to pay its expenses but also to "provide for the payment of all the public debt" which was then "redeemable." Indeed, in 1832 the government had paid $18,000,000 in principal and interest.[27] Moreover, even though the recently enacted 1832 tariff, not yet in effect, was sure to cause a "falling off in the revenue" in 1833, funds would nonetheless remain sufficient to meet all expenses and "for the redemption and purchase of the remainder of the public debt." In fact, he proudly announced that on January 1, 1833, a few short weeks away, "the entire public debt of the United States . . . will be reduced to within a fraction of $7,000,000." More than two million of this amount was not "of right" redeemable until January 1, 1834, and well over four million until January 2, 1835. Yet Jackson still hoped that the Sinking Fund Commission, authorized to buy back debt at market prices, would be able to extinguish the entire debt in 1833.[28]

Jackson remained focused on the debt. "I can not too cordially congratulate Congress and my fellow-citizens on the near approach of that memorable and happy event—the extinction of the public debt of this great and free nation." Adhering "to the wise and patriotic policy marked out by" the Redemption Act of 1817, "the present Administration has devoted to" debt elimination "all the means which a flourishing commerce has supplied." Tariff revenues, in other words, combined with "a prudent economy," in federal spending, had permitted a dramatic reduction—$58,000,000—of the national debt during his four years in office. Moreover, this paring down of the debt had been accomplished without cutting appropriations for defense and other needs.[29]

Jackson then connected approaching debt freedom to the tariff question: "The final removal of this great burthen,"—the national debt—". . . presents the occasion for such further reduction in the revenue as may not be required" for national purposes. He "earnestly recommended" tariff reduction "to remove those burthens" which fell "unequally" on the country.[30] Specifically, he suggested "adaptation of the revenue to expenditure." This was basically South Carolina's view. Indeed, such an "adjustment" was necessary "in justice to the interests of the different States, and even to the preservation of the Union itself." Protection was only justifiable, as he had said on earlier occasions, to counteract discriminatory trade laws of other countries and to assure the domestic production of defense needs.[31]

Protectionism, Jackson pointed out, had both positive and negative consequences. It had, for example, stimulated domestic manufactures, something from which all Americans benefited. At the same time, however, it promoted "discontent and jealousy" among "a large portion of our countrymen" and now endangered "the stability of the Union." Accordingly, protectionism could not be the permanent policy of the government. "Nothing could justify it but the public safety."[32] At the moment, however, high tariffs were undermining the public safety, and "manufacturing establishments can not expect that the people will continue permanently to pay high taxes for their benefit" when government did not need the money.[33] "Is it not enough that the high duties have been paid as long as the money arising from them could be applied to the common benefit in the extinguishment of the public debt?"[34] For Jackson the time had come, because of approaching national debt freedom, to reduce the tariff beyond the level reached earlier that year. It could be done immediately, because Jackson still expected that debt elimination would occur in early 1833. His remarks were conciliatory, aimed at mollifying South Carolina. In essence, Jackson told the nation and South Carolina what his administration was willing to do to head off a crisis.

Six days later, however, Jackson told South Carolina what he was not willing to let that state do: nullify federal law. In a Proclamation to the People of South Carolina, December 10, 1832, he made his view utterly clear. He attacked the constitutional theory espoused by South Carolina's leadership as false and inconsistent with the historical record. He denounced nullification as treason. Reminding South Carolina that he was sworn to make sure that the laws were "faithfully executed," he warned that he would live up to that pledge. The Constitution vested him with the authority to suppress rebellion. South Carolina, he said, was flirting with disaster. Enough time remained for the state to backtrack, and he hoped that it would. But if it did not, he would fulfill his responsibility.[35] In a single December week, Jackson defined the limits—somewhere between the carrot and the stick—within which a lawful and peaceful resolution of the crisis would have to take place.

The proclamation focused on the constitutional issue. It was on that level, after all, that South Carolina had justified its case for nullification. But beyond the abstract constitutional debate lay this public financial reality: Jackson's "memorable and happy event"—national debt freedom—now stood at risk. Congress had not appropriated funds for the invasion of South Carolina, and if such a military operation became necessary, how much would it cost? Would the federal government be compelled to resume borrowing? Would Jackson acquiesce in a bond sale? Or would he prefer to retreat toward free trade in order to preserve the union and fulfill his pledge to eliminate the national debt? From this perspective, South Carolina's nullification of the tariffs was nothing more than hostage-taking. The hostage, of course, was the timely payment of the national debt.

Jackson was fully aware of this dimension to the crisis. In his proclamation he alluded to the financial implication of nullification. "If South Carolina considers the revenue laws unconstitutional and has a right to prevent their execution in the port of Charleston, there would be a clear constitutional objection to their collection in any other port; and no revenue could be collected anywhere. . . ."[36] Put simply, if South Carolina got away with nullifying the tariff laws, then other states would do the same thing. A domino effect would not only erase the prospect of debt freedom but also bankrupt the government. Without a source of revenue, the government's credit would evaporate. Unable to sustain itself by taxation or by borrowing, the union would unravel.

Congress also worried about a domino effect. In the House of Representatives Jabez W. Huntington of Connecticut made the same point but in a different way. Needling his colleagues from South Carolina, he said, "Suppose" that protection was suddenly abandoned, inducing economic calamity throughout the New England and Middle Atlantic states, and those states, "through conventions," addressed Congress in these words: "Unless you repeal this bill immediately we shall secede from the Union."[37] What then? In the upper chamber a senator put the problem this way: "[O]nce surrender to a State, under her threat of a dissolution of the Union, and the Union is not worth preserving, it is virtually dissolved. Every refractory State would catch and rely on the example, and whenever a mere and ephemeral majority in a state becomes refractory, she may set you at defiance, compel you to renounce the principle of which she complains, or the Union is dissolved."[38] On February 8, 1833, Senator George M. Dallas of Pennsylvania presented the problem succinctly and powerfully. "If the position now taken by South Carolina . . . be sustained by the connivance of this body [the Senate], your revenue is lost; not a part of the revenue, but the whole of your revenue, is gone." He warned, "The extinguishment of the revenue is the necessary consequence of adopting this doctrine [nullification], and is, in itself, a superabundant, a strong, if not an imperative call on those who are managing the concerns of the American people to prevent such a contingency."[39]

The administration and members of Congress were not alone in worrying about a domino effect if South Carolina got away with nullifying the tariff. In January, for example, the *North American Review* addressed the matter directly. Successful nullification meant that federal revenue would decline "almost to nothing," resulting in "an annual deficit of nearly the whole amount necessary to defray the expenses of the Government, and pay the interest and principal of the debt." The *Review* added, understatedly, the obvious: "The ordinary resource in cases of deficit is a loan, but it may well be doubted whether, under the circumstances supposed, the credit of the Government would be particularly good."[40] Nullification, in short, represented a financial as well as a constitutional threat to the United States. President Jackson was not about to bow to the pressure. In fact, on January 16 he asked Congress to authorize the use of force to collect the revenue.

The federal government faced grave perils, as did South Carolina. If secession and possible civil war constituted that state's overt threat, then the overthrow of the revenue system and Monroe's schedule for debt elimination constituted the unspoken threat. In fact, Jackson's hope to accelerate that schedule and pay off the debt in 1833 immediately became a casualty in the contest between South Carolina and the national government. Uncertainty with respect to the volume of federal revenue both before and after the adoption of a new tariff in 1833 discouraged the Sinking Fund Commission from trying to buy back bonds at market prices.

On December 27 Gulian Verplanck of New York, chairman of the House Ways and Means Committee, introduced a tariff bill that embodied Jackson's annual message recommendation. It proposed reducing rates to 1816 levels in two years. Although not a free trade measure, it offered South Carolina rapid and radical tariff reduction. Beginning in 1835, no import duty would exceed 20 percent.[41] The two-year transition assured that the reduction would occur after the scheduled 1835 elimination of the national debt. The administration was being conciliatory, but on Jackson's terms.

The Verplanck bill touched off a long, often acrimonious, sometimes tedious, debate. Various amendments were offered and discussed. Representatives from the manufacturing states had many objections to the proposal, but they all boiled down to two. First, they complained that the bill took them by surprise. After all, they had revised the tariff at the preceding session—the 1832 tariff—and that revision had not gone into effect yet. Now, under the Verplanck bill, drastic cuts were to occur in two short years. Manufacturers would be unable to adjust their operations to such drastic reductions in so brief a period. Northeastern representatives predicted widespread business failures, severe unemployment, and the utter ruin of their section of the country. Second, they protested that the bill's sponsors were shamelessly capitulating to South Carolina's threats.[42]

Yet, oddly enough, South Carolina itself abandoned the Verplanck bill and instead endorsed a plan proposed by Henry Clay in February. Under the Clay plan, tariff reduction would occur over a ten-year period. All rates above 20 percent in the 1832 tariff would be reduced by 10 percent in two-year intervals beginning in 1834, with sharp reductions reserved for the final 1840-1842 time frame. In 1842 no import duties would exceed 20 percent.[43] These elements constituted the core of the so-called Compromise Tariff of 1833. It meant that the 1832 tariff, which South Carolina had declared null and void, would, in fact, operate for one year, after which the scheduled compromise reductions would begin. When Calhoun, on February 12, announced his support for the Clay bill, its passage was assured.[44] Apparently all the principals were satisfied. Friends of the tariff secured ten more years of protection, and reestablishment of the 1816 rates in 1842 did not reject in principle the policy of protection. Indeed, the 1816 revenue law had been passed for protection. The nullifiers, accordingly, did not win free trade, but they did secure sharp downward revision of the tariff over a decade. Neither the advocates nor the opponents of protection secured all they wanted. However, on a separate but related matter, they did. The scheduled reductions under the Clay compromise rendered certain that no revenue shortfall would interfere with the scheduled elimination of the national debt in 1835. Jackson's "memorable and happy event" would still arrive on time. On March 2 Jackson signed the Compromise Tariff into law. South Carolina rescinded the Ordinance of Nullification but, to make a point, nullified instead the now unneeded Revenue Collection Act, or Force Act, which Congress had passed in February and which the president also signed on March 2. But this latter action was moot, a mere gesture. The Force Act was not going to be implemented. The Nullification Crisis was over.

Resolution of the crisis under Clay's formula raises a question first addressed by James Parton, Jackson's nineteenth-century biographer. Why did South Carolina abandon the Verplanck bill? After all, it promised the same sharp rate reductions in two years which Clay's bill provided in ten. "The nullifiers in Congress," Parton wrote, "could have carried the Verplanck bill if they had given it a frank and energetic support."[45] They did not, but why not? Parton attributed Clay-Calhoun cooperation to their shared enmity for President Jackson, the complex politics surrounding appointments to the select Senate committee created to consider the Clay plan, Jackson's attempts to influence those appointments, and the pressures on Calhoun to settle the tariff issue.[46] Since Parton, historians have largely ignored this matter.

Politics, of course, were involved, but the status of the national debt factored into those politics. Clay's behavior is relatively easy to understand. Having lost the 1832 presidential election, he no longer had reason to delay or oppose timely debt payment. At the same time he had little to gain from the Verplanck bill because it would hurt manufacturers whom he wanted to protect. Coming up with a different formula that Calhoun could accept would enhance his reputation as a compromiser, seemingly save the union, and perhaps prepare the way for a future presidential bid.

Calhoun's behavior is less transparent. The Verplanck bill gave to South Carolina most of what it demanded. Yet it is important to remember that in 1816 South Carolina had accepted protectionism because increased federal revenues allowed a rapid pay-down of the national debt. Monroe's 1824 announcement that the debt would be paid off at the end of 1834 meant that serious downward revision of the tariff was warranted. The modest reductions included in the 1832 tariff disappointed Calhoun and the South Carolina leadership: Hence the Ordinance of Nullification, threatening the revenue system and the timely extinction of the debt on January 1, 1835, in order to pressure the government into more substantive tariff relief. From this perspective South Carolina's defiance of federal policy exposes a contradiction. The state held debt freedom hostage at the same time that it demanded, or said it demanded, free trade, which, however, depended upon securing debt freedom.

South Carolina's abandonment of the Verplanck bill in favor of the Clay compromise suggests an answer to this problem. South Carolina was engaging in a common ploy: Demand everything, but settle for less. But the Verplanck bill, as it turned out, by yielding to so much of South Carolina's demand, actually went further than South Carolina really wanted to go. Why? Because embedded in the Verplanck bill was the possibility—the risk—that after 1835 the government would face revenue shortfalls that would require either raising the tariff again or contracting new debt. Neither alternative was in South Carolina's long-term interest. Accordingly, the gradual reduction of the tariff over a decade was more likely to achieve the state's ultimate objective: free trade. Calhoun was an intelligent man and likely understood this. On March 1, 1833, as the Senate prepared for its final vote on the Clay compromise, Calhoun reiterated his support for the bill. "To many of the details of the measure," he objected, "but . . . was willing to take it with its faults, as a peace-offering."[47]

If this explanation enjoys any merit, then it raises two other questions. First, if the Verplanck bill portended future upward tariff revision or new public debt, or both, then why did Jackson support it? There are at least two answers to this question. One is that passage of the bill would not interfere with debt extinction on January 1, 1835. On Jackson's watch debt freedom would take place, and he would get credit for it. If the Verplanck measure generated future fiscal problems, then his successor or later successors would have to deal with them. Vice President Van Buren, whom Jackson trusted implicitly, was possibly, if not likely, one of these. Indeed, Van Buren, who advised the president during the Nullification Crisis, later wrote: "The administration and its friends in the existing Congress did not possess the power to pass Verplank's bill or any bill for the reduction of the tariff that would be satisfactory to South Carolina."[48] The second half of Van Buren's observation is, of course, patently false.

Congress passed Clay's compromise, and it proved satisfactory to South Carolina. The first half of Van Buren's statement is dubious at best. James Parton, it will be recalled, believed that with unity and determination South Carolina could have carried the Verplanck bill into law. Nonetheless, if Van Buren persuaded the president that the measure could not pass, then Jackson would have had no alternative but to do what he ultimately did—sign the Clay Compromise Tariff into law.

The second and more important question that South Carolina's abandonment of the Verplanck bill raises is this: If South Carolina declined to fight for the Verplanck bill, then how credible were its threats to resist forcibly the collection of customs duties in the state? Why choose the more desperate measure? Indeed, had South Carolina pressed for a vote on the Verplanck bill and it failed to pass, then it would either have had to back up its threats or eat crow. In fact, however, South Carolina did not want to confront either of these alternatives. Its actions and not its rhetoric make this clear. In January 1833, it began to retreat. It postponed the effective date of nullification from February 1 to March 4.[49] By that date, however, Inauguration Day, the Compromise Tariff had ended the crisis. South Carolina avoided both military conflict and humiliation. This reality raises a final question: Had South Carolina been bluffing all along?

Bluffers, by definition, do not announce that they are bluffing. Yet at the time there were some who believed that that was exactly what South Carolina had been doing. Vice President Van Buren was one of them. "South Carolina has not, and will not secede," he assured Jackson. "She will . . . postpone the operation of her ordinance, of this there cannot be reasonable doubt. It would be worse than madness in her to refuse to do so. . . ."[50] Joel R. Poinsett, a prominent South Carolina opponent of nullification and Jackson's point man in Charleston, also believed that the nullifiers were bluffing. Reporting to Jackson on the state's efforts to raise volunteers, Poinsett observed: "The recruiting in town [Charleston] goes on slowly. In the Country we understand five thousand Volunteers have offered their services to the governor. They have been assured however . . . that there would be no fighting. . . . That They had only to put on a bold front and the government of the union would at once yield to their demands."[51] Indeed, it seems that South Carolina was ill prepared to defend itself against the United States Army. Military preparation was a last-minute affair. In December 1832, for example, two weeks after Jackson's proclamation, Governor Robert Y. Hayne promised to supply weapons to volunteer units, but a month later, James H. Hammond, a leading nullifier, reported from the large Barnwell District that his several volunteer units still lacked weapons.[52] This reality was likely the situation throughout the state, undermining the credibility of the belligerent rhetoric in which South Carolina's leaders were engaging. To be sure, the suspicion that South Carolina would never implement its Ordinance of Nullification apparently had wide currency. A settler in Maury County, Tennessee, for example, wrote to Representative James K. Polk: "The South Carolina Heresy is all the talk, at first I confess I was a good deal concerned for fear our Blessed Union might be dissolved, but the more I reflect on the absurd position taken by that State the more I am disposed to consider it a mere Braggadocia."[53]

Empty bravado? Reckless bluff? Other reasons lend credence to this view. First of all, no other southern, tariff-aggrieved state allied itself with South Carolina, much less nullified the laws or pledged military support for their sister state. South Carolina stood alone, poorly prepared, against the might of the United States. Simply put, South Carolina stood no chance of success in an armed conflict with the national government. The nullifiers had to know this.

Moreover, William W. Freehling's now classic study of the nullification crisis, *Prelude to Civil War,* establishes the important fact that South Carolina whites, a minority in most of the state's nineteen districts, lived in chronic fear of slave uprisings. Their apprehension became acute after discovery of the Denmark Vesey plot in 1822.[54] If Freehling is right—and he is—then South Carolina's nullification and secessionist threats seem hollow. After all, what would invite a slave insurrection more than a federal army marching through South Carolina to suppress a white rebellion?

Yet South Carolina played its hand well and walked away from a high-stakes game a winner. It got most of what it wanted, on terms that were acceptable, and it avoided armed conflict as well as embarrassing surrender.

Successful bluffers do not always admit that they had been bluffing. South Carolina's leaders did not. In fact, the leadership did not know the extent or the depth of its bluff. On January 8, 1833, as House debate on the Verplanck bill got underway, Representative Tristam Burges of Rhode Island proposed creating a special committee of twenty-four, one member from each state, to "examine into and report" on a very long and precise set of questions concerning the sources of federal revenues, the specifics of imports and exports, commodity prices in England and France, and much more. The scope of Burges' resolution was so lengthy and broad that it had no hope of adoption. It would have bogged the Treasury Department down in a seemingly never-ending search for data, and, when the information was presented to the committee for review, even more time would be lost. In brief, the resolution was impractical. Yet item I of the resolution was exceedingly important and easily attainable. It required the proposed special committee to "report to this House the amount of money paid by the people of each State of the United States, viz: 1st. On all goods, wares, and merchandise imported into said state from foreign countries."[55] The House of Representatives would have been wise to call for at least this information. Instead, it began debating the Verplanck bill completely uninformed regarding each state's contribution to federal coffers. Under the circumstances this was no minor matter. South Carolina had been complaining for years that it (and the other southern exporting states) paid more than its fair share to the federal treasury. Calhoun had made this point in his *Exposition*, and the assertion came up again and again during earlier tariff debates.[56] South Carolina's conviction that it paid an inordinate share of federal taxes through the tariff emboldened it to threaten withholding those funds to secure tariff reduction. South Carolina believed that it had enough revenue muscle to confront the government with possible postponement of extinguishing the national debt that Congress and the administration would yield to its demands. Congressional willingness to accommodate the nullifiers suggests that other states believed that South Carolina had enough clout at the treasury to delay the elimination of the national debt.

The question of state contribution to the treasury reemerged in House debate on January 15. Rufus Choate of Massachusetts called for reconsideration of the Burges resolution in order to "call out all the evidence . . . contained in the treasury and the custom-houses." Such evidence, Choate declared, would show that the "allegation of the planting states, that they are taxed more than a constitutional proportion by a protective tariff" was false.[57] Choate's plea, however, was ignored. Congress debated the Verplanck bill and then the Clay compromise bill without knowing what South Carolina (or any other state) paid annually in import taxes. This ignorance, as it turned out, strengthened South Carolina's hand.

What precisely was South Carolina's contribution to tariff revenues? The answer to this question remained unavailable for a dozen years after the nullification crisis was resolved, but the 1845 annual report of the secretary of the treasury published the amount each state paid in customs duties between 1800 and 1844. The data for South Carolina are revealing (see Table 1 below). They indicate that South Carolina paid only 3.23 percent of all tariff dollars collected between 1816 and 1833. Indeed, the trend over that eighteen-year period was that the Palmetto State paid less and less. In the crisis years 1832-1833, it accounted for less than 2.0 percent of federal tariff revenues. Denying this amount to the federal treasury might not have had any impact whatever on the timely extinction of the national debt, particularly since the treasury recorded a surplus of nearly $11,000,000 in 1833.[58] The problem was that at the time no one knew this, including public officials in South Carolina. The threat to debt payment seemed real but was not. Moreover, according to the 1830 census, the white population of South Carolina, the overwhelming majority of

TABLE I

South Carolina's Share of Federal Tariff Payments, 1816–1833
Total Customs Receipts Duties Collected in South Carolina (%)

Year	Federal Tariff Annual Total ($)	South Carolina Duties Collected ($)	Percentage of Federal Tariff
1816	36,307,000	1,474,474	4.06
1817	26,283,000	1,145,677	4.35
1818	17,176,000	1,308,104	7.61
1819	20,284,000	813,829	4.01
1820	15,006,000	613,697	4.08
1821	18,004,000	595,317	3.30
1822	17,590,000	794,004	4.51
1823	19,088,000	765,899	4.01
1824	17,878,000	732,076	4.09
1825	20,099,000	661,327	3.29
1826	23,341,000	573,707	2.45
1827	19,712,000	592,025	3.00
1828	23,206,000	450,967	1.94
1829	22,682,000	490,750	2.16
1830	21,922,000	497,397	2.26
1831	24,224,000	505,050	2.08
1832	28,465,000	523,031	1.83
1833	29,033,000	401,634	1.38
Total	400,300,000	2,938,965	3.23

Sources: *Historical Statistics,* 711; *NASP,* vol. 8, *General Reports,* 133. This latter reference is identified in the Secretary of the Treasury's Report, December 3, 1845, as "Table G: Comparative statement of duties on imports into South Carolina."

tariff-paying consumers, stood at 257,863, or 2.0 per cent of the entire United States population of 12,866,000.[59] South Carolina was indeed paying its fair share of the tariff and perhaps even less. Again, at the time no one knew this. Accordingly, from a public finance perspective, South Carolina bluffed its way through the nullification crisis, itself unaware that its contribution to federal revenues and debt reduction was marginal. In the end, South Carolina only seemed to take the payment of the national debt as a hostage in the contest over the tariff. The reality was quite different. Unverified assumptions, however, often present themselves as facts.

❧

The Nullification Crisis concerned the national debt. South Carolina had always shared in the republican consensus that eliminating the debt was essential to liberty. Yet nullifying revenue laws contradicted that goal, and the contradiction exposes the truth: South Carolina took debt extinction hostage not because of states' rights theory but because it recognized that the debt issue, virtually sacred as it was, constituted the most powerful lever with which to pry tariff reform from Congress and the administration. Threatening secession was mere rhetoric; money was the real issue. Simply put, South Carolina was bluffing, and the tactic succeeded. The bluff worked even better than South Carolina knew because the state's tariff contributions to the federal treasury, rather than oppressively high, were actually marginal but in accord with the size of its free population. Ignorance inadvertently allied itself with the national consensus in favor of debt extinction to assure a compromise settlement to the crisis. In the end, South Carolina secured tariff reform and extinction of the debt. Jackson's "memorable and happy event" remained on schedule for New Year's Day 1835.

SEVEN

AWAITING DEBT FREEDOM, 1833–1834

JACKSON'S SECOND INAUGURAL CEREMONY, MARCH 4, 1833, differed sharply from the one four years earlier. No "open house" celebration at the executive mansion was planned, and the "severity of the cold" and "very high" winds forced the oath-taking into the House chamber.[1] There the Old Hero delivered his second inaugural address. He briefly reviewed the secessionist danger the nation had recently passed through and stressed the importance of the union to the preservation of liberty.[2] "I shall continue," he declared, "to exert all my faculties to maintain the just powers of the Constitution and to transmit unimpaired to posterity the blessings of our Federal Union."[3] He reaffirmed his commitment to "simplicity and economy in the expenditures of the Government" and pledged "to raise no more money from the people" than was necessary to fulfill the responsibilities the Constitution imposed on the federal authority.[4] National debt freedom would remain on schedule, and no new taxes would be levied. In other words, Jackson defended the recent Compromise Tariff.

❧

While Jackson accepted peace with South Carolina, he rejected it with respect to the Bank of the United States. His reelection encouraged him to escalate the war he had begun against the "monster" bank the preceding July. He believed that Clay, Biddle, and other Bank of the United States proponents had introduced the recharter bill four years early on the assumption that he, rather than risk throwing the economy into turmoil as the election neared, would sign the measure. To Jackson, this tactic bordered on extortion, and, of course, he refused to bend under pressure. His veto then became the principal issue of the campaign, and Clay had hoped to ride it to victory. Jackson, interpreting the election result as a mandate to destroy the Bank once and for all, shortly after the inauguration began planning to strangle it to death by removing the federal deposits. As Jackson had told Van Buren earlier: "The Bank is trying to kill me . . . but I will kill it."[5]

The Bank, in the meantime, gave Jackson additional reasons to destroy it, because, the veto notwithstanding, it was not planning to go down without a fight. After Secretary McLane and the administration acquiesced in the three-month postponement of the July 1832 debt payment, Biddle, it seems, chalked that matter up as a victory—a small one, perhaps, but a victory nonetheless. Shortly afterward, another opportunity to play the same game presented itself. In July, McLane informed Biddle that the government planned to pay off two-thirds of the remaining three-percent debt on October 5 and the remaining one-third on January 5, 1833.[6] Biddle now resolved to delay payment again, not as he had last time by convincing the secretary of the inexpediency of the proposal but by covertly arranging to delay the payoff.

Briefly put, Biddle sought to postpone the presentation of European held bonds worth about $5,000,000 until October 1, 1833. To accomplish this goal he sent Thomas Cadwalader, a member of the Bank of the United States Board of Directors and a close personal friend, to London to negotiate an agreement with the House of Baring, the British bank, by which the latter would buy up the American bonds and hold them until October 1833. In effect, Baring would proxy for the Bank of the United States. Such an arrangement, however, was very risky for Biddle because the Bank of the United States charter prohibited it from investing in the national debt. If the House of Baring acted as a stand-in for the Bank, would the arrangement not violate the spirit—if not the letter—of the charter? In any event, Cadwalader and the Barings agreed upon a contract. The latter would offer 91 cents on the dollar to European holders of the three-percent bonds, and, come October 1, 1833, cash them in at face value. The Barings would earn profit, and the Bank of the United States would retain the use of five million dollars' worth of taxpayer money for its own purposes.[7]

All of this, of course, was to be accomplished secretly. The House of Baring, however, had to publicize its offer to the bondholders, and, accordingly, it printed and distributed a circular announcing its terms. Unfortunately for Biddle and the Bank of the United States, one of these documents fell into the hands of the *New York Evening Post*. On October 11, 1832, just weeks before the election, the *Post* published it.[8]

Exposure of this operation deeply embarrassed Biddle. On October 15 he wrote to McLane, explaining that Cadwalader had gone to London to arrange an entirely different deal but had violated his instructions. Biddle disavowed the contract Cadwalader had negotiated in order to distance himself and the Bank from the apparent and perhaps illegal scheme to delay payment on the national debt. Yet it seems likely that Biddle had the Barings contract in his possession "weeks before" the *Post* published the circular, in which case disavowal came only after exposure.[9]

Biddle's scheme backfired. None of this sat well with the administration. Roger B. Taney later recalled that "when the transaction came to the knowledge of the President he was exceedingly indignant."[10] This characterization of Jackson's reaction probably understates the matter. Jackson was likely livid. Why? Because even granting Biddle the benefit of the doubt regarding the disavowal, one fact remained. The "object of the arrangement was to prevent the government from paying five millions of its debt," enabling the Bank to use that much of the "public money for an entire year."[11]

For what purpose would the Bank use that money? Jackson learned later, in August 1833, that the Bank's ordinary expenses for "stationary and printing" began to grow after his first annual message had questioned its legitimacy. By election year 1832, these expenses had increased by a factor of six. Jackson was convinced that "stationary and printing" served to cover Bank expenditures to defeat him. In short, Jackson believed that the Bank of the United States was using the government's own money to overthrow his administration.[12]

The Bank's effort to postpone payment on the national debt and, as Jackson saw it, to use the money, or at least part of it, to unseat him sealed the Bank's fate. Biddle had attempted to delay payment on the three-percents until October 1, 1833. Jackson now determined to seize upon that very same date not only to start killing the Bank of the United States but to rub Biddle's face in its ashes.

❧

Months of deliberation and preparation passed before the president struck. Finally, on September 18, 1833, he assembled his cabinet and read a lengthy paper explaining the action he was about to take. After briefly reviewing the objections to the Bank that he had articulated in his veto message, Jackson argued that the Bank had violated its charter over and over again by involving itself in politics and thereby threatening the integrity of republican government. Among the Bank's political misdeeds, according to the president, were actions that obstructed his administration's efforts to extinguish the national debt. Even though the Bank's charter was nearing expiration and it "was aware that it was the intention of the Government to use the public deposit as fast as it has accrued in the payment of the public debt, yet did it extend its loans" between January 1831 and May 1832 from about $42,500,000 to about $70,500,000—"an increase of $28,025,766.48 in sixteen months."[13] Why the credit expansion? According to Jackson, "the leading object of this immense extension . . . was to bring as large a portion of the people as possible under its power and influence. . . ."[14] The Bank had transformed itself into a great political machine responsible to nobody.[15] Moreover, this credit expansion countered government policy regarding the debt and demonstrated the Bank's "faithlessness as a public agent" in making debt payments; "the bank had extended its loans more than $28,000,000, although it knew the Government intended to appropriate most of its large deposit during that year in payment of the public debt."[16] Accordingly, the Bank knew that "it would not be able to pay over the public deposit when it would be required by the Government."[17] Jackson then recounted what happened when Treasury Secretary McLane "informed the bank that it was his intention to pay off one-half the 3 percents" on July 1, 1832, "which amounted to about $6,500,000." Biddle, it will be recalled, claiming that he wanted to assist New York's credit-pressed merchants, had encouraged McLane to postpone the payment until October 1. In exchange the Bank of the United States would pay the additional quarterly interest itself. Hence, postponement would not cost the government anything.[18] McLane agreed.

The Bank's scheming, according to Jackson, did not end there. He explained to the cabinet what the Cadwalader mission had been about. Knowing "that at the end of that quarter the bank would not be able to pay over the deposits, and that further indulgence was not to be expected of the Government," Biddle pursued another course.[19] He sent "an agent" to London "secretly to negotiate with the holders of the public debt in Europe." The agent's mission was to "induce" those bondholders "to hold back their claims for one year" by promising them "an equal or higher interest" than what the government paid. If this arrangement succeeded, then the Bank of the United States would "retain the use of $5,000,000 of the public money, which the Government . . . set apart for the payment of that debt." Only when elements of this operation leaked to the press did the Bank try to backtrack and disavow violations of its charter. Nevertheless, Jackson said, "[i]n this scheme the bank was partially successful" because "to this day the certificates of a portion of these stocks have not been paid and the bank retains the use of the money."[20]

Although Jackson had a variety of reasons to remove the federal deposits from the Bank of the United States, what could have provoked him more than unwarranted interference with the timely payment of the national debt? (South Carolina, after all, had incurred presidential wrath by pursuing a similar tactic during the recent Nullification Crisis.) To his cabinet Jackson declared: "This effort to thwart the Government in the payment of the public debt that it [the Bank of the United States] might retain the public money to be used for their private interests . . . would have justified the instant withdrawal of the public deposits."[21] Now, Jackson said, the day of reckoning was at hand, and on October 1, 1833, a short two weeks away, the process of drawing down the federal revenues in the Bank of the United States would begin. Incoming revenues would be deposited in selected state banks. American public finance was to undergo an immediate and radical restructure. For this reason alone the removal of the deposits was controversial. Jackson's statement, Amos Kendall later recalled, "underwent the severest criticism."[22] But it hardly mattered. Jackson's will prevailed.

Yet there was also a legal issue. The law establishing the Bank of the United States reposed authority for deposit removal in the secretary of the treasury. William J. Duane, recently appointed to that post, believed Jackson's decision was unjustifiable because it was financially reckless and illegal. He refused to implement the directive. Jackson fired him. Attorney General Roger B. Taney took Duane's place and ordered deposit removal.

Financial panic and political uproar resulted. Biddle, confronting the gradual diminution of the deposits, called in loans and created a severe credit crunch. The business community howled, laid off workers, and watched the economy slide into recession. National

Republicans and Democrats who found the president's action unpalatable drew together under a new party label—Whig—and protested against what they denounced as arbitrary and illegal executive power. Indeed, in early 1834, led by Henry Clay, the Senate formally censured Andrew Jackson for unconstitutional conduct.[23]

Nevertheless, despite economic and political crisis, debt freedom remained on schedule. As January 1, 1835, drew nearer, awareness that a large federal budgetary surplus loomed commanded increasing congressional attention. It was within this context that the status of the public lands and the disposition of the revenue earned from their sale became urgent issues.

Few public questions were as longstanding and as complex as the federal lands in the new western states. The issue concerned not only the law but also tightly intertwined regional, economic, and political interests so complicated that a national consensus to address it remained elusive.[24]

The legal status of these lands antedated the Constitution. Originally claimed by Virginia, New York, and several other states, they were ceded to the United States in the early 1780s in order to provide stability to the Articles of Confederation. But all the state cessions were made on the understanding that, as the Virginia deed said, the lands would serve "as a common fund" for the benefit of all current and future states.[25] The deeds transferring state title to the Confederation provided the legal foundation for the famous Land Ordinances of 1785 and 1787. After adoption of the Constitution in 1788, the deeds and the Land Ordinances remained in effect under Article IV, Section 3. In 1790, it will be recalled, Congress appropriated the "proceeds" from the sale of those lands exclusively to the payment of the national debt.[26] This measure fulfilled the "common fund" obligation of the cession deeds, but land sale revenues were not deposited in a special Treasury account or in any way kept separate from tariff or other revenue sources.

During the Federalist era, the public lands generated little revenue.[27] However, as Native American claims were extinguished and as the American population grew, the early decades of the nineteenth century witnessed expansion into the regions north and south of the Ohio River and the creation of new states with extensive federal holdings within them. A fundamental question arose: Should those lands be sold at modest prices to encourage settlement or should they be sold dearly to maximize revenue? This question, seemingly simple, entailed numerous difficulties. A few examples: Would cheap land rapidly drain population from east to west? If so, would not property values in the old states suffer? Would not developing business confront high labor costs? Would not the federal government have to depend on high tariffs to meet its responsibilities?[28] By the time Andrew Jackson became president in 1829 these and other related problems remained unresolved. Yet time was running out. The year of debt freedom—1835—lay on the short horizon. What was to be done with land revenues, whether large or small, when debt freedom was achieved and the law of 1790 became obsolete? Would they foster a federal surplus?

In his first annual message to Congress in 1829, Jackson discussed the future surplus, recommending its distribution to the states, but he did not address the public lands question.[29] Congress, however, did, and approaching debt freedom counted as a major factor in its debates. On December 17, for example, Representative Jonathan Hunt of Vermont offered a resolution that the Committee on Public Lands "inquire into the expediency of appropriating the nett annual proceeds" of land sales "to the several states" for education and internal improvements. The ratio of representation in the House would serve as the distribution formula.[30] But William D. Martin of South Carolina immediately moved to amend Hunt's proposal. Reminding Congress that from time to time over the years it had "donated" land to the western states for roads, canals, schools, asylums, and other purposes, Martin suggested that the Public Lands Committee account for those land grants by subtracting their value from the sums that would otherwise be due recipient states before distribution began.[31] Martin, of course, was simply pointing out the obvious: that states which had secured federal land grants in the past would, under Hunt's resolution, secure benefits at the expense of those which did not.

Hunt's resolution and the Martin amendment triggered a lengthy debate that inevitably raised questions about the impact of the proposed distribution upon the timely payment of the national debt. Martin himself expressed concern about applying to other purposes revenue that was pledged to debt reduction.[32] He was not alone. Spencer Pettis of Missouri worried that an "immediate distribution would embarrass the Government" in "paying off" the national debt.[33] For this reason he opposed the Hunt resolution and the Martin amendment. Both, he thought, were premature. "When the public debt shall have been paid," Pettis said, "it will be time enough to make this inquiry" into the viability of distributing land sale revenues.[34] Rollin Mallory of Vermont agreed. No distribution should be made, the New Englander believed, until the national debt was actually extinguished. "When that payment shall have been accomplished," he asked, "what shall then be done with the public lands? That is the question."[35]

As December drew to an end, James K. Polk proposed tabling the Hunt resolution indefinitely, because even its supporters acknowledged that no distribution could occur until the debt was paid.[36] Buchanan of Pennsylvania, James Blair of South Carolina, and others agreed: The debt had to be paid first.[37] Although it consumed valuable House time, in the end the Hunt resolution went nowhere because actual elimination of the national debt had higher priority than disposition of any subsequent surplus.

The 1829 House debate on the public lands has largely been forgotten, and for good reason. The Senate debate on the same subject, dominated by Daniel Webster and Robert Y. Hayne of South Carolina, generated an extraordinary elucidation of the meaning of the Constitution and the nature of the union under it. Webster articulated the nationalist perspective while his opponent represented the states' rights school. Yet the debate had nothing to do with the distribution of land sale revenues. Rather, it emerged from a resolution offered by Samuel Foot of Connecticut on December 29, 1829, to limit the sale of public lands to those already on the market "at the minimum price."[38] This proposal exposed divergent sectional interests. The West, for example, complained that it was an attempt to slow their region's growth and development in order to assure the North a large supply of cheap labor. The South complained that Foot's resolution was, among other things, an attempt to shrink land sale revenues in order to perpetuate high tariff rates for northern manufacturers. The North denied ill will against any section, arguing that the glut of public land on the open market did not serve the national interest.[39] The Webster-Hayne debate probed these issues and more: the division and separation of powers, slavery, internal improvements, and, of course, the national debt.

Senator Hayne believed that the status of the public lands was a matter of grave importance to the American people. If the federal government retained possession of them *ad infinitum,* counting them as a long-term source of income, then the United States would, in effect, maintain an independent revenue beyond the control of taxpayers. "I distrust . . . the policy of creating a great permanent national treasury, whether to be derived from public lands or from any other source . . . ." because "an immense national treasury would be a fund for corruption."[40] A huge surplus, in other words, would serve the same evil purpose as a huge debt. But, fortunately, Hayne said, "[t]he time has not yet arrived when the question" of what to do with the public lands had to be decided.[41] "The public debt must be first paid."[42] It was enough to deal with one problem at a time.

In his reply, Webster addressed the debt aspect of the public lands issue. "Among other things, the honorable member [Hayne] spoke of the public debt. To that he holds the public lands pledged, and has expressed his usual earnestness for its total discharge." Webster declared that he too wished to see the debt eliminated and had, ever since coming to Congress, always voted for measures to reduce it. "But," he added, "I have observed that, whenever the subject of the public debt is introduced into the Senate, a morbid sort of fervor is manifested in regard to it, which I have been sometimes at a loss to understand." After all, he explained, "[t]he debt is not now large, and is in a course of most rapid reduction. A very few years will see it extinguished." Yet there was "so much anxiety to get rid of it." Why? Webster believed he knew the answer to that question. The national debt, he said, served as a "tie, holding the different parts of the country together. . . ." Americans collectively were obligated to their creditors, and that obligation bonded the people into one. He did not characterize the debt as a national blessing, but he did say that it was "not to be lamented."[43] By implication Webster attributed disunionist sentiments to Hayne.

Hayne deftly rebutted the allegation. He observed that Webster "took occasion to intimate" that zeal for debt freedom "arises from a disposition to weaken the ties which bind the people of this union." Yet, while the senator from Massachusetts "deals us this blow," he declares himself at the same time to favor debt extinction. Could Webster have the matter both ways? Hayne felt "bound to conclude" that Webster "will be found acting with those with whom it is a darling object to prevent the payment of the public debt."[44] Hayne, of course, was referring to the internal improvers and others who, guided by the notion that "liberty is power," would "bankrupt the treasury of the world" to fulfill their ambitions.[45] Surely no one missed the reference to the Adams agenda.

In the end the twenty-first Congress adjourned its first session without doing anything regarding the public lands. The issue, however, did not go away, and, as the day of debt freedom drew nearer, it resurfaced; and it resurfaced in connection with the anticipated post-debt federal surplus.

❦

In his second annual message to Congress, Jackson reaffirmed his commitment to distribute the surplus to the states.[46] This portion of his remarks was assigned to a select House committee for review and evaluation. Under the chairmanship of James K. Polk, it reported on

January 28 the following year a negative critique of the distribution proposal.[47] Over subsequent weeks the Polk report generated some heated debate, but it ultimately went nowhere.[48] After all, the debt had not yet been paid off, and there was no surplus to distribute. But, importantly, Jackson's proposal and Polk's report concerned a surplus generated from all, not just one, revenue sources.

The Senate too took up the issue, but from an angle reminiscent of Jonathan Hunt's resolution in the House three years earlier. On April 16, 1832, Henry Clay introduced a bill to distribute the proceeds of the sales of the public lands to the states. It aimed, in other words, to distribute the revenue derived from one specific source. The states were to apply the funds not only for internal improvements and education but also for the colonization of free blacks to Liberia.[49] Clay's bill maintained the longstanding price of $1.25 per acre and provided, prior to the actual distribution, a ten-percent rebate on the net revenue to the states in which the lands were located. Enactment, of course, would reduce federal revenues and shrink the looming surplus and at the same time promote programs to which Clay was committed. (Clay was a founding member of the American Colonization Society.) Yet the bill had little chance of success: This was the congressional session that had to deal with the 1832 tariff and the Bank of the United States recharter bill. Distribution would have to wait, and Clay probably knew it. He himself was busy running for president. In fact, the bill got bogged down in politics, and, although it passed the Senate, the House wound up postponing its consideration until the next session.[50] In short, no sense of urgency concerning the future surplus had yet emerged.

Indeed, Jackson did not directly address the coming surplus in his December 1832 message to Congress. Rather, it will be recalled, in language conciliatory to South Carolina, he discussed the need of limiting government revenue to operational needs once the debt was extinguished.[51] Nor did he refer to the surplus in relation to the public lands. "Among the interests which merit the consideration of Congress after the payment of the public debt, one of the most important . . . is that of the public lands."[52] He recommended that the lands be sold "at a price barely sufficient to reimburse to the United States the expense of the present system and the cost arising under our Indian compacts."[53] Cheap land would, of course, promote western settlement—but not a surplus.

Yet in 1833, with the Bank bill vetoed, Jackson reelected, and the Compromise Tariff in the works, Clay reintroduced his measure. It came up for debate in January, consumed a great deal of Senate time, and was passed by the upper chamber before the end of the month.[54] The House, however, debated the bill for many weeks. It amended the measure by dropping the provision concerning the colonization of free blacks and by increasing the rebate from 10% to 12.5% and, on March 1, three days before Congress was set to adjourn, voted 96 to 40, to approve.[55] The next day the Senate, by a vote of 23 to 5, agreed with the House and approved the amended bill.[56]

Because of his earlier statements regarding distribution, Jackson was expected to sign the measure into law. But to the dismay of many, he pocket-vetoed the bill. Clay, of course, was angry. He was particularly disappointed that the House's late action on the bill had allowed the president to avoid the Constitutional obligation to present his objections in writing. He believed that Congress had the votes to override a formal veto. "I believe that we should have passed the Land bill by Constitutional majorities, if it had been returned," he wrote Biddle, "but the President pocketed it."[57] For Clay this was no minor matter. Indeed, he believed that addressing the public land question and the anticipated surplus was of such importance that the veto prevented his retirement. "Had the Land bill passed," he wrote Samuel Southard, "I should certainly not have returned to Washn. The state of that measure creates some doubt whether it is not my duty to go back once more."[58] Clay likely overstated the role the land bill played in his decision to retain his senate seat, but, whatever his motivations, when Congress convened in December he was at his desk in the capitol building. Awaiting him was not only the crisis engendered by the President's removal of the government's deposits from the Bank of the United States but also a written explanation for the pocket veto of the bill to distribute land sale revenues the previous March.

Jackson had seemingly flip-flopped on the distribution matter, and the president was well aware of this widespread perception. Accordingly, he wanted to explain why the land sale-distribution bill failed to win his approval. On December 4, 1833, the day after he submitted his fifth annual message to Congress, a written explanation of the pocket veto arrived at the Senate. Jackson excused the pocket veto on the ground of necessity: The bill had come to him at the very last minute. "The brief period then remaining before the rising of Congress and the extreme pressure of official duties unavoidable on such occasions did not leave me sufficient time for that full consideration of the subject which was due to its great importance."[59] He reviewed the history by which the public lands in the West had become the property of the United States. The cessions by Virginia and other states had been made on the condition that the lands serve "as a common fund for the use and benefit" of all the states, present and future, and that that agreement, though entered into under the Articles of Confederation, was binding under the Constitution. Yet the bill enacted by Congress surrendered one-eighth of the revenue earned from sales to the states within which the land was located, leaving only seven-eighths for proportional distribution to all the states. Accordingly, to Jackson, the bill violated both the original agreement and the Constitution.[60] He elaborated on these points.

Jackson reminded the Senate that the law of August 4, 1790, pledged the proceeds of land sales to debt reduction.[61] Yet circumstances had changed. "The debt for which these lands were pledged," he wrote, "may be considered as paid, and they are consequently released from that lien." But that pledge, he correctly said, had "formed no part of the compacts with the States, or of the conditions upon which the cessions were made." Rather, that pledge, the 1790 law, "was a contract between new parties—between the United States and their creditors." Accordingly, paying off the national debt did not extinguish the original compacts of cession. Rather, they remained "in full force, and the obligation of the United States to dispose of the lands for the common benefit is neither destroyed nor impaired."[62] But since discharging the debt would in the very near future no longer constitute the "mode" for serving the common good, "the only legitimate question which can arise is, In what other way are these lands to be . . . disposed of for the common benefit of the several States?"[63] The land sale-distribution bill violated the common good intent of the cession agreements and the Constitution, Jackson asserted, by granting an eighth of the proceeds to the states in which the lands were located before the general distribution.[64]

Furthermore, the bill required the states to spend the distribution rebate on education and internal improvements. But, Jackson argued, if federal moneys could not be appropriated for purely local projects, as his Maysville veto had made clear, or for state educational pursuits, then Congress could not appropriate federal dollars to the states on the condition that the states expend them on these matters. Again, in this way the bill violated the Constitution.[65]

Jackson saved his most severe objection to the end. He acknowledged that the post-debt era promised "a surplus of moneys in the Treasury" and that returning it to the people was the right and proper thing to do. Moreover, since returning it to individual taxpayers was impossible, the next best thing to do was to return it to the states where "the more immediate representatives of the people" could use it for the betterment of those to whom it belonged without restriction.[66] These observations essentially restated the views he had expressed in his 1829 and 1830 messages to Congress.

But, Jackson asserted, the land sale-distribution bill "assumes a new principle. Its object is not to return to the people an unavoidable surplus of revenue paid in by them, but to create a surplus for distribution among the States."[67] What did he mean? According to Jackson, the practice of the government from its inception was to deposit all federal revenues in the Treasury without reference to their source. In other words, there were no separate funds; all revenues were mixed.[68] The land-sale distribution bill, he believed, changed that longstanding practice. "It seizes the entire proceeds of one source of revenue and sets them apart as a surplus, making it necessary to raise the moneys for supporting the Government and meeting the general charges from other sources." Even the costs of administering the land office system would be imposed on other revenues, namely, of course, the tariff. The bill did not return to the people an incidental surplus; rather, it "compels" them "to pay moneys into the Treasury for the mere purpose of creating a surplus for distribution" to the states.[69] The danger was clear. As states looked more and more for the annual distribution, the less and less they would have to tax to maintain their own operations. State dependence upon distribution funds would diminish the power and influence of the various state governments and expand the authority, power, and influence of the federal government. The land sale-distribution bill threatened "consolidation."[70]

"Money is power," he declared, mockingly reminding the Senate of John Quincy Adams's alternative definition of power and at the same time suggesting that the land sale-distribution bill, if it became law, would pull the nation in the direction that Adams had tried to lead it. The distribution, as designed by Clay, led only to corruption.[71]

Finally, while the bill might tempt the states, according to Jackson, it offered no real benefits at all, especially for the western states in which the public lands were located and to which a one-eighth premium was promised. The welfare of the new western states was better served in other ways. "Their true policy consists in the rapid settling and improvement of the waste lands within their limits," Jackson wrote. "As a means of hastening those events, they have long been looking to a reduction in the price of public lands upon the final payment of the national debt. The effect of the proposed system [Clay's land sale-distribution bill] would be to prevent that reduction."[72] Assigning a specified element of revenue for distribution implied increased federal dependence on the tariff system and perhaps even renewed borrowing. Clay's bill was, in short, inconsistent with the goal of debt freedom. For this as well as for other reasons, it was doomed before it even reached Jackson's desk.

❦

The year 1833 ended without legislation regarding the public lands or disposition of the revenue from their sale. Indeed, no legislation concerning the post-debt surplus was enacted. Instead, the year closed with Congress in an uproar over Jackson's removal of the government's funds from the Bank of the United States and their deposit in selected state banks, a presidential decision rooted in part upon Biddle's perceived attempt to manipulate the timely payment of the national debt to his and the Bank's advantage and the administration's disadvantage.

The following year Congress consumed much of its time on matters unrelated to debt extinction and the surpluses that were sure to follow. The so-called "Panic Session" devoted endless hours to the question of whether the credit contraction in the money market was Jackson's responsibility for removing the federal deposits, or Biddle's for needlessly choking the economy in order to secure restoration of the funds and recharter of the Bank. In the White House, Jackson fumed over the Whig-dominated Senate's censure of his conduct. In short, both Congress and the executive expended their energies on matters that had nothing to do with the extraordinary situation that the nation would soon confront: debt freedom and huge surplus revenues. But by December the mood changed. The severity of the panic and the disenchantment it fostered within the business community finally compelled Biddle to ease up on credit, and confidence began to grow. And 1835, of course, offered another reason for optimism.

EIGHT

DEBT FREEDOM AND THE MEANING OF JACKSONIAN DEMOCRACY

In December 1832, at the height of the Nullification Crisis, President Jackson predicted that eliminating the national debt would constitute a "memorable and happy event."[1] Two years later, on December 1, 1834, he enjoyed the satisfaction of announcing in his sixth annual message that national debt freedom was but one month away. He mentioned it rather matter-of-factly. After reviewing federal revenues and expenditures during the preceding eleven months, he said: "Thus it appears that after satisfying" current appropriations, "and after discharging the last item of our public debt, which will be on the 1st of January next," a large balance would remain in the Treasury.[2] Jackson did not gloat. Rather, he asserted that debt freedom provided an opportunity to resolve problems that had perplexed the union for years. "Free from public debt, at peace with all the world, and with no complicated interests to consult in our intercourse with foreign powers, the present may be hailed as the epoch in our history the most favorable for the settlement of those principles in our domestic policy, which shall be best calculated to give stability to our Republic and secure the blessings of freedom to our citizens."[3] What did Jackson have in mind? First and foremost was continued retrenchment. "Among these principles, from our past experience, it can not be doubted that simplicity in the character of the Federal Government, and a rigid economy in the administration, should be regarded as fundamental and sacred."[4] Unnecessary federal spending meant either increased taxes, new debt, or both, exacerbating problems caused by the debt then being eliminated. He was specifically referring to the crisis over nullification. "All must be sensible," Jackson said, "that the existence of the public debt, by rendering taxation necessary for its extinguishment, has increased the difficulties which are inseparable from any exercise of the taxing power; and that it [the debt] was, in this respect, a remote agent in producing those disturbing questions which grew out of the discussions relating to the tariff."[5] Then came a caution, if not a warning. "If such has been the tendency of a debt incurred in the acquisition and maintenance of our national rights and liberties, the obligation of which all portions of the Union cheerfully acknowledged, it must be obvious that whatever is calculated to increase the burdens of Government without necessity, must be fatal to all our hopes of preserving its true character."[6] Unnecessary federal expenditures—for internal improvement, for example—threatened the union. New debt could unravel the Constitution. "While we are felicitating ourselves, therefore, upon the extinguishment of the national debt, and the prosperous state of our finances, let us not be tempted to depart from those sound maxims of public policy, which enjoin a just adaptation of the revenue to the expenditures that are consistent with a rigid economy, and an entire abstinence from all topics of legislation that are not clearly within the constitutional powers of the Government and suggested by the wants of the country."[7] Strict government economy, according to Jackson, also promoted prosperity and patriotism. "Properly regarded," he said, "under such a policy, every diminution of the public burdens arising from taxation, gives to individual enterprise increased power, and furnishes to all the members of our happy Confederacy new motives for patriotic affection and support."[8] Finally and "above all," the president observed, retrenchment's "most important effect will be found in its influence upon the character of the Government, by confining its action to those objects which will be sure to secure to it the attachment and support of our fellow-citizens."[9] Jackson's remarks on debt freedom were, in brief, sober and cautionary.

Secretary of the Treasury Levi Woodbury's report came the next day. His revealed that at the beginning of 1835 the Treasury would hold a balance of more than $6,736,000.[10] Regarding the debt, Woodbury reported that "[a]ll the four and a half per cents, outstanding at the commencement of the present year, have been redeemed, except the sum of $443.25."[11] Enough money, however, had been placed in the Bank of the United States to cover that remaining payment. Moreover, between July and December 1834, Treasury agents had succeeded in purchasing at par nearly $500,000 of the five-percent debt created in 1821.Whatever remained would be promptly paid four weeks later, on January 1, 1835. Unlike Jackson, Woodbury could not resist some boastfulness. "Thus," he wrote, "before the end of the year, the whole [debt] will be either paid, or money provided to pay it; and the United States will present that happy, and probably, in modern times, unprecedented spectacle, of a people substantially free from the smallest portion of a public debt."[12] Even the bitterly anti-Jackson *United States' Telegraph* editorialized as much as two years earlier: "It must certainly be gratifying to the people of the United States to know, from official authority, that the Government is free from debt."[13]

On New Year's Day 1835, the prediction former president Monroe had made in 1824 was realized. The United States was debt free. Celebrations marked the occasion, especially among Jackson Democrats, who recognized that Debt Freedom Day missed the twentieth anniversary of the victory at New Orleans by only one week. The most conspicuous party was held in Washington at Brown's Hotel on January 8. Celebrants drank to Jackson's victory over the British and his victory over the public debt. Dinner was served to more than 200 guests. Vice President Van Buren was there. So too were Thomas Hart Benton, James K. Polk, and other leaders of the Democratic Party. Jackson himself did not attend but sent a toast to be read to the celebrants: "*The Payment of the Public Debt.* Let us commemorate it as an event which gives us increased power as a nation, and reflects luster on our Federal Union, of whose justice, fidelity, and wisdom, it is a glorious illustration."[14]

Not everyone celebrated, however. An administration opponent like John Quincy Adams remained at home and sulked. He wrote dryly in his diary: "The Jackson Republicans of both Houses of Congress had a dinner at Brown's Hotel to celebrate conjointly the victory of New Orleans and the extinction of the national debt, both of which they hold as belonging to the glorification of Andrew Jackson."[15]

Debt freedom, in some circles at least, became the subject of dinner conversation. Harriet Martineau, for example, the English political economist and social commentator, arrived in the United States in January 1835. In Washington she was the guest, along with others, of Secretary of State John Forsyth and his wife. She sat beside Henry Clay during a ham-and-turkey dinner and "consulted a great deal" with him about the public debt. Clay, of course, explained that the United States national debt had recently been paid off, and she expressed the hope that the British national debt might "soon be paid off too."[16] In February Martineau visited the aging ex-president Madison at his Virginia home and discussed the elimination of the debt with him.[17] It is not unreasonable to assume that many such conversations took place around the United States in the immediate aftermath of debt extinction. The nation's financial situation was, after all, unique.

Martineau, it is worth noting, was not the only foreign visitor to take interest in American national debt freedom. For some it meant different things. Simon Ferrall, for example, an English tourist in the early 1830s, was deeply impressed by anticipated American debt freedom. "The national debt will be totally extinguished in four years," he wrote, "when this country will present a curious spectacle for the serious consideration of European nations."[18] The United States, in other words, could serve as a model for other countries. Stephen Davis, a Scottish traveler in 1832 and 1833, considered the nation's "national debt" as virtually "extinguished" and that, as a result, the United States "would unquestionably soon become rich."[19] Michel Chevalier, a French visitor, observed: "The public debt is now paid." For him, however, this financial situation undermined the union. Debt freedom, he wrote, "is one federal tie the less."[20] Charles Lyell, who came to the United States in the early 1840s, remarked that since the federal debt was "entirely paid off in 1835," the effect was to raise "the character of American securities throughout Europe."[21] Diverse opinions characterized foreign understanding of the meaning of American debt freedom.

❧

For Andrew Jackson, however, simple clarity characterized what debt freedom meant.[22] In his first inaugural he explained that the national debt was "incompatible with real independence."[23] Debt meant dependence upon creditors, an obligation of the majority to a minority, a burden on the many to the advantage of a few. Eliminating this contradiction of democratic-republican tenets was not Jackson's only purpose. Debt freedom, he asserted, would also "counteract that tendency to public and private profligacy" which government extravagance "is too apt to engender."[24] Public debt, in other words, constituted a moral as well as a political danger. It raised the specter of unrestrained self-indulgence and unembarrassed vice. Borrowing tempted government to overspend and to expand beyond its legitimate sphere. Debt, in brief, corrupted government in the classic Walpolean fashion or by other means. It encouraged government to exercise power that it did not legally possess. Historically, power targeted individual liberty. Because public indebtedness was the mother of abusive power, eliminating the debt made liberty safe and secure, and making liberty safe and secure was Jackson's purpose from the beginning of his terms in office. Accordingly, debt extinction factored into all the great public policy decisions of his administrations. It explained, as the flip side of constitutional issues, his position on internal improvements, the recharter of the Bank of the United States, the Nullification Crisis, the removal of the government deposits in the Bank of the United States, and the sale of the public lands. Debt freedom, in fact, unified Jackson's policies on diverse issues. It accounted for a lot.

Yet debt freedom entailed much more. It was a core element of what is commonly called Jacksonian Democracy.[25] The relationship between public indebtedness and political and moral corruption had, of course, been an essential ingredient in republican ideology since the Revolutionary era. By Jackson's day it was firmly rooted in the Jeffersonian tradition. Indeed, Thomas Jefferson had elevated the American farmer to special civil status because he was naturally free and naturally virtuous—the ideal, incorruptible citizen. Jefferson's observation has become immortalized: "Those who labor in the earth are the chosen people of God, if ever he had a chosen people, whose breasts he has made His peculiar deposit for substantial and genuine virtue." But "dependence begets subservience and venality, suffocates the germ of virtue, and prepares fit tools for the designs of ambition."[26] By promoting vice, dependence undermined the moral foundation upon which freedom stood. Jackson's awareness of the threat the debt posed was anchored securely in the Jeffersonian worldview. Eliminating the debt would mold the entire nation into the image of Jefferson's farmer—self-sufficient, morally upright, and secure in its liberty: In brief, a "chosen" nation. This conception was essentially what Benton meant, it will be recalled, when he said that paying off the national debt would make the United States "wholly free."[27]

National debt freedom involved more than casting the nation in the role of Jefferson's husbandman. It implied small government, or, to paraphrase Henry David Thoreau's paraphrase of Thomas

Jefferson, a government that governed less rather than more.[28] Debt freedom enhanced personal liberty because individuals were less and less likely to encounter federal power. Tax burdens, for example, would shrink because principal and interest payments were no longer needed. Government revenues would serve government operations only, and Americans would keep more of the fruit of their labor. This aspect of debt freedom bore enormous consequence. South Carolina employed it as a weapon in the Nullification Crisis. Here debt freedom and states' rights theory intersected. Restricting federal expenditures to revenues implied a decreasing federal and an increasing state role in the lives of the American people. This reality helps to explain South Carolina's willingness to accept a compromise but protectionist tariff in 1833. Securing debt freedom meant that time was on the side of states rights advocates.

Another dimension of debt freedom directly affected long term government-business relationships. Before the Maysville Road veto, the federal government had from time to time invested public money in corporate stock. The most notable of these purchases was its acquisition of twenty percent of the outstanding shares in each of the Banks of the United States. The first bank investment yielded a significant profit before the government completely divested its holdings in 1802.[29] Under Nicholas Biddle's management, the second Bank of the United States generated approximately $500,000 per year in dividend revenue to the government.[30] Although the most prominent, these were not the only federal investments in corporate stock. The government also bought shares in various canal companies as a way of promoting internal improvements. Interestingly, this method raised no concerns. In fact, in early 1825 the Committee on Roads and Canals reported to the House of Representatives: "The committee cannot conceive how the General Government can aid in the internal improvements of the country . . . with greater propriety than by subscriptions to companies incorporated by the respective states."[31] However, unlike the bank investments, the canal investments lost money, costing the public almost $1,850,000 in the decade and a half after 1825.[32] If the financial goal of public policy was to eliminate the national debt, then such investments did not serve the public interest. Jackson's Maysville Road veto made this clear.

The president, however, elaborated more fully his thoughts on public investment in the private economy in his December 1830 message to Congress. Objecting to means as well as substance, he challenged the "practice which has obtained to some extent . . . that of subscribing to the stock of private associations. Positive experience, and a . . . thorough consideration of the subject, have convinced me of the impropriety as well as inexpediency of such investments." He argued that they did not benefit all the American people as the Constitution required, asserting that they instead led to federal consolidation of power at the expense of the states. He pointed out that appropriating taxpayer dollars to private companies placed "a portion of the public funds" under the "management and control" of "an authority unknown to the Constitution, and beyond the supervision of our constituents." He added: "This mode of aiding" companies involved in improvement projects "is . . . deceptive, and in many cases conducive to improvidence in the administration of national funds."[33] Unprofitable companies in which the United States held stock kept coming back to Congress for more money, and Congress, hoping to save prior investments, was inclined to appropriate the solicited funds. Jackson offered an example. "The bill authorizing a subscription to the Louisville and Portland canal," then before Congress, "affords a striking illustration of the difficulty of withholding appropriations for the same object, when the first erroneous step has been taken by instituting a partnership between the Government and private companies. It proposes a third subscription on the part of the United States, when each preceding one was at the time regarded as the extent of the aid which Government was to render. . . ." The same reasoning, of course, could be applied to all for-profit enterprises, not merely those employed in infrastructure development. Jackson concluded, saying that all appropriations for improvement projects should be "deferred until the national debt is paid."[34]

The Maysville Road veto, and the subsequent broader policy statement of 1830 concerning federal investments in private companies, bore an important result. They divorced government from the business sector. With the sole exception of several stock purchases in the Chesapeake and Ohio Canal Company between 1829 and 1833, ever since the Jackson era the government of the United States has not invested taxpayer dollars in corporate securities.[35] The origin of this longstanding policy rests as much in the Jacksonian determination to extinguish the national debt and to avoid future borrowing as in its concern about constitutional propriety. To risk the public's money in the stock market was to risk perpetuating the debt or raising taxes, neither of which Jackson approved. Had the pre-Jackson policy of investing federal funds in corporate stock endured, it is interesting to speculate what the face of American capitalism would look like today. In any event, *laissez-faire* realities characterized the Jacksonian economy, and it arrived at that condition more from deference to debt freedom than to Adam Smith. Indeed, the Jacksonian commitment to debt freedom had little, if anything, to do with economic theory. Revolutionary-era republicanism did.

Besides the divorce of government and business, Jacksonians were unsure exactly what conditions debt freedom would create. For some, this uncertainty justified postponing legislative action on the bill to recharter the Bank of the United States. Representatives John C. Bell and Augustus Clayton, it will be recalled, had taken this position during the bank debate.[36] But, although the Bell-Clayton line of reasoning failed to delay congressional action, it is nonetheless revealing. No one, it was true, could predict what the specifics of debt freedom would be, but, at the same time, no one doubted that the specifics—whatever they were—were going to be beneficial. America would become a better place. Debt freedom meant progress. In this sense, the determination to eliminate the public debt constituted one of the great reform movements with which the Age of Jackson is associated. The drive to extinguish the debt, in fact, shared some of the characteristics of abolition, temperance, education reform, and the other leading causes of the era. All identified themselves with freedom—freedom from debt, freedom from bondage, freedom from alcohol addiction, freedom from ignorance, and freedom from other dependencies. All rooted themselves in morality: debt corrupted, slavery was sin, intemperance affronted both God and man, and ignorance played into the hands of Satan. All were driven by a sense of urgency. These evils had to be conquered now, not at some unspecified time in the distant future. However, unlike abolitionism and other crusades of the era, which required the time, labor, and funds of private citizens organized in voluntary associations, the crusade to liberate the nation from debt was led by the government itself, especially the executive branch, which used all its constitutional muscle to assure success. This reform effort was, in other words, a top-down undertaking, much like Jackson's pursuit of "rotation in office" (the "spoils system," to its critics), to democratize the federal civil service.

Other parallels are worth noting. For example, one of the first reform movements to organize during the era was dedicated to abolishing imprisonment for debt, and it reflected evolving American attitudes toward debt.[37] To wage the War of 1812, the United States had been compelled to borrow and thereby increase its national debt. The alternatives were military defeat and, possibly, loss of national independence. Necessity, not some moral defect embedded in republicanism or the Constitution, had justified raising the debt level. The moral danger that national indebtedness represented was derived not from its origin but from its increase and perpetuation after the necessity ended. Reflecting this understanding, after the Treaty of Ghent more and more Americans reassessed the meaning of individual indebtedness. While earlier generations had attributed unmet financial obligations to moral turpitude—dishonesty, fraud, intemperance, laziness, and other failings—and had assigned recalcitrant debtors to jail, the War of 1812 generation increasingly recognized that individuals often fell into debt from unavoidable and overwhelming circumstances. Necessity, in other words, was often the mother of individual indebtedness, just as it had been of national indebtedness during the recent conflict with England. Questions arose: Did imprisoning debtors make sense? Or should debtors be accorded the opportunity to emulate their government and to pursue, through their own hard work, honest and consistent debt reduction? The Jeffersonian tradition, always in favor of liberty and virtue, suggested the answer. Eliminating imprisonment for debt became the republican thing to do.

The idea that eliminating imprisonment for debt would foster a freer and more benevolent society relates to a second and more significant parallel to the Jacksonian determination to extinguish the public debt. The era's great protestant religious revival—the so-called second Great Awakening—sought to settle humankind's account with God. Charismatic preachers like Charles Grandison Finney insisted that mankind's sinfulness necessitated "redemption," a financial as well as a religious term, and that individual and collective acts of benevolence to uplift society from its multiple depravities led to redemption. Making the world a better place satisfied and gratified the will of Jesus the Redeemer. Mankind, by doing God's work here on earth, extinguished its debt to the Almighty and secured eternal salvation. Debt freedom imbued the religious as well as the political spirit of the Age of Jackson.[38]

In any event, as national debt freedom drew nearer and nearer, American politicians became increasingly inclined to boast about their national financial situation. In 1833, for example, T. M. McKennan, a Pennsylvania representative, declared debt freedom an "extraordinary and astonishing spectacle." He asserted that "the extinguishment of the public debt will be hailed by our citizens as an era of exhultation, and of mutual congratulation."[39] Senator Isaac Hill of New Hampshire concurred: "[T]he extinction of our national debt presents this nation in an attitude to excite the admiration of the world," he maintained. "There is probably on record no other instance of the kind."[40] According to Augustus Clayton of Georgia, debt elimination "makes this nation the envy and admiration of all other nations."[41]

Indeed, to the generation of the 1830s, paying off the national debt demonstrated not only the success of republicanism but also its superiority over other forms of government. No other nation had ever eliminated its debt and liberated its people from its burdens. Moreover, the Founders, for all their extraordinary success in transforming republican theory into reality—the Constitution and its separation of powers, the Bill of Rights, and more—had been unable to secure debt freedom. This essential element of true republicanism had remained beyond reach until the Jacksonians came to power. Their generation achieved what their parents and grandparents could not—all the more reason for effusive national pride. The previously unattainable was attained on January 1, 1835. If, as the historian Marvin Meyers has argued, Jacksonian Democracy constituted a nostalgia for the seemingly lost values of the very early republic, then the Jacksonians had good reason to pride themselves on accomplishing what their forebears could not.[42] Debt freedom seemed to prove that the United States was not only free and virtuous but also unique and special in ways no other nation could match. It meant that the United States was indeed God's chosen nation. The elimination of the national debt confirmed American exceptionalism.

Debt freedom also implied a new international role for the United States. As early as 1827, a writer for the *North American Review* observed that the United States "has already risen as if by magic from the state of extreme exhaustion, to which she was reduced in 1815, to a high degree of prosperity; she is rapidly throwing off the burden of her public debt, and providing for the increase of her navy and fortifications, with a liberality from which freer and more favored nations, might derive a useful lesson." Debt freedom enhanced national security. "A nation thus circumstanced has nothing to fear from the aggressions of any continental power."[43] Writing at about the same time, James Fenimore Cooper, the distinguished author, also perceived the national security implication of debt freedom. "[T]he debt will be entirely extinguished in a few more years," he wrote, and a "fair proportion of the moneys that shall then remain will, beyond a doubt, be used in fostering so interesting an arm of the public defence as the navy."[44]

Debt freedom provided more than defense. It offered an opportunity for the United States to participate more fully and effectively in world affairs. It allowed departure from the isolationism recommended by George Washington in his Farewell Address. James A.

Hamilton, for example, son of the eminent treasury secretary and confidante of Andrew Jackson, believed that debt freedom and overflowing federal coffers justified establishing more United States diplomatic missions abroad. Moreover, according to Hamilton, debt freedom warranted greater American energy in foreign affairs. The United States could exercise its exceptionalism by becoming the beacon of freedom in the world. "We have no right," he said, "to hold back in the great struggle for the political regeneration of the world."[45]

Andrew Jackson needed no advice on the foreign policy implications of debt freedom. When France reneged on its obligation under an 1831 treaty to compensate for American shipping losses during the Napoleonic Wars, Jackson was assertive, even, some said, belligerent. Indeed, in the same 1834 message to Congress announcing debt freedom, he recommended, as we shall see, retaliatory measures against France, raising the prospect of war.[46] Debt freedom, in short, encouraged American boldness in foreign affairs. It helped sow the seeds that Manifest Destiny reaped a decade later, and American territorial expansion westward ultimately provoked the several crises that led to Civil War.

Despite its various contributions to American values, however, Jacksonian Democracy was both racist and sexist. It included and applied only to white men. At the state level, for example, northern free blacks either lost the right to vote or had it severely restricted; Native Americans and white women could not vote at all.[47] At the national level matters were no better. In fact, approaching national debt freedom victimized both Native and African Americans, and ignored women altogether.

Early in his administration, as is well known, Jackson advocated the removal of Native Americans from southern states where they resided to regions beyond the Mississippi River. Arguing that the Choctaw, Cherokee, and Creeks faced extinction unless they traded their Georgia and Alabama holdings for trans-Mississippi lands, Jackson said that "[h]umanity and national honor demand that every effort should be made to avert so great a calamity."[48] Yet coercion should be avoided. "This emigration should be voluntary," he declared, but Native Americans who chose to remain in Georgia and Alabama had to accept and obey state laws.[49] In 1830 Congress enacted the president's recommendation, appropriating $500,000 for relocation.[50] What ensued is a familiar and tragic story. Thousands died in the removal process.[51] A half-million dollars was an inadequate sum for a project of such magnitude. Yet the willingness of the president to spend such a sum derived not only from the pressure that the states, especially Georgia, were imposing on the administration but also from the fact that larger and larger sums were available as the national debt was paid down. Interestingly, in May 1830 the Choctaws proposed a treaty for their own removal, which Jackson submitted to the Senate for its advice and consent. They sought a sizable sum, but Jackson, committed to retrench on everything else, told the Senate in his message accompanying the draft treaty: "It will be seen that the pecuniary stipulations are large; and in bringing this subject to the consideration of the Senate I may be allowed to remark that the amount of money which may be secured to be paid should . . . be viewed as of minor importance."[52] The point is that on Indian removal, for Jackson, money was no object. On this issue he was a spender and not a retrencher, probably because he sympathized with southern whites who wanted to grab Indian lands for cotton development. In any event the Senate, for a variety of reasons, declined to consider the Choctaw treaty.[53]

The negative implication for African Americans is clear. Indian removal widened the area of slavery. But there was more. While Georgia and other southern states might cheer Indian removal, they were at the same time aware that if the federal authority could colonize Native Americans in the West, then government might also colonize free blacks to Africa. Indeed, great interest existed, even in the upper slaveholding South, to deport free blacks to West Africa. Motivation ranged from unvarnished racism to humanitarian concern.[54] The principal institutional advocate of free black repatriation was the American Colonization Society (ACS), many of whose founders in 1816 were prominent slaveholding statesmen—James Monroe, Henry Clay, John Fenton Mercer, and Bushrod Washington, to name a few. ACS, in other words, had access to powerful men at the nation's capital. In fact, in January 1817, John Randolph of Roanoke, a representative of no mean prestige, introduced into the House a petition from the new organization's Board of Managers for federal assistance in its effort. In short, ACS sought American tax dollars to promote and implement colonization.[55] Congress did not appropriate any funds, probably because the Redemption Act was not yet passed and because legislators from the Deep South were hostile to any federal involvement in state racial relationships. Many feared that colonization was but a precursor to emancipation.[56]

Two years later, however, in 1819, Congress passed "an Act making an appropriation for the suppression of the slave trade." This legislation, intended to tighten enforcement of the 1808 ban on the international commerce in people, empowered the president to authorize armed vessels to cruise the American and African coasts to intercept violators, to return all captives to Africa, to appoint an "agent or agents" to receive returnees in Africa, and to prosecute offenders of the 1808 law. To carry the measure into effect Congress appropriated $100,000.[57] From time to time this legislation was renewed and updated. In 1828, for example, Congress appropriated another $30,000 for suppression of the illegal trade.[58] These sums were assigned to the Department of the Navy, which bore the costs of enforcement.

The agency created by the 1819 measure was established at Liberia, the colony founded by ACS, and Africans repatriated under the suppression laws were sent there. Much of the navy's enforcement activities, therefore, entailed interaction with ACS at Liberia, and the latter wound up on the receiving end of some of the federal appropriations because the government agents purchased food and other supplies from ACS. Every year, of course, the secretary of the navy reported to the president and to Congress the activities of his department, and in 1830 Secretary John Branch devoted considerable space to the navy's operations along the African coast. He revealed that since 1819 252 individuals, illegally enslaved, had been "removed to the settlement provided by the Colonization Society."[59] He added that over the same time period the navy had spent $264,710 in implementing the suppression laws. He explained that while "the authority given to the President was limited to the support" of the illegal captives "until their removal to the coast of Africa, and to the delivering of them to the care of the agent," actual practice had gone beyond those restrictions.[60] "A liberal interpretation of the law might permit some allowance . . . for their [the returned Africans] maintenance after being landed. . . ." But, Branch wrote, those brought to Liberia were afforded provisions for as long as a year. In addition, they were provided housing, arms and ammunition, fortifications, and vessel construction—"in short, . . . all the aids required for the founding and support of a colonial establishment."[61] He concluded: "This latitudinous interpretation of the law has resulted in the heavy expenditures" spelled out in his report and accompanying documents. Branch observed that "[t]here is no power expressly vested in the Executive to provide, after . . . delivery, either for their support or protection." His department was, therefore, going to change policy and apply strict construction to the 1819 law. "Understanding the law in the limited acceptation . . . it will in future be executed accordingly, and every effort made by the Department to confine the application of this fund within the pale of its provisions."[62] In effect, the Jackson administration abandoned funding for the suppression of the slave trade. ACS, of course, lost an important source of its revenue.[63]

In 1830 the experiences of Native Americans, Africans, and African Americans intersected not only on the cynicism and hypocrisy of the Jackson administration with regard to racial minorities but also on the matter of money and the pay-down of the national debt. The president, eager to remove Native Americans from the southeastern states, was more than willing to spend taxpayer dollars on colonizing them west of the Mississippi River. Steady debt reduction made the funds available without throwing debt freedom off schedule. Jackson exempted Native American removal from retrenchment. At the same time, however, he slashed appropriations for the suppression of the slave trade and, by doing so, threw blacks repatriated to Africa onto their own meager resources to survive and eliminated a major source of ACS's revenue. Jackson, of course, opposed the goals of the ACS and did not exempt it from retrenchment, even though the organization's revenue from the Navy Department was earned in exchange for goods and services. A result was, by implication, that whatever the administration saved through strict interpretation of the 1819 law to suppress the slave trade helped subsidize Indian removal. The year 1830, which witnessed passage of the Indian Removal Act and modification of the navy's role in suppressing the illegal traffic in slaves, demonstrated that the white male majority used approaching debt freedom not to liberate racial minorities but to oppress them further.

The experience of white American women differed sharply from that of Native Americans and blacks. The debt freedom dimension of Jacksonian Democracy did not victimize them. Rather, it ignored them or passed them by. The Jacksonians simply did not count them as part of the political community. National debt freedom may have put more money into the their purses, at least for a time, and in the midst of the emerging market revolution this circumstance may have improved the quality of life among white women. Yet this possibility constitutes speculation. But another matter is distinctly clear. Women, aware of the social and political equality characterizing white male society, were inspired and energized by Jacksonian Democracy's many manifestations. They participated in the various crusades of the era—abolitionism, temperance, peace, education, and other reform movements—and became increasingly conscious of their capacity to change the condition of things. In 1848, at Seneca Falls, New York, they declared their determination to overcome sexist oppression, organized, and struggled to secure full rights as citizens.[64]

NINE

SURPLUS, DISTRIBUTION, AND THE END OF DEBT FREEDOM

On December 31, 1834, the very eve of debt freedom, John C. Calhoun was brooding, as he had been for some time, over the immediate impact of the unique financial condition the United States was about to enter. He wrote to his friend Samuel D. Ingham, Jackson's former treasury secretary, that "I have been long satisfied, that almost every political disorder may be traced to the fiscal action . . . of the Gen[era]l Gover[n]ment. . . ." A huge revenue surplus was imminent, transforming the federal government into an "instrument of corruption and power" that threatened "the overthrow of our institutions and liberty." In other words, Calhoun worried that an overflowing national treasury created the same danger as a perpetuated national debt. It threatened not only to consolidate federal power at the expense of the states but also to concentrate power in the hands of the president at the expense of Congress. After all, since the removal of the deposits from the Bank of the United States and their disposition in state banks chosen by the Jackson administration, the federal revenues were beyond the reach and regulation of the national legislature. Accordingly, they were subject to the will and the whim of the president. "The evil," Calhoun wrote, "lies in an excess of revenue unfixed as to its objects, and almost unrestrained in its final exercise by the Executive." He lamented that the "Simple remedy" to the surplus problem was "to reduce the amount" of the federal revenue, but "this remedy, as simple as it is, cannot be applied. . . ." Why not? Because cutting revenue meant cutting the tariff. But "[t]he compromise," he wrote, "cannot be touched. . . ."[1] The Compromise Tariff of 1833 had become sacrosanct, at least to Calhoun.

Calhoun obsessed over the surplus issue. Little more than a week after debt freedom was achieved he was harping on the same subject. "I have no doubt, that the disease, under which the country is labouring, is excess of revenue, expended on objects depending almost wholly on the will of a mercenary majority, moved by the will of the Executive."[2] Yet Calhoun was not alone in his concern over the surplus. Henry Clay's land bill two years earlier had aimed, among other things, to curtail the inevitable post-debt surplus but had wound up vetoed in Jackson's pocket. Others also worried about the accumulating millions in the treasury. As the second session of the twenty-third Congress got down to serious business after New Year's Day—debt freedom day—the surplus quickly emerged as a major issue. Unlike in 1817, when a prevailing consensus to eliminate the national debt resulted in passage of the Redemption Act, the bitter partisanship in 1835 rendered agreement on what to do about the surplus exceedingly difficult to secure.

❧

The administration, of course, had its own ideas regarding the surplus, and they emerged as a result of an unanticipated foreign policy crisis. In his December 1834 message to Congress—the one in which he announced debt freedom—Jackson laid out the problem to Congress. In 1831 his minister to France, William C. Rives of Virginia, concluded a treaty with the Paris government resolving a longstanding issue between the two countries, compensation for spoliations against United States commerce during the Napoleonic era. Under the treaty, France agreed to indemnify Americans who had suffered "unlawful seizures, captures, sequestrations, confiscations or destruction of their vessels, cargoes, or other property" at the hands of the French military between 1800 and 1817. The amount agreed upon was twenty-five million francs, payable in six equal annual installments beginning one year after each country had ratified the agreement.[3]

Ratifications were exchanged in Washington on February 2, 1832. Accordingly, the first installment was due on February 1, 1833. As it turned out, however, the "perfect confidence" that the administration had had in French compliance was "wholly disappointed." The French Chamber of Deputies had failed to appropriate the money.[4] Indeed, in April 1834, the French legislature simply refused to pay. In July a newly elected Chamber of Deputies did the same thing.[5]

What was to be done? Jackson, unsurprisingly, rejected "acquiescing in the refusal to execute the treaty" and said that any "further negotiation on the subject" was "equally out of the question."[6] He was taking a tough stand. "It is my conviction that the United States ought to insist on a prompt execution of the treaty. . . ." Moreover, if refusal or delay was the response, then the United States should "take redress into their own hands." International laws "provide a remedy." It was a well established "principle," he asserted, that, under such circumstances, the "aggrieved" nation "may seize on the property belonging to the other, its citizens or subjects, sufficient to pay the debt without giving just cause of war." He recommended passage of legislation "authorizing reprisals upon French property" if the next session of the Chamber of Deputies failed to fulfill its commitments under the treaty.[7]

Congress, however, demurred. In January 1835, the Senate voted against reprisals at that time, and the House took no action at all on the matter.[8] Nevertheless, Franco-American relations were not only unsettled but deteriorating. Jackson's confrontational posture regarding France's failure to meet its obligations under the Spoliations Treaty suggested that the United States might be on the road to war against France. This possibility defined the administration's policy toward the revenue surplus.

On February 9, during a debate over executive patronage, Benton, surely speaking for the administration, commented that the "public debt is paid," and "some surplus" would be the result. What should be done with it? According to the Missouri senator, the French crisis made the answer to that question obvious: The surplus should be spent on defense. "[L]et the national defense become the next great object" of public commitment, just as debt freedom had been, "and all spare money go to that purpose."[9] The Whig-dominated Senate did not welcome Benton's remarks. After all, throwing millions into defense would not only encourage greater presidential belligerence in dealing with France, but it would also promote rather than curtail the power of Andrew Jackson.[10] Yet the Senate did vote to fund the annual Fortifications bill as it did every year.

In the Democratic-controlled House of Representatives, however, the Fortifications bill underwent serious alteration. Democrats tacked on an amendment that added three million to the ordinary appropriation, a sum "to be expended, in whole or in part, under the direction of the President . . . for the military and naval service, including fortifications and ordnance, and increase of the navy," so long as the country needed "such expenditures" before "the next meeting of Congress."[11]

Whigs were outraged. They denounced the House amendment as extraordinary and the appropriation as excessively large. Worse, they charged that the amendment effectively transferred the war-making power from Congress to the president. Senator Benjamin Leigh of Virginia could not adequately express his "astonishment." Here was a recipe for monarchy. The House amendment "might almost as well say that the President should be made Consul for life, or Emperor of the American people."[12] Samuel Southard of New Jersey agreed. The amendment, he said, reposed too much power in the hands of

Andrew Jackson. "[I]f the President wanted a war with France, he could readily bring about such an event" if the amendment was passed.[13] Webster demanded that the Senate object "at once" to the amendment.[14] It did so, by a vote of 29 to 19.[15] The Senate then returned its original Fortifications bill to the House. A subsequent House-Senate Conference Committee recommended changes in the Senate bill, but it did not matter. In the end, the House failed to act on the measure, and Congress wound up adjourning without passing any Fortifications bill at all—despite the ongoing crisis with France.[16] That failure, of course, simply added to the expanding surplus.

In his December 1835 annual message, Jackson informed Congress that the French crisis had deepened during the preceding months. The French ministry, he reported, had "decided to consider" his "conditional recommendation of reprisals" the year before as "a menace and an insult which the honor" of their country "made it incumbent on them to resist."[17] As a consequence, France had broken diplomatic relations and had presented the American minister, now Edward Livingston, his passport. Yet, the president explained, the government in Paris knew that the Senate had rejected enacting reprisals and that the House had done nothing at all on that subject. Accordingly, the French finance minister had recommended and a committee of the Chamber of Deputies had proposed a measure to pay the United States what the Spoliations Treaty required.[18] Indeed, the French crisis had seemed close to resolution. But, as the French appropriation bill neared passage, an amendment was added that "the money should not be paid until the French Government had received satisfactory explanations of" Jackson's remarks in his message to Congress a year earlier.[19] To Jackson, this demand constituted an unwarranted intrusion into the domestic affairs of the United States Government and, even worse, a demand for an apology. This, Jackson vowed, he would never do.[20] In short, unless France retreated from its insistence upon an apology, war seemed unavoidable.

From the standpoint of military preparedness, especially in light of the failure of the Fortifications bill the preceding March, the United States was far from ready for war against France. On the other hand, unlike in 1812 when financial resources for war against Great Britain were lacking, in 1835 the federal treasury was overflowing. Jackson alluded to this reality. As a consequence of debt freedom, "there will be a balance in the Treasury at the close of the present year"—only three weeks away—"of about $19,000,000." He was confident that "after meeting all outstanding and unexpended appropriations," approximately $11,000,000 would remain on hand. Moreover, he predicted that in 1836 revenue from all sources would amount to roughly $20,000,000.[21]

Impending war, the surplus, and the relationship between the two were on everyone's mind. On January 11, 1836, debate on these matters got into full swing in the Senate. Benton, picking up where he had left off in 1835, introduced a resolution that "the surplus revenue of the United States . . . ought to be set apart, and applied to the general defence and permanent security of the country."[22] The resolution called upon the president to provide specific information concerning defense needs and their probable costs. The Senate took up the resolution the following day, and Benton, as usual, spoke at length in its favor. The country stood in danger, he asserted, and it was the obligation of all nations to defend themselves. Yet "[t]he United States were not in a state of defence, and it was their duty to attend to that object." Indeed, he said: "The present time was the proper time." After all, he continued, "The public debt was paid, a large surplus revenue was accumulating, and the country was every way prosperous." He rejected, alluding to the Clay plan, proposals to distribute any of the surplus to the states. Rather, he was "in favor of setting" the excess revenues "apart, and dedicating them to the defence of the Union." "Formerly," he continued, "and by a law as old as the republic, these surpluses were all set apart, and constituted a separate fund, called the sinking fund, and inviolably applied to the sacred purpose of extinguishing the national debt. By this means the debt has been paid." Benton insisted that it was now time for "reviving and continuing this policy, with a change of object, from the debt to the defences of the Union." He wanted "to see all the surplus revenue take that direction, until the country was as secure from receiving, as it is averse from offering, offence."[23]

Benton had made his point, but brevity was not among the Missouri senator's virtues. Sixty French warships, he asserted, were already approaching the United States, and the peril the nation faced was imminent and dire.[24] He criticized the Senate for, among other things, rejecting the House amendment to the Fortifications bill the preceding session.[25] He denounced any distribution of the surplus to the states as "incompatible" with the nation's defense.[26] He insinuated that failure to dedicate the surplus to defense would amount to a dereliction of duty by the Senate.

Benton's declarations, explicit and implicit, drew an immediate and sharp response from his colleagues. Webster, Benjamin Leigh, William C. Preston of South Carolina, and John M. Clayton of Delaware defended the Senate's action on the Fortifications bill, blaming the House of Representatives for springing the large discretionary appropriation to the president on the Senate by surprise and without spelling out how the money would be spent and without War Department justifications for the sum. Moreover, if indeed a French fleet had embarked toward American waters, then why had the president not alerted the Congress to the danger?[27] Angry Senators finally assented to Thomas Ewing of Ohio's motion to adjourn without taking up the question on Benton's resolution.[28]

Two days later, however, the Senate returned to Benton's resolution, and the Whigs lambasted the Missourian. Ewing led off, sarcastically wondering aloud what Benton meant by "surplus." After all, he explained, a surplus was what remained after all the needs of the public had been met. Accordingly, if national defense required expenditures, then the money spent for that purpose could not be considered surplus at all.[29] Ewing, of course, was having fun at Benton's expense, but his mocking humor soon yielded to the seriousness of the issue. Ewing, for example, pointed out that it was the responsibility of the president, not the senator from Missouri, to define national defense needs. Why had the president not done so? For Ewing the reason seemed clear. "I am opposed," to Benton's resolution because "[i]ts prime object does not seem to be the defence of the country, but the expenditure of the surplus revenue. It is not offered because a fort is wanting here, or a fleet there. . . . It is because we have plenty of money, and this is a good way to get rid of it." Ewing maintained that it would take years to spend down the surplus on defense projects and that, in the interim, only the stockholders in the deposit banks who would invest it for their personal profit would benefit from the excess of revenue. In the process they, of course, would become beholden to Jackson and the Democratic Party for their good fortune. Throwing the surplus at the military, in other words, simply redounded to the power of the White House. It was for that very reason that the Senate's rejection of the House version of the Fortifications bill in 1835 had been wise.[30]

Others followed Ewing in rebuking Benton. Robert H. Goldsborough of Maryland denounced the Missouri senator's charge that the Senate had failed in its obligation to the nation as "unjust and gross."[31] Alexander Porter of Louisiana defended the Senate against Benton's "grave charges" and challenged the allegation that a French fleet was *en route* to the United States.[32] Webster reviewed the history of the Fortifications bill and blamed the House of Representatives for its failure.[33] Benton stood virtually alone. Only Alfred Cuthbert of Georgia came to his defense, arguing that the country had nothing to fear from President Jackson but everything to fear from the "moneyed aristocracy" which sought to dominate the nation.[34]

A few days later, on January 18, Jackson sent a special message to Congress updating it on the French crisis, together with documents regarding the controversy that he had promised to provide in his "state of the union" message five weeks earlier. He reported that although the French government had appropriated the indemnity funds, it nevertheless refused to pay until Jackson offered "regrets" for his 1834 remarks to Congress. The accompanying thirteen documents supported Jackson's view that France's conduct insulted the honor of the United States. The president recommended retaliation by denying French vessels and products access to American ports and by making "large and speedy appropriations for the increase of the Navy and the completion of our coastal defenses."[35]

Jackson's message and documentary evidence proved timely with respect to the Senate debate. Surely they relieved some of the pressure on Benton by demonstrating how real the danger of war was. They also encouraged senators friendly to the administration to speak out. "It is now made clear as a sunbeam," Buchanan of Pennsylvania said. "The money will not be paid . . . unless the Government of the United States" shall present to France "a degrading apology."[36] Buchanan agreed with Jackson. Closing American ports to French ships and risking war were preferable to national dishonor. But not all agreed. Calhoun, for example, now had more to brood about than just the surplus. He regretted the deterioration of Franco-American relations and held Jackson responsible for the crisis.[37]

In the meantime, Great Britain had been following very closely the unfolding Franco-American drama. Enjoying friendly and important commercial relationships with both countries, it feared that war between the United States and France would disrupt trade and perhaps create other negative but unanticipated problems. Accordingly, the government in London sought a solution to the crisis. In late January 1836, Charles Bankhead, Britain's Charge d'Affaires in Washington, acting under instructions, presented a paper to Secretary of State John Forsyth. In it he explained that his government "witnessed with the greatest pain and regret" the current impasse between Washington and Paris and, for that reason, was offering to mediate the dispute.[38] The United States accepted, and Britain's effort quickly bore fruit. On February 15 Bankhead informed the State Department that Jackson's most recent annual message had clarified the American position and had satisfied French concerns. Consequently, "the French Government is now ready to pay" the first installment on the American indemnity.[39] On February 22 Jackson informed Congress that Great Britain's intervention had preserved the peace.[40] Abruptly and unexpectedly, the French crisis ended.

Great Britain's apparent role as *deus ex machina* in ending the Franco-American war scare did more than preserve the peace. It also rendered moot Benton's resolution to spend down the surplus on defense. Indeed, it separated the defense and surplus issues altogether. Congress could now focus on the latter question without the distraction of national security concerns. Yet the only serious proposal before Congress dealing with the surplus was Clay's ongoing effort to distribute land-sale revenues to the states.

On December 29, 1835, just three weeks after Jackson's annual message, Henry Clay had introduced a modified version of his 1833 land bill.[41] The most important alteration reflected the then-boiling French crisis. The bill provided that, in the event of conflict, distribution of the land revenues to the states would cease and the funds would be "applied to the prosecution of the war" instead.[42] The measure also reduced the dividend that the states rich in public lands would receive before the general distribution.

Clay's 1833 bill had allowed a 12.5% award; his 1835 bill allowed only ten percent. The remaining revenue would then be distributed to all the states according to the federal ratio.[43] Clay was confident that, if confronted with another veto, he had enough votes in Congress to override it. After all, the matter had greater urgency in 1835 than it did in 1833. Land sale revenues had risen dramatically in two years and were ballooning the surplus. In 1833 land sale revenues amounted to $3,968,000; in 1835, however, they jumped to $14,758,000, and by the end of 1836 they threatened to exceed an astonishing $24,500,000.[44]

The Senate addressed the distribution bill at the same time that it was dealing with Benton's resolution to spend the surplus on defense. (This fact constituted the reason why Benton denounced distribution while promoting defense spending.) Yet Benton and most Democratic senators either overlooked or ignored that Jackson had already distributed the surplus, not to the states, of course, but to selected state chartered banks—the administration's so-called "pets."

This distribution formula did not return the public's money to the people but to privately owned corporate entities which used the funds, surplus or not, for private profit. This reality was inconsistent with the public image of the "People's President," and Henry Clay promoted his land bill by, in part, noting this contradiction. On April 26, for example, on the Senate floor he asked rhetorically: "What was the state of the Treasury?" Relying on the reports of the secretary of the treasury, Clay answered his own question. More than $40 million of taxpayer dollars was disbursed among thirty-four state chartered banks. Collectively, those banks held only about $11 million in specie [gold and silver] reserves. Yet their liabilities totaled about $90 million.[45] They had loaned out the federal deposits without the authority of Congress and to people "unknown" to the secretary of the treasury. This situation did not serve the American people. Pressure existed in the money market, Clay asserted, and an explosion was bound to happen. "Look now at the state of the currency; confidence in it was already diminishing . . . while bank issues had enormously increased."[46] If an explosion like the Panic of 1819 occurred, then the American people as well as the Treasury could be utterly ruined. It was unwise, Clay believed, to leave the people's money in "repositories that were insecure and unsafe." What should Congress do? Surely every senator present knew what Clay's answer to that question was: Shrink the surplus by distributing the revenues earned from the sale of the public lands.[47]

The next day Benton shot back. Noting that the Senate had not yet passed any of the usual appropriations for the civil and military establishments, he charged that the failure was deliberate, designed to make the surplus seem especially large. The larger the pie, in other words, the larger the distributed pieces the states would receive under Clay's bill. "The distribution bill," he declared, "was now the antagonist, not of fortifications only, but of every bill for the service of the country." Passing appropriations bills, he shouted, "tended to diminish the mass of money for distribution."[48] Accordingly, he said, nothing had been done—"all the heavy appropriations have been kept back"—in order to create the appearance of a surplus. Even senators weary of Benton's endless declamations must have suddenly sat up and paid attention. Benton, who three months earlier had demanded that the surplus be spent on defense, now denied that any surplus existed at all. He claimed that it was merely a fiction manufactured for partisan purposes and that consideration of Clay's bill should be postponed until after all necessary appropriations had been made. His motion to postpone failed, 26 to 20.[49] But Benton did not give up. He moved to table Clay's bill and to address the Fortifications bill instead. This proposal was also defeated, 26 to 20.[50] Still Benton persisted. The next day he argued that if land sale income was subtracted from total government revenue and distributed to the states, then the burden of all federal expenses would "fall upon the customhouse." Result? "[T]here would soon be a *deficit* in the Treasury which must be filled by loans or taxes." Renewed government borrowing was not, of course, a desirable option for good republicans. Therefore, "[r]evival of the tariff would then be inevitable."[51] Benton, in other words, accused Clay of subtly undermining the 1833 Compromise Tariff. His tactic aimed at detaching Calhoun from Clay.

The debate dragged on as other Senate critics expressed their views. Thomas Morris of Ohio, for example, argued that "[t]he tariff, upon the payment of the national debt, should have been reduced to the wants of the Government," thereby drying up any surplus.[52] Perceptively, he added that distribution would likely further fuel inflation by making easy money easier.[53] Others objected that distribution would promote corruption and even disunion because it would "absorb all other considerations."[54] The states' appetites for federal revenue would override the national interest. Distribution, opponents said, would undermine the division of powers between the federal and state governments.[55] The threat of corruption that the national debt had once posed had now reemerged in the form of a surplus and its possible distribution. Nevertheless, on Wednesday, May 4, 1836, the Senate passed Clay's land bill by a vote of 25 to 20. Significantly, John C. Calhoun voted with the opposition.[56]

In the meantime, the House of Representatives was considering a similar measure. Introduced in mid-March by Clay's fellow Kentuckian, Representative Sherrod Williams, it came to the floor on March 21. Another Kentuckian, Chilton Allan, spoke in its favor, describing distribution of land revenues as "a subject of higher importance than any which was ever submitted to the deliberation of Congress." Yet he quickly abandoned hyperbole and got to the point: "I rejoice that the attention of Congress has been . . . brought directly to the question, what shall be done with the thirty millions of dollars now in the Treasury over and above the wants of the Government, and the millions of surplus destined hereafter to come into the Treasury?"[57] Although he regretted that the House had been in session "nearly four months" without addressing the surplus, the time had finally arrived to deal with "the subject . . . which has been at the bottom of all the political movements which we have witnessed for more than a year."[58] Allan's subsequent speech in defense of distribution was probably the most important the House heard on the subject that session. It split the Jacksonian majority, leaving the diehard anti-distribution purists in a minority. The House ultimately supported distribution. For this reason Allan's speech is worth reviewing.

"The excellent law of 1817," he said, "for the payment of the national debt, having accomplished its object, we find our Treasury overflowing. It now devolves on the present Congress to decide how this treasure can be most beneficially used for our country." He continued, "Sir, we are thrown here at a most important point of history. Our country is in a situation hitherto unknown [national debt freedom]. . . . The weighty contest now depending before Congress and before the nation is, whether the thirty millions of dollars, which is the produce of the honest labor of our constituents, shall be returned to their pockets, or devoted to the schemes of official ambition on the eve of a presidential election."[59]

Allan's reference to the upcoming 1836 presidential campaign suggested where his argument was going. The Kentuckian ripped into the Jackson administration, accusing it of hypocrisy, deception, and abuse of power. He reminded the House that in his 1829 annual message Jackson had recommended that the post-debt surplus be distributed among the states. Yet, in 1833, when Congress enacted legislation to accomplish that goal, "it was met by another veto."[60] Now, Allan said, the administration wanted to spend the surplus on the military. But why? Because expanding the military and entering into defense contracts would enlarge the federal patronage, and the surplus millions in the Treasury's accounts at the deposit banks would sustain it. The money and the government hirelings together would subvert the "freedom and purity of elections."[61] Allan, in effect, was accusing the administration of doing what the administration had accused the Bank of the United States of doing when the latter controlled the federal deposits: namely, interfering in free elections. Now, however, the power of the patronage and the surplus would be deployed to elect the heir-apparent, Vice President Martin Van Buren.

Allan was far from finished. He accused the Jackson administration of misleading the country on the soundness of the currency. By destroying the Bank of the United States the president had "struck down the best currency in the world . . . everywhere preferred to gold and silver." Even so, the elimination of the Bank of the United States did not promote a metallic currency. Instead, "banks and bank notes and paper money have more than doubled," and he presented statistics to support his claim. The result, he thought, was both clear and inevitable: Inflation and the collapse of the economy. "All men of forecast know that, upon the first great reverse in our commercial relations, we are destined again to experience all the train of calamities which will flow from the depreciation of the millions of paper money now in the hands of the people."[62]

Allan also charged that the president had broken one of his most solemn pledges to the nation, the promise of economy in government. The Jacksonians, he alleged, "before they came into power, and when they were seeking votes, told the people . . . That the expenditures of the Federal Government were prodigally, dangerously, wastefully extravagant; and that, if they were invested with power, they would speedily introduce such a system of reform and retrenchment as would bring back the Government to the Jeffersonian economy." These promises, repeated over and over again in 1828, fooled the people, but "[w]e have seen seven years glide way, and the first effective movement for retrenchment has not yet been made."[63] Instead, and Allan again offered statistics to document his point, the costs of government had increased sharply during the Jackson era compared to the preceding two administrations—Monroe's second term and Adams's tenure. Nor, Allan said, could Jackson justify the increased expenditures on the aggressive pay down of the national debt. According to Allan, the Monroe and Adams years had disposed of more of the debt than the Jackson administration, even though "we have seen public festivals and rejoicings upon the point of the transcendent merit of having paid the public debt." No president, he said, could take credit for extinguishing the debt "more than the man in the moon." Credit belonged to the Congress of 1817, which passed the Redemption Act and to "the people of the United States, whose industry and enterprise filled the public Treasury."[64]

Allan was not yet done. He proceeded to outline the alternatives Congress faced regarding the surplus: to leave it in the Treasury, to absorb it by increasing expenditures, or to distribute land sale revenues to the states. He presented detailed arguments against the first two options and defended the third as the only suitable and just solution to the matter.[65]

Allan's lengthy address was surely partisan, but it articulated themes that dominated the House debate about the surplus for the next month or so. If, for example, the Treasury retained the proceeds from the public lands, then millions of taxpayer dollars would wind up in the vaults of the deposit or "pet" banks. While the people would earn no interest on the deposits, the banks' stockholders would turn a profit on them by loaning the funds out. Moreover, under existing conditions the Congress had no control over the public revenues. Only the president, through his treasury secretary, did. Would the administration abuse its authority over the revenue to expand its own power and to influence the 1836 election? In short, was leaving the public funds in the Treasury in the public interest?

The second option, spending down the surplus for defense or for any other purpose, also failed to serve the public interest, especially after the war scare with France vanished. Such an effort would only increase executive patronage and thereby endanger the integrity of the constitutional separation of powers. For Representative Allan, the distribution of the land sale revenue represented the only viable option. It returned to the people what was rightfully theirs.

Jacksonians in the House found themselves on the defense, even though they were among the majority. The reason was that many from the western states who stood to gain from the distribution united with the opposition on this issue. In other words, the Democrats split, and administration loyalists found themselves on weak ground. Some vainly insisted on spending the surplus on defense.[66] Poor Representative Ratliffe Boon of Indiana found himself parroting Senator Benton's most recent claim that there was no surplus to distribute.[67] Still others tried to bury the bill by sending it to the Ways and Means Committee, then chaired by C. C. Cambreling, a Jackson insider and confidante.[68] But the case for distribution of land sale revenues seemed solid.

❧

Calhoun, of course, followed the debates on the surplus closely and from time to time made his own views known. He opposed spending it on defense, and he argued that retaining it in the government accounts in the deposit banks was inherently inflationary, a "folly" which "must in the end prove fatal."[69] On March 14, for instance, he urged Congress to address the surplus question during that session because the country's currency was "diseased," the reason why so much of it was then being invested in the public lands.[70] Three days later he reiterated this view. "Some honest and equitable manner of getting rid of this surplus revenue must be devised." Delay was not an option. "Something must be done, and done speedily. . . ." Otherwise, "a wound will be inflicted on our currency and our country, from which neither will recover." Why not? Because "[a]ll who have any of this worthless capital . . . will be rushing to invest it in the public lands."[71] The government would be trading its most valuable asset for depreciating dollars.

At the same time, whatever confidence, if any, Calhoun might have had in Clay's land bill as a solution to the surplus problem withered quickly and in the end, it will be recalled, he voted against it. He confessed that he entertained some constitutional doubts about Clay's bill but that those concerns were moot because the bill would not pass both houses of Congress and that, even if it did, it would certainly encounter a Jackson veto.[72] Then, of course, there was Benton's argument that distributing the revenue from land sales would impose all federal expenses on the customs houses. In that event, any emergency could force an increase in the tariff or renewed government borrowing. To Calhoun neither alternative was palatable.

In the final analysis, however, Calhoun's critique of the matter went deeper than spending the surplus on defense, inflation, or implications for the tariff. For him the very relationship between the surplus and the deposit banks constituted the heart of the problem. As matters stood, the government's funds, including the growing surplus, were lodged in state banks chosen by the Jackson administration. As a consequence, those banks enjoyed the privilege of loaning out or otherwise investing taxpayers' dollars for their own private profit. They did not even pay interest on the deposits. Accordingly, the officers and stockholders of the chosen banks were necessarily beholden to the administration. By implication, individuals and businesses, including newspapers, which depended upon loans and credits from the deposit banks were likewise beholden to the administration. These circumstances, simply put, expanded the power of Andrew Jackson, his administration, and the Democratic Party. They corrupted the constitutional system of checks and balances and threatened American liberty. An American "Robinocracy" was emerging, but not from perpetual national indebtedness. It was emerging instead from an overabundance of revenue under the control of the executive branch, which distributed it in a fashion to perpetuate its own power. Almost twenty years earlier Congress had enacted the

Redemption law to prevent corruption of the constitutional order by eliminating the national debt in 1835. Now, as far as Calhoun was concerned, the time had again arrived for Congress to save the Constitution from debasement. The time had come to both eliminate the surplus and reestablish control over the public funds. Calhoun believed he had a solution to the problem. He wrote Samuel D. Ingham in early April: "I see but one alternative left, to advance the money to the States to be returned whenever the government shall require it, without interest; or in other words, (for such would be the effect) to make the States instead of the State banks the depository of the public funds."[73]

Jacksonians, of course, were themselves not content with the *status quo*. Earlier in the year Benton had worked hard to spend down the surplus on defense, and in the House others worried about the superabundance in the Treasury's accounts at the deposit banks. Indeed, on May 3, when a bill came up in the Senate to regulate the public deposits, Silas Wright, the staunch Jacksonian from New York, offered an amendment requiring the secretary of the treasury to invest all balances in excess of seven million dollars in state bonds. On Calhoun's request, the matter was postponed until the ordinary appropriations for civil and military establishments had been addressed.[74]

The matter did not arise again until May 25, when Calhoun was permitted "by common consent" to modify "the public deposits bill by adding new sections" to it. But what Calhoun proposed was more than a mere modification. Rather, it was a radical single solution to the surplus and deposit questions. It spelled out in detail what Calhoun had suggested to Ingham six weeks earlier. It proposed to distribute to the states as callable loans the entire federal surplus, whatever the source—public lands or tariff. Finally, it imposed tough regulations on the deposit banks and, if passed, would transfer control over the public money from the executive to the legislative branch of the government.

Unsurprisingly, Calhoun's sweeping proposal not only swallowed up Clay's land revenue bill but also triggered a debate that consumed most of what was left of the congressional session. It encountered numerous objections, but from only a handful of senators. Benton and Mississippian Robert J. Walker complained that consideration of the bill should be postponed until the Fortifications bill, still pending, had been dealt with.[75] Wright argued that the public money in the deposit banks was safe but that the growing surplus was encouraging speculation in the public lands. His plan, he insisted, to invest any surplus more than $7 million in state bonds was the best solution to the inflation problem.[76] His idea went nowhere, but opponents piled on objection after objection: that the bill should be divided into separate measures, one for distribution and another to regulate the deposit banks; that the measure would destroy the states, reducing them to mere appendages of the federal authority; that the so-called "loan" was not a loan but a giveaway. These and other arguments, however, failed.[77] On June 18, 1836, the Senate approved Calhoun's bill 40 to 6.[78] Four days later, after passing a minor amendment, the House concurred, passing the measure by a vote of 155 to 38.[79] Reluctantly, Jackson signed it into law a few days later.[80]

The Deposit Act of 1836 recaptured congressional control over the public money. The law required the secretary of the treasury to employ as federal depositories only banks that were incorporated under the legal procedures of the entity (state, territory, or District of Columbia) within which they operated, provided that no public deposit exceeded three-fourths of the capital stock investors had actually paid. This provision aimed at assuring that every qualifying bank had sufficient assets to sustain the dollar value of the deposits.[81] To qualify as public depositories, chartered banks had to document their worthiness to the treasury secretary. Appropriate evidence included copies of charters, lists of boards of directors, financial statements, and the like. Once approved, the deposit banks accepted obligations in exchange for custodianship and use of taxpayers' money. They had to file, for example, frequent general financial statements as well as weekly statements on the federal deposits. In addition, they had to agree to transfer funds and make payments on behalf of the United States government without charging fees, commissions, or claiming allowances for differences in exchange rates. In short, the

1836 law required the deposit banks to perform all the "duties" and services formerly imposed on the Bank of the United States.[82]

There were other important conditions. To retain their status as federal depositories, qualifying banks had to redeem their notes in specie (gold and silver) on demand, refrain from issuing notes in denominations less than five dollars, and refuse to accept notes less than five dollars for payments to the United States.[83] The purpose was to prevent a profusion of unsupported bank notes, which could undermine the purchasing power of the paper currency or, in other words, promote an inflationary spiral. Because of the inflationary dangers, the law also authorized the secretary of the treasury to demand, if necessary, any participating bank to improve its note/specie ratio to assure the safety of the public money.[84] Any deposit bank which failed to abide by the law's regulations would forfeit its holdings to other banks. As for the deposit banks already operating under Jackson's aegis, their contracts would remain in force until the secretary of the treasury implemented the new law.[85]

The secretary's oversight responsibility was great. The act required him to report to Congress at the outset of every session the number and names of the deposit banks and, very importantly, the amount of the federal deposits in each. Moreover, whenever in any quarterly period the federal deposit exceeded one-fourth of a bank's paid-in capital, then the bank was obliged to pay 2% interest on the excess, calculated *per annum* on the annual average of excess. If interest was due, it was the secretary's job to make certain that it was credited to the government's account.[86] Finally, the law rendered it illegal for the deposit banks to transfer funds to other banks simply to accommodate them or to sustain their credit. Legal transfers were restricted to disbursements on behalf of the government and to maintenance of the three-fourths ratio of government funds to capital stock.[87]

Article XIII of the law focused not on deposit bank regulation but on the surplus. (Under existing conditions the surplus wound up in the deposit banks, and this reality constituted the link between both matters.) It provided that on January 1, 1837, any balance in the Treasury above $5 million, retained as a contingency fund, would be deposited with the states as loans. The funds would be distributed according to the number of senators and representatives a state had in Congress. To receive the funds, the law required that each state's treasurer or designee had to give to the secretary of the treasury a signed "certificate of deposit." The CDs would pledge the states to the "safe keeping and repayment" of the money whenever the United States needed it. The distribution, in other words, was structured as a loan to the States and callable "for the purpose of defraying any wants" of the national treasury "beyond . . . the five millions" held in reserve. If any state refused the deposit, then its share would be allocated to the other states. If the secretary of the treasury called the loan, the summons would be in "rateable proportions" and never exceed $10,000 in any one month; and Treasury was required to give thirty days' notice for each additional $20,000.[88] Equal disbursements would be made on the first day of each quarterly period, starting January 1, 1837, and continuing through June 1842.

Now it was Jackson's turn to brood. Although he disapproved of the Deposit Act, he had not vetoed it, probably fearing that a rejection of the distribution would redound against Van Buren in the upcoming election. Yet there was much to worry about. Sales of the public land had reached a frenzied pace. Speculation in them was bubbling their value far above what they had traded for just two years earlier. Did the buying wave, Jackson wondered, indicate that the money market was losing confidence in the multiplicity of state bank notes that were flooding the country? Was the money stock depreciating and, if so, would the forthcoming distribution of the surplus aggravate the inflation? More to the point, was the government exchanging its most valuable asset, the public lands, for increasingly worthless dollars? Of equal importance were related questions. Would not currency depreciation shrink the value of the government's holdings in the deposit banks and diminish the value of the surplus scheduled for distribution? These were matters of the utmost concern.

In the summer Jackson decided to stop the speculation in the public lands. He directed Treasury Secretary Woodbury to restrict their sale to specie payments only. On July 11, 1836, the so-called Specie Circular went out to "all receivers of the public money and . . . the deposite banks," ordering them not to accept paper money for land purchases after August 15 but only gold and silver coin.[89] Ostensibly, the directive was issued on account of "complaints" concerning "frauds, speculations, and monopolies" regarding land purchases and the alleged role of "bank credits" in facilitating these "dangerous" practices.[90] Easier and easier credit, it seemed, was expanding the money supply beyond banks' capacities to sustain their obligations. The value of the federal deposits as well as the entire money stock stood at risk.

Demanding specie for the public land imposed an immediate brake on speculation, but the circular's impact could not be confined to one facet of the overall economy. After all, by Jackson's era the national economy was a complex and dynamic mechanism, and a sudden and radical change in one of its elements necessarily affected other parts of it, including the psyche of the business and investing communities. From this perspective the most striking fact about the Specie Circular is this: The president of the United States, on his own authority, had demonetized bank notes—the common medium of exchange throughout the nation—with respect to a particular kind of real estate, the public land. Yet if the president could demonetize the country's currency for one purpose, then he could do it for others as well. If the money market was already nervous about the soundness of the currency, then the Specie Circular was unlikely to inspire long-term confidence. Although it took time for the full implication of the circular to sink in, a long, slow shiver set into the money market.

In the meantime, the presidential election preoccupied the nation. As Jackson wanted, the Democratic Party nominated Van Buren as its candidate. The Whigs, on the other hand, failed to unite around a single nominee and instead fielded three regional candidates, a tactic which, at best, would toss the election into the House of Representatives but which, more likely, would assure Van Buren's victory. It did. In November, Vice President Van Buren was elected to succeed General Jackson, and the Old Hero enjoyed the satisfaction of knowing that the people approved of his leadership during the preceding eight years and that Van Buren would adhere to the policies he had pursued. Jackson's administration now entered its twilight.

The transition proceeded smoothly, but anxiety about the economy weighed heavily on the retiring president. In his eighth and last annual message to Congress, December 5, 1836, he addressed his concerns. With the first installment of the distribution less than a month away, Jackson wondered what would happen if an unanticipated revenue shortfall required a call for "a portion of the funds deposited with the States." The problem was, as Jackson saw it, that even though the Deposit Act only loaned the surplus to the states for safekeeping, the fact was that the law had been promoted—"extensively spoken of"—as an unrestricted grant to the states "without regard to the means of refunding it when called for." Such a "suggestion," the President asserted, constituted the height of irresponsibility and a "violation of public faith and moral obligation."[91]

Jackson also told Congress that he had devoted his "most anxious reflection" upon "the intimate connection" between the Deposit Act and "the financial interests of the country." "The experience of other nations," he explained, "admonished us to hasten the extinguishment of the public debt; but it will be in vain that we have congratulated each other upon the disappearance of this evil if we do not guard against the equally great one of promoting the unnecessary accumulation of public revenue." Spending money for the sake of spending it was "the parent of profligacy, . . . no people can hope to perpetuate their liberties who long acquiesce in a policy which taxes them for objects not necessary to the legitimate and real wants of their Government." Although the debt-free condition of the country was "Flattering," nevertheless "it can not be disguised that there is a lurking danger" wrapped up in the post-debt surplus. Yet the reality was that "there will continue to be a surplus beyond the wants of the Government" and that Congress "should be employed in devising some more appropriate remedy than" distributing it to the states.[92]

(For Jackson, the solution was clear: reduce the tariff to the government's needs.)[93]

Any distribution, the president warned, was dangerous. When the surplus emerged after debt freedom, it wound up in the state banks his administration had selected as depositories—in effect a distribution, not to the states, of course, but to "sundry banks." What happened? "The banks proceeded to make loans upon this surplus, and thus converted it into banking capital, and in this manner it has tended to multiply bank charters and has had a great agency in producing a spirit of wild speculation."[94] Jackson, it seems, believed that any distribution of the surplus, whether to banks or states, was inherently inflationary.

Jackson had long doubted the efficacy of paper money. He believed that the only currency consistent with the language and meaning of the Constitution was specie. The value of gold and silver coins was intrinsic and stable. The value of paper money was neither. He observed that the "progress of an expansion, or rather a depreciation, of the currency by excessive bank issues is always attended by a loss to the laboring classes." He went on to describe a process that came close to predicting the calamity that would strike the country in less than six months. The profusion of paper "banished" specie to foreign countries. "The next step is a stoppage of specie payment—a total degradation of paper as a currency—unusual depression of prices, the ruin of debtors, and the accumulation of property in the hands of creditors and cautious capitalists."[95]

These concerns, the president explained, justified his Specie Circular. "The effects of an extension of bank credits and over issues of bank paper have been strikingly illustrated in the sales of the public lands." By the summer of 1836 revenue from that source had reached "an unprecedented amount." But, Jackson complained, "these receipts amounted to nothing more than credits in a bank." Why? Jackson now pointed his finger at the heart of the problem: "The banks lent out their notes to speculators. They were paid to the receivers and immediately returned to the banks, to be lent out again and again, being mere instruments to transfer to speculators the most valuable public land and pay the Government by a credit on the books of the banks." But the credits were worthless because they exceeded the banks' capacities to discharge. "The safety of the public funds and the interest of the people . . . required that these operations should be checked."[96] Hence the Specie Circular. Yet Jackson did not perceive that his effort to restore confidence in the currency also undermined it at the very same time. The Specie Circular was a double-edged sword.

Much of Jackson's analysis was compelling, but his warnings about the distribution of the surplus and the soundness of the currency went unheeded. On January 1, 1837, the distribution went into effect. After reserving $5 million for contingencies, the Treasury Department disbursed $9,367,215, to the states, the first quarterly installment of the surplus. Equal disbursements were due on the first of April, July, and October.[97] Each state's share was determined by its number of Electoral College votes compared to the total number. Each state was free to decide how to use the money. For the time being all seemed well. When a complex bill overriding the Specie Circular arrived on Jackson's desk on March 3, the day before Van Buren's inauguration, he pocket vetoed it.[98] This action, however, was not his last presidential deed.

The next day Jackson, emulating George Washington, published a farewell address to the nation. He thanked his countrymen for the confidence they had reposed in him and expressed satisfaction that he was leaving office with the nation "prosperous and happy, in the full enjoyment of liberty and peace."[99] He praised the country's accomplishments and warned of the dangers that both sectionalism and consolidation posed.[100] Then he addressed the cluster of issues concerning finance, substantially repeating the forebodings he had articulated in his last annual message. He argued that the federal taxing authority was restricted to the needs of government only. For that reason he had vigorously and successfully defeated efforts for federally funded internal improvements. That "decision," he said, accounted for "the rapid extinguishment of the public debt" and the ensuing surplus. The surplus, however, represented danger. The government had no right to tax the people to create an overflowing treasury for the purpose of distribution, a policy which must "inevitably lead to corruption, and . . . end in ruin."[101] Again he warned of the dangers of a paper currency and how it benefited only a small well-to-do minority to the disadvantage of most Americans. The latter's "interests," he said, "can not be effectually protected unless silver and gold are restored to circulation."[102] Specie would prevent the unwarranted expansions and violent contractions of the paper money system.

Jackson's warnings were again ignored. The nation, after all, remained prosperous, and Martin Van Buren, taking the presidential oath the same day the farewell address was published, was optimistic that the humming economy he inherited would persist. His inaugural address emphasized the glories of forty years under the Constitution. "[W]e present an aggregate of human prosperity surely not elsewhere to be found."[103] This great achievement, he boasted, defied much of the common wisdom around the world a half century earlier. The American experiment, it was said, was doomed to fail. The American people "would not bear the taxation requisite to discharge an immense public debt . . . and pay the necessary expenses of the Government." Yet, Van Buren said, "[t]he cost of two wars has been paid, not only without a murmur, but with unequaled alacrity."[104] As long as the people remained faithful to the principles of the Constitution, a bright future lay ahead.

But Van Buren, like Herbert Hoover nine decades later, did not know that the sun was setting, not rising, on American prosperity. The causes of the 1837 Panic and subsequent depression remain controversial, but several elements seem clear.[105] The Specie Circular pulled gold and silver westward from eastern banks, undermining their capacity to maintain healthy note-specie ratios. At the same time, financial difficulties in Great Britain compelled English holders of American debt to summon those loans, and in May the resulting domestic and international pressures forced several New York deposit banks to suspend specie payments, that is, the conversion of their notes into gold and/or silver coin upon demand.

The shock reverberated throughout the nation, and soon banks all across the United States were defaulting. Businesses closed. Workers lost their jobs. As disposable income shrank, consumer purchasing did too, and tariff revenues dropped sharply. Van Buren summoned a special session of Congress to address the emergency, but before it met in September the second installment of the distribution went out to the states on April 1 and the third on July 1—a combined disbursement of more than $18 million. By the time Congress met, government revenues were falling short of expenditures. Accordingly, Congress canceled the fourth installment of the distribution, due October 1, but it did not recall any portion of the "loan" to the states that the distribution legally constituted. Jackson had been right. The distribution had simply been a giveaway. Instead, Congress did something else. It approved issuing $10 million in treasury notes. In other words, the government of the United States was borrowing again, and it has been borrowing ever since. The era of national debt freedom ended swiftly and suddenly in the aftermath of the Panic of 1837. Had the post-debt surplus not been distributed, or distributed in a different fashion, then conceivably the period of debt freedom might have lasted longer. As it was, however, that long sought Jacksonian reform, national debt freedom, endured for only two years and ten months—January 1835 to October 1837, "one brief, shining moment" in American history.[106]

National debt freedom, to be sure, ushered in no Camelot-like republican utopia, but that is not to say, despite the period's brevity and virtual disappearance from our memory, that it lacked consequences. In fact, it contributed to or reinforced several aspects of American political culture. As we have seen, for example, the anticipation of debt freedom helped stoke the reemergence of a two-party system after a decade of one-party rule during "the era of good feelings." The suspicion that John Quincy Adams was going to abort the Monroe schedule for debt freedom and become America's Robert Walpole had a lot to do with that development, but, be that as it may, we have lived with a two-party political system ever since. Indeed, it is a salient characteristic of our democratic politics.

Moreover, anticipating and then securing debt freedom underscored the collective American commitment to individual liberty despite slavery, the oppression of Native Americans, and the second-class status of women. Once approaching debt freedom helped cast the nation into the image of Jefferson's free and virtuous farmer, liberty's benefits could not be confined to white men only. Various reform movements arose to make the nation, in Benton's phrase, "wholly free," and not simply with respect to indebtedness. To this day reformism to liberate Americans from the vestiges of racism, sexism, nativism, and other "isms" hostile to liberty endures as one of the legacies of the Jacksonian era.

Debt freedom, Americans in the Jacksonian era believed, would improve the material quality of life in the United States. It would reduce taxes, increase disposable income, reduce the privileges of the creditor class, and, in general, generate greater equality as well as liberty. From this perspective securing debt freedom was itself a major reform, but one that was driven by the government itself—a top-down rather than a bottom-up undertaking. As part of that effort Jackson broke what was, by his day, a longstanding, uncontroversial tradition that dated back to Alexander Hamilton's tenure as secretary of the treasury: the idea that government and the private sector were partners in national development. But Andrew Jackson believed that that partnership contradicted the goal of national debt freedom because it put taxpayer money at risk in the securities markets. As a result, he effectively separated government from business enterprise. The conviction that government ought not involve itself in the marketplace remains alive and well in the United States today and constitutes a bequest from the Jackson era to our own. Indeed, the nature of American capitalism today owes much to Jackson's elimination of the national debt in 1835.

In addition, since no other nation had ever extinguished its entire debt, Americans of the Jacksonian era generally believed and their politicians bragged that the United States was somehow special—God's "chosen nation." Debt freedom, it seemed, demonstrated the superiority of American republicanism over other forms of government, proving American exceptionalism. The United States had a unique role to play in God's providential plan. The concept of American exceptionalism also remains vital in the United States today.

In Jackson's era debt freedom and the notion of American exceptionalism together encouraged an energetic foreign policy. Not only did America's "destiny" in the Western Hemisphere become "manifest," but also the financial affordability of an assertive role on the international stage was realized. The idea that the United States had a mission in the world and the wherewithal to achieve it endured into the post-debt freedom era and into more recent times—from Woodrow Wilson making "the world safe for democracy" in 1917 to George W. Bush declaring war on global terrorism in 2001.

Lastly, but importantly, the achievement of debt freedom in 1835 offers a unique perspective on the Age of Jackson. It imbues all the great policy issues of his day with coherence. It unifies them. It binds together under one umbrella issues as disparate as internal improvements, the recharter of the second Bank of the United States, the removal of the federal deposits from the Bank of the United States, the South Carolina Nullification Crisis, the sale of the public lands, and others. Nevertheless, whatever its historiographical explanatory power, the 1835 victory over national indebtedness is worth remembering in view of our current debt problem.

EPILOGUE: THEN AND NOW

Americans living in the Jacksonian era not only welcomed debt freedom but took pride in its achievement. No other nation had ever paid off its public debt. The country's success in this matter demonstrated the vitality of American republicanism and the benefits of liberty. For this reason, many Americans believed, the United States became the envy of the world, a role model for other nations to emulate—especially the European powers, whose citizens and subjects bore heavy taxes to sustain the perpetuated debts of corrupt regimes. Debt, after all, concentrated power in the executive authority by granting it the means to undermine the independence of legislatures through bribery and patronage. It led to tyranny. By eliminating its debt, the United States had removed this threat to its constitutional order. It had saved the constitutional separation of powers—the system of checks and balances—from corruption. The United States became, in Senator Benton's phrase, "wholly free." In other words, in Jackson's day, the national debt was perceived primarily as a political and constitutional problem, not as a financial or economic problem.

⁂

We have come a long way since the Age of Jackson. Nowadays, we mainly perceive the national debt as a financial and economic danger and not as a political and constitutional threat. The nation has borne a public debt since October 1837. Indeed, it has factored into government finance for so long that its once-feared governmental implications have evaporated. The president of the United States has not bought up Congress, and the office of the presidency has not metamorphosed into kingship. The anxieties about national indebtedness that gripped both the revolutionary generation and the next have long been forgotten. Recalling them now renders such ideas absurd.

Until recently, even the financial and economic implications of our national indebtedness had lost much of their power. We now know, for example, that the debt Andrew Jackson was so determined to eliminate actually promoted American economic development, transforming the United States from a nation of farmers into, ultimately, an industrial giant. (Alexander Hamilton's assertion that the national debt could become a "national blessing" turned out to be true.)[1] By the 1930s, when the Great Depression laid the giant on its back, Franklin Roosevelt's New Deal espoused deficit spending to revitalize the economy. Most Americans, in the midst of economic calamity, did not worry about accumulating debt. In fact, American attitudes toward national indebtedness changed remarkably in the century between Jackson and Roosevelt. Whoever shrugged off the debt with the now famous quip that "we only owe it to ourselves" summed up the new mood. Andrew Jackson might have rolled over in his grave.

After World War II the United States, locked in the Cold War with the Soviet Union and confronted with social problems that needed to be addressed, spent heavily on defense (including, of course, the Vietnam War), Medicare, Medicaid, education, and more. As a result, the debt grew. During the first year of Ronald Reagan's administrations, the debt exceeded, for the first time ever, one trillion dollars. By the time Reagan retired, the debt had grown beyond 2.5 trillion. Under George H. W. Bush, the debt ballooned to more than four trillion. The Republican Party, it seemed, which had long accused the Democrats of "taxing and spending," had become the party of "borrowing and spending."

Nevertheless, the debt problem was far from hopeless. In 1992, it will be recalled, Ross Perot, the Texas billionaire, mounted a third-party presidential campaign mainly on a single issue: the spiraling growth of the national debt. The United States, he warned, was heading toward insolvency. At the polls Perot performed much better than most other third-party candidates had in the past, and the Democratic victor, Bill Clinton, apparently absorbed the message that made Perot's candidacy credible. During Clinton's eight years, growth in the debt slowed as a result of treasury surpluses, and in the year 2000, for the first time in a long time, the debt actually shrunk. Anticipated future federal surpluses put the national debt on the road to extinction by 2010, or 2013 at the latest. The Treasury, in fact, discontinued the long bond. Another 1835 appeared on the horizon.

Unanticipated events intervened, however. The first was the election of George W. Bush as president, apparently a true believer in "borrow and spend." His administration proceeded to cut taxes without matching cuts in expenditures. This approach to government finance assured renewed borrowing. The massacres of 9/11 made matters worse. In the wake of the attacks, Bush declared a Global War on Terror and in 2003 attacked Iraq. Yet he sought no sacrifice from the American people, through taxation, to finance the war against Al Qaeda and the Taliban in Afghanistan or Saddam Hussein and the subsequent insurgency in Iraq. Instead, he borrowed. As a result, when he retired, the national debt stood at 10.5 trillion—a huge sum, still growing.

It is important to remember that national indebtedness transfers expenditures to future taxpayers. In Jackson's day, Henry Clay argued that borrowing for infrastructure projects like roads and canals was fair because future generations who bore part of the cost would also enjoy the benefits of their use. Similar reasoning justified borrowing for New Deal projects—dams, highways, bridges, tunnels, all of which the next generation or two which helped pay for them would utilize. But it is difficult to discern, at least at this juncture, what benefit, if any, the next couple of generations will get from the war in Iraq.

It is also instructive to remember that no foreign misadventures engulfed the Jackson presidency and that even the Old Hero, the alleged "military chieftain," sheathed his saber after rattling it at France in 1835. Jackson, of course, was committed to debt freedom. George W. Bush was not.

Moreover, with respect to the current public debt, we can find little solace in the notion that "we only owe it to ourselves." Unlike the debt that Andrew Jackson eliminated, much of today's debt is held by foreign governments, banks, and businesses. Principal creditors are China, Japan, the oil-exporting countries, the United Kingdom, and many others, including Russia. The amount owed to foreign entities exceeds five trillion, or roughly a third of our total national debt. The nature and scope of this indebtedness is unprecedented and what it means—for good or ill—remains unclear.

Yet the general public is becoming increasingly mindful that the bloating debt represents a financial and economic problem, which must be addressed sooner or later. Failure invites calamity.

The magnitude of the debt already affects the quality of our lives. In 2010, for example, interest on the debt accounted for approximately 6% of all federal expenditures. This amount represented hundreds of billions of dollars. In 2013 interest on the debt amounted to almost $416 billion, or approximately 11.8% of all federal expenditures that year. As the debt grows, and especially if interest rates rise, debt service will command more of taxpayers' money. The impact is obvious: less and less will be available for other needs. Put simply, growing interest obligations squeeze budget money out of defense, social programs, education, and other necessities. If not checked, this process must undermine the standard of living to which we are accustomed. On this point it is worth remembering that in Jackson's day no so-called "entitlements" existed. Congressional legislation established Social Security a century later, and Medicare and Medicaid a century and a third later. For this reason the term "entitlement" is a misnomer because laws can be changed, even repealed. Indeed, over the years Congress has amended and modified provisions of the "entitlements" and will likely have to do so again if our fiscal problems persist. "Entitlement" beneficiaries will experience a decline in the quality of their lives.

The only true "entitlement"—both in the Jackson era and now—is to bondholders. Government borrowing is secured not by legislation but by contract between the creditor and the United States Treasury. Congress cannot amend, modify, or nullify these contracts, and a substantial body of law upholds the rights of creditors. Their contracts literally "entitle" them to interest on their loans and return of principal upon maturity.

Yet, if debt growth remains unchecked, at some point lenders may become skeptical about the United States' capacity to sustain its mountainous debt. It is impossible to know when such a moment may arrive. Anything might trigger it—a debt to Gross Domestic Product ratio of 150%, a calamitous terrorist attack, fear that American monetary policy is fueling inflation and devaluing the debt—anything could induce the country's creditors to demand higher and higher interest rates or to cease lending altogether. Such a prospect threatens our way of life. High interest rates would put heavy pressure on many businesses to maintain profitability, forcing layoffs. As unemployment grew, consumer demand would fall, forcing more layoffs, generating a downward spiral into deflation. Would the government, perhaps unable to borrow, have the resources to meet unemployment insurance payments? Social Security payments? Compensation for the military? The list can easily be extended.

If unable to borrow, the government would find it impossible to revive the economy through deficit spending and stimulus packages. The only option left would be to increase the money supply, but this medicine could be as bad as or even worse than the illness. The degree of the subsequent inflation is impossible to gauge. Hyperinflation would, of course, be the worst possible case. Prices for ordinary necessities like food, clothing, and housing would soar; people on fixed incomes would be wiped out; life savings would melt down to a pittance. The once-almighty dollar would lack any value at all. Multiple variations of these scenarios are conceivable. None is good. All raise the specter of widespread misery, civil disorder, and the possible collapse of our institutions.

Fortunately and obviously, we have not—the Great Recession notwithstanding—collapsed into deep economic depression or drifted into wild inflation.

The long-awaited era of debt freedom turned out to be remarkably brief; only two years and ten months. To contemporaries this reality must have been disappointing and discouraging. After all, the fruits of debt freedom—firm checks and balances on power, limited government, the security of individual liberty, minimal taxes, and more—were supposed to endure for the long-term. In effect, American debt freedom was to demonstrate the superiority of republican institutions over all other forms of government. But the effort failed, done in by the Panic of 1837 and the subsequent depression.

The reasons for the economic crisis of 1837 remain controversial. Some historians view it as the product of the movement of specie from east to west in the wake of the Specie Circular; others see it resulting from imbalances in international trade; recently, one scholar has argued that it was a function of local capitalist culture within the United States interacting with the more mature and national capitalism of Great Britain.[2]

Whatever the precise economic causes, American political failure contributed to the financial crunch that struck the Van Buren administration during its first months. It will be recalled that when Congress enacted the 1817 Redemption law, the Jeffersonian Republicans constituted the only national political party. The Federalist Party was dead. Accordingly, the Redemption Act took shape in a non-partisan environment. Genuine consensus existed to eliminate the debt, and Congress put together the plan by which to do it. The plan was well thought out, viable, and ultimately successful. The Redemption Act serves as an example of how pure republican legislation was to be crafted: lawmakers selflessly acting for the public good. Political parties and self-interested politicians had no place in a republican universe.

This, of course, was not the case as debt freedom and its converse, surplus revenues, approached. A new party system emerged during Adams's administration and was fully blown by Jackson's second term. Although the Founders would not have had it happen that way, debt freedom arrived in the midst of intense and bitter political competition between the Democrats and the Whigs. So too, of course, did the federal surpluses. Unlike in 1817, however, when consensus prevailed, no consensus existed regarding what to do about the overflowing treasury. Clay's public land bill, for example, could not survive presidential vetoes. Nor, as the French crisis revealed, could a foreign policy emergency foster a consensus to spend the surplus on defense. Indeed, the immediate reduction of tariff revenues to suffocate the surplus, the obvious solution to the problem, was not seriously considered. The 1832 Verplanck tariff bill, by proposing immediate and radical reductions on import duties, implicitly promised strangulation of the surplus at its source. Everyone, however, abandoned it. The Clay Compromise Tariff, which was adopted instead, postponed sharp reductions for nearly a decade, assuring accumulation of a surplus. In addition, the compromise quickly acquired an aura of untouchability, which only complicated the matter. Even John C. Calhoun, it will be recalled, opposed tampering with it. In the end, Congress voted by heavy majorities to distribute the surplus to the states—but the House and Senate tallies in favor of the measure disguise an important reality. Calhoun introduced the Deposit and Distribution bill on May 25, 1836; the Senate approved it on June 18, and the House on June 22. Congress addressed the Distribution question, a matter of extraordinary significance to the entire nation, for less than a month. Did the brief debate on this important issue reflect shared wisdom—consensus—or political expediency? While the majorities in both chambers might suggest the former, the truth is that individual representatives and senators would have had a difficult time justifying to their constituents voting "no" on a generous federal handout. Political self-interest, not patriotism, explains the enactment of the Deposit and Distribution bill. Even Jackson, who disapproved of the measure, reluctantly signed it, either because the votes in both houses could override his veto or because a veto might imperil Van Buren's chances in the upcoming election. Perhaps both of these considerations factored into his thinking.

It comes down to this: the Distribution was rushed through Congress and signed by the president for partisan purposes. Serious analysis of the distribution's likely impact was missing from the debate. Would the federal surplus, although ostensibly only a loan to the states, simply wind up in state accounts—in the same so-called "pets" which then also held the non-surplus revenue of the national government? Would not some of the deposit provisions of the law require increasing the number of state banks holding federal revenues? Would not the infusion of all this revenue into state banks encourage them to expand their note issues? If so, would that not foster inflation? Would the distribution, in other words, undermine the national economy? These and other relevant questions failed to get a fair hearing in the bitterly partisan atmosphere of Washington, D.C. in 1836. For this reason alone, Congress bears some responsibility for the financial collapse of 1837.

The same contentious partisanship that characterized Congress in the Jacksonian era also characterizes Congress today. It is the reason why a large majority of Americans hold the national legislature in low esteem. Conservative Republicans and liberal Democrats relentlessly blame each other for the mess in which we find ourselves, and nothing seems to get done; or it gets done poorly. President Barack Obama has worked hard to overcome party divisions and to find common ground upon which to begin consensus-building. He has had little success promoting bipartisanship, but unless the heat in Congress gets turned down, the general welfare will be overlooked.

We will get partisan measures loaded, like the Distribution of 1836, with unintended consequences. Until and unless both parties can achieve consensus on what to do about the debt problem, either nothing will get done or whatever gets done will, at best, be ineffective, and, at worst, unleash a myriad of new problems.

Indeed, we have already experienced, as a result of irresponsible partisanship, close encounters with disaster over the debt issue. In August 2011, Republicans in the House of Representatives toyed with defaulting on the debt, leading Standard & Poor's to lower the government's credit rating from Triple-A to AA+. This was unprecedented. Never before had the nation's credit rating taken a hit. Nonetheless, in October 2013, the Republican majority in the House once again flirted with default while it shut down the government for sixteen days. Neither action, of course, helped spur economic growth, and, although Congress voted for a clean debt-ceiling measure in February 2014, where we go from here remains unclear.

It is worth noting that in the era of Andrew Jackson the very idea of defaulting on interest or principal payments on the national debt was unthinkable. South Carolina, it is true, took debt freedom as a hostage in its effort to secure free trade. Henry Clay and Nicholas Biddle, it will be recalled, also tried to delay debt freedom, each for his own purpose. But delaying debt freedom did not entail default. They were and are different things. In short, no Democrat and no Whig, despite the bitterness of their interactions, ever considered default an option. Once again, we have come a long way since the Age of Jackson.

❧

Despite what some economic historians may believe, no reliable formula exists to compare the purchasing power of the 1816 dollar and the 2014 dollar. Accordingly, there is little to gain by matching dollar-for-dollar the national debt then and the national debt now. In 1816 the debt peaked at $127 million; today's debt stands at more than seventeen trillion. To the post-War of 1812 generation, the former seemed a colossal amount; today the latter seems a *supercolossal* amount. The best that can be done is to measure the debts as percentages of Gross Domestic Product (GDP), the total value of goods and services generated by the national economy in a given year. If Thomas Senior Berry's calculations are reasonable estimates, the GDP in 1816 totaled $1.5 billion.[3] Accordingly, the $127 million in national debt represented 10.95% of the GDP. Today we would consider this a remarkably healthy ratio. After all, today (May 13, 2014) the debt stands at more than $17 trillion. Current estimates of GDP for 2014 hover at less than that amount. Accordingly, by the end of 2014 debt will represent more than 100% of GDP. This debt/GDP ratio constitutes a serious threat to the quality of life we have enjoyed since the end of World War II. (It translates into a debt of more than $54,000 for every man, woman, and child in the United States today; the 1816 debt, *per capita*, amounted to about $14.55.) A strong rebound from the current economic crisis is essential to solving this problem. If a powerful recovery fails to materialize and the nation slides into deep deflation (or, quite possibly, severe inflation), then the national debt will emerge again as a political and constitutional problem of the highest priority—but for reasons very different from those of the Jacksonian period. The disorders in Greece in the spring of 2010, the product of that country's overextended debt, suggest what those reasons might be. But, once again, unless Congress overcomes its penchant for partisan bickering and addresses the issue honestly and for the sake of the public good, a solution will remain elusive.

The Panic of 1837 brought the era of debt freedom to a quick end. Yet, although brief, the period of debt freedom was not without distinctive features. One notable characteristic was the sudden rise in federal revenues from the sale of the public lands. In 1834, on the eve of debt freedom, the treasury secured $4,858,000 from the sale of public lands. In 1835, debt freedom year, it drew in $14,758,000. In 1836 the sale of public lands earned the treasury an astounding

$24,877,000. Over two years, revenue from the public lands more than quintupled.[4] What caused this "bubble?" Several factors explain this phenomenon. First, the elimination of the national debt and the distribution of the surplus to the states meant that the country was going to be awash in money. Secondly, the destruction of the second Bank of the United States meant that the one institution with the capacity to check the growth of the money supply no longer played that role. Furthermore, since federal law set the price of public land at $1.25 per acre, and since Americans were moving west in considerable numbers, speculators found buying land at the minimum price for resale to settlers at a later date an attractive investment, especially since the volume of money on hand at the state banks suggested that bank notes might depreciate. Converting paper into real estate for future profit seemed a smart thing to do. Jackson, as we have seen, considered these operations scams on the public, and he ended it with his Specie Circular. Yet the order requiring specie for land accelerated the erosion of confidence in bank notes, and in May 1837, when panic struck, state banks, including those with federal deposits, suspended specie payments—that is, the conversion of their notes into gold and silver coin upon demand. Confidence in the entire system collapsed. Credit markets froze. Major bankruptcies ensued. Unemployment was rife. Tariff revenues declined sharply, and Van Buren, unwilling or unable to recall the distribution "loans," was forced into government borrowing.

In 2007 another "bubble" in the economy—this time in housing—burst, not by preemptive government action as in 1836 but on its own accord. Bubbles always burst.

In its aftermath, the Bush administration failed to act until the credit markets froze. In the fall of 2008 Treasury Secretary Henry Paulson and Fed Chairman Ben Bernanke seemed to be flailing as AIG, Fannie Mae, Freddie Mac, and major banks faced insolvency. Some got bailed out; others did not. The United States slipped into the worst economic crisis since the Great Depression.

The incoming Obama administration faced an enormous problem, but had only one real option to address it: to offer additional bailouts and to provide stimulus, especially through construction, to breathe life back into a moribund system. Only the government could command the enormous resources needed to impose sufficient demand on the productive system to get the economy humming again. The downside, of course, was that this effort entailed increasing an already staggering national debt. Obama's effort has not yet fully run its course, but the economy finally seems to be on the rebound: Production is up, joblessness is down, budget deficits are shrinking, and the stock market is bullish. If the recovery endures, the condition will be set for addressing the debt problem. If the recovery stalls and fails, the debt will continue to grow. Like other bubbles, it too will burst. The consequences will not be pretty.

All this leads to one last important matter, one already alluded to—*leadership*. The United States secured debt freedom in 1835 because Andrew Jackson, as we might say today, never "took his eye off the ball." He was determined to eliminate the national debt in 1835, if not earlier. Accordingly, that priority meant not only effective enforcement of the 1817 Redemption Act but also avoiding policies or programs that might incur new debt: Hence, for example, his veto of the Maysville Road bill and his tough stand in the Nullification Crisis. Indeed, his public policy decisions (except when it came to race) were consistently on the side of debt freedom. There were, of course, no public opinion polls in Jackson's day, no scientific way to assess the public's mood on specific issues. Accordingly, when he vetoed the bank recharter bill or removed the federal deposits from the Bank of the United States, he risked making more enemies than friends. But he took those risks for what he believed was a greater good. Jackson was, in other words, more than just a politician. As a leader and a statesman, Jackson was determined to secure debt freedom and deliver its benefits as his legacy to the American people.

Consistent and effective leadership today is essential to extract us from the quagmire of debt into which we have fallen. President

Obama has been working hard to stir economic recovery, without which the debt problem cannot be addressed. Now deep into his second term, his steadfastness seems to be paying off. If it is, the $17 trillion in debt will slowly be pared back. If the age of Andrew Jackson has anything to offer in the way of guidance while addressing our current debt problem, it is that leadership characterized by vision, consistency, and determination is the pathway to success.

ACKNOWLEDGMENTS

This work has been in progress for a long time, and I have incurred many debts in bringing it to fruition. First, I thank the Felician College administration and its Faculty Development Committee for their steady support. Sabbatical in the spring 2007 semester and several summer research stipends were vital for the book's completion.

I also thank the members of my department—Robert Ingoglia and Maria Vecchio—for their boundless moral support, but most especially my former longtime departmental chair, Sasha Sinkowsky, who facilitated my efforts in a hundred ways. To her I am particularly grateful.

I would be remiss if I omitted Paul Glassman, Director of the Felician College Library, and his predecessor, Stephen Karetzky, together with current and former library staff—especially Rosalind Bochynski, Bonnie Fong, Elisabeth Gatlin, Joanne Karetzky, Mary Lynne Parisi, and Mary Zieleniewski, all of whom helped me with interlibrary loans, microfilm editions of Jackson-era newspapers, microfiche resources, and other needs. I thank all of them.

The Gilder Lehrman Institute also earns my gratitude for inviting me to participate in its June 2003 summer seminar at Columbia

University, entitled "Political History of the Early Republic: New Challenges, Old Strengths." Led by Joyce Appleby, this enriching experience deepened my understanding of the era that this book addresses. I thank Professor Appleby and the other seminar members.

I owe a special debt to the Economic and Business Historical Society (EBHS), which over the last decade, allowed me to present earlier versions of several chapters at its annual conferences. I invariably received valuable feedback from EBHS officers and participants. I especially want to thank Stephanie Crofton, Ranjit Dighe, Lynne Pierson Doti, Jane Knodell, Wade Shilts, Jamie Stitt, Jason Taylor, and Robert E. Wright. An early version of chapter 8 was published on the Internet as well as in the 2007 edition of *Essays in Economic and Business History.* The latter, "The Elimination of the National Debt in 1835 and the Meaning of Jacksonian Democracy," won EBHS's James Soltow Award. Special thanks go to EBHS for allowing me to reproduce portions of that essay here, especially in chapter 8.

Others to whom I owe special thanks include my friend and former colleague George Castellitto, who critiqued several chapters and helped me deal with a number of computer issues. I must also thank Robert Ingoglia and Alex Iuculano for their help on computer-related problems and Nicholas DeSantis, my nephew, for his photography. I also thank Dick Gersh, Marc LaBella, Louise Mayo, and David Weinberg, each of whom read all or portions of the manuscript and provided valuable commentary. I am, however, most especially grateful to Thomas R. Chevraux of Canton, Ohio, my very good friend since our Peace Corps service in Jamaica in the 1960s, for his close reading of the entire manuscript and his rigorous critique. His insight and advice have been invaluable.

I would also like to thank Bruce H. Franklin of Westholme Publishing, my copy editor Alex Kane, and Trudi Gershenov for her cover design.

My wife Carolyn, of course, merits special thanks for her support of this project, especially since it took so long to complete. I know that there were times when it was not easy. I am also grateful to both of my sons, Philip and David, for their encouragement and moral support throughout this endeavor. Lastly, but very, very far from least, I thank my daughter Elizabeth, to whom this book is dedicated, not only for her unflagging interest in my work but also for her strength and courage in the face of adversity. She is and always will be the proverbial apple of my eye.

NOTES

Chapter One: Crisis and Promise, December 1824–March 1825

1. For the weather in the fall of 1824, see Joel W. Hiatt, ed., *The Diary of William Owen from November 10, 1824 to April 20, 1825* (Indianapolis: Bobbs-Merrill Company, 1906), 7-55, *passim.* William Owen was son of Robert Owen, the prominent socialist.

2. For the election of 1824, see Sean Wilentz, *The Rise of American Democracy: Jefferson to Lincoln* (New York and London: W.W. Norton & Company, 2005), 240-57 and Daniel Walker Howe, *What Hath God Wrought: The Transformation of America, 1815-1848* (New York: Oxford University Press, 2007), 203-11. Also useful is Eugene H. Roseboom, *A History of Presidential Elections* (2nd ed., New York: Macmillan Company, 1964), 77-88.

3. For the importance of boarding house arrangements on the politics of the period, see James Sterling Young, *The Washington Community, 1800-1828* (New York: Columbia University Press, 1966), 98-106, 123-24, 132-34, 139-41.

4. Gaillard Hunt, ed., *The First Forty Years of Washington Society in the Family Letters of Margaret Bayard Smith* (New York: Frederick Ungar Publishing Co., 1965, reprinted from the first edition, 1906), 165.

5. For a solid overview of Monroe's administrations, see Noble E. Cunningham, Jr., *The Presidency of James Monroe* (Lawrence: University Press of Kansas, 1996). Cunningham, however, offers just one sentence on Monroe's announcement that the debt would be eliminated in a decade. On his anticipation of retiring, Monroe wrote Thomas Jefferson in October 1824: "I shall be heartily rejoiced when the term of my service expires, & I may return home in peace with my family. . . ." in Stanislaus

Murray Hamilton, ed., *The Writings of James Monroe* (7 vols.: New York and London, G. P. Putnam's Sons, 1898-1903), VII, 43.
6. Monroe subsequently described his role in the 1824 contest this way: "Nor did I ever express any preference to anyone in favor of either of the candidates, wishing to deal with all impartially. . . . I was not the partisan of any of the candidates." James Monroe to T. Ringgold, May 8, 1826, in Hamilton, ed., *Writings of James Monroe*, VII, 82.
7. Charles Francis Adams, ed., *Memoirs of John Quincy Adams* (12 vols., Philadelphia: J. B. Lippincott & Co. 1874-77), VI, 428. Hereafter, simply Adams, *Memoirs.*
8. *Ibid.,* VI, 431.
9. *Ibid.,* VI, 438.
10. *Senate Journal,* 18:2, 28.
11. James D. Richardson, ed., *A Compilation of the Messages and Papers of the Presidents, 1789-1897* (10 vols.; Washington: Bureau of National Literature, 1896-99), II, 817. Hereafter simply cited as *Messages and Papers.*
12. *Ibid.,* II, 823.
13. *Ibid.,* II, 823.
14. William H. Crawford, "Report on the State of Finances," December 31, 1824, 18:2; *Register of Debates*, Appendix, 18:2, 40.
15. *Albany Argus,* December 14, 1824.
16. Adams, *Memoirs,* VI, 440.
17. For an analysis of how Clay's supporters worked in his behalf in 1824, see Robert V. Remini, *Henry Clay: Statesman for the Union* (New York and London: W.W. Norton & Co., 1991), ch. 14.
18. *Ibid., passim.*
19. *Ibid., passim.* For a sample of foreigners' commentary on Clay, see William Faux, *Faux's Memorable Days in America* in Reuben Gold Thwaites, ed., *Early Western Travels* (32 vols., Cleveland: Arthur H. Clark Company, 1904-07), XII, 28-30 and Sir Charles Augustus Murray, *Travels in North America During the Years 1834, 1835, & 1836* (London: R. Bentley, 1839), 135-36.
20. Henry Clay to George McClure, December 28, 1824 in James F Hopkins, ed., *The Papers of Henry Clay* (12 vols., Lexington: University of Kentucky Press, 1959-1992), Vol. 3, 906. Hereafter, *Clay Papers.*
21. Adams, *Memoirs,* VI, 446-47.
22. *Ibid.,* VI, 448-49. Adams ordinarily frowned on campaigning for office as unrepublican. In this instance he apparently made an exception.
23. *Ibid.,* VI, 452-53.
24. *Ibid.,* VI, 455.
25. *Ibid.,* VI, 456-57.
26. *Ibid.,* VI, 457-58.
27. *Ibid.,* VI, 464. For the lobbying in which the other candidates engaged to win

Clay's support, see James Parton, *Life of Andrew Jackson* (3 vols., New York: Mason Brothers, 1860), III, 55-65.
28. *Ibid.,* VI, 464-65.
29. *Ibid.,* VI, 465.
30. Henry Clay, "Address to the People of the Congressional District," March 26, 1825, *Clay Papers,* IV, 146.
31. "Appeal to the House," February 3, 1825, *Ibid.,* IV, 53.
32. Adams, *Memoirs,* VI, 484.
33. Clay to George Thompson, January 15, 1825, *Clay Papers,* IV, 19.
34. *Register of Debates,* Appendix, 18:2, 83-90.
35. The House received the report on January 3, 1825, *Journal of the House of Representatives,* 18:2, 100.
36. "Report of the Committee of Ways and Means on the State of the Public Debt. . . ," January 12, 1825, *Register of Debates,* Appendix, 18:2, 72-73.
37. "An Act . . . to borrow a sum not exceeding twelve millions of dollars. . . ," *Ibid.,* Appendix, 18:2, 119-20.
38. *Register of Debates,* House of Representatives, 18:2, 66.
39. *Ibid.,* 67.
40. "An Act Making Provision for the Debt of the United States," August 4, 1790, *Statutes at Large of the United States* (18 vols., Boston: Little, Brown and Company: 1845-1873), 1:2, 144. Hereafter, simply *Statutes at Large.*
41. "Report of the Committee on Roads and Canals," February 6, 1825, *Register of Debates*, House of Representatives, 18:2. Appendix, 76. According to the bill, the states could buy federally held shares on demand, allowing them to substitute themselves for the federal government at whatever point in the process they might choose. This provision constituted a sop to those who questioned federal authority to fund internal improvements. Nonetheless, the committee asserted that it was "unnecessary . . . to make any effort to ascertain where the true line" between federal and state authority "lies." Instead, the bill distinguished between two categories or "classes" of projects. The first consisted of those "passing through different states . . . not interested in a degree sufficient to induce them to undertake the perfection of the work, or any considerable part of it." Such works were simply federal responsibilities. But the second "class" of projects were those on which "the General Government and the states can act conjointly" because both had an interest in fulfillment. How would federal-state cooperation be achieved? Quite simply by federal subscription to the stock of "companies incorporated in the respective states, for internal improvements." The committee's bill, therefore, aimed at facilitating second class and not first class projects. "It is a plan of encouragement," the committee reported, "and its operation, will not interfere with objects of the first class." The measure aimed at "the actual execution of internal improvements." It would "excite the states to incorporate companies for such objects as will be, in a degree, National, and sufficiently so as to induce

Congress to countenance them." Interestingly, the committee perceived no problem in the federal government's purchase of stock in private companies. To the contrary, it declared: "The committee cannot conceive how the General Government can aid in the internal improvements of the country . . . with greater propriety than by subscription to companies incorporated by the respective states." *Ibid.*, 76.

42. *Ibid.*, 80.

43. *Ibid.*, 76.

44. Hunt, ed., *The First Forty Years of Washington Society,* 175, 186.

45. *Ibid.*, 186-87.

46. *Journal of the House of Representatives,* 18:2, 129.

47. *Ibid.*, 18:2, 143.

48. *Register of Debates,* House of Representatives, 18:2, 361-63, 420.

49. *Ibid.*, 18:2, 515.

50. John C. Fitzpatrick, ed., *The Autobiography of Martin Van Buren* (Annual Report of the American Historical Association for the Year 1918: Washington, D.C.: Government Printing Office, 1920), 150. Hereafter, simply Van Buren, *Autobiography.*

51. *Ibid.*, 150-52.

52. James Fenimore Cooper, *Notions of the Americans: Picked Up by a Travelling Bachelor* (2 vols., New York: Stringer & Townsend, 1850), II, 176.

53. Hunt, ed., *The First Forty Years of Washington Society,* 187.

54. For Wright's presence, see Daniel Feller, *The Jacksonian Promise: America, 1815-1840* (Baltimore and London: Johns Hopkins University Press, 1995), 11-12.

55. *Register of Debates,* House of Representatives, 18:2, 526.

56. *Ibid.*, 18:2, 525.

57. *Ibid.*, 18:2, 526.

58. Hunt, ed., *The First Forty Years of Washington Society,* 187.

59. *Register of Debates,* House of Representatives, 18:2, 526.

60. All this was according to rule number 5.

61. *Register of Debates,* House of Representatives, 18:2, 527.

62. *Ibid.*, 18:2, 527; Cooper, *Notions of the Americans,* II, 178.

63. Cooper, *Notions of the Americans,* II, 178; *Register of Debates,* House of Representatives, 18:2, 527.

64. *Register of Debates,* House of Representatives, 18:2, 527.

65. A few days later Van Rennselaer offered an excuse for his vote, which is excluded from the narrative because it lacks credibility. According to Van Buren, a night or two after the election, he and Van Rennselaer were walking together to visit Mrs. Stephen Decatur. Van Rennselaer used the occasion to explain to Van Buren why he had changed his vote. He admitted that the meeting with Clay and Webster had upset him, and that when he took his seat in the House "he dropped his head upon the edge of his desk and made a brief appeal to his Maker for his guidance . . . and when he removed his hand from his eyes he saw on the floor directly below him a

ticket [ballot] bearing the name of John Quincy Adams." Taking this circumstance as a response from heaven, he deposited that ticket in the ballot box. In other words, God made him do it. This story is difficult to believe. Why would a ballot with Adams's name on it be lying on the floor below the New York delegation's table? The voting had not yet even begun. (Van Buren, *Autobiography,* 152.) More likely, Van Rennselaer wanted to justify his action to defuse the social ostracism he was sure to face by his messmates. Years later, in 1849, Clay visited Van Buren at his home in upstate New York. Van Buren told Clay Van Rennselaer's story. Clay, who "listened with great interest," probably found the story amusing (*Ibid., 153).* According to Thurlow Weed, the New York politico, Van Rennselaer had actually decided to vote for Adams a few days before the balloting. Weed's source for this information was Representative Albert H. Tracy. (Harriet A. Weed, ed., *Autobiography of Thurlow Weed,* (2 vols., Boston: Houghton, Mifflin and Company, 1884), I, 462.

66. Hunt, ed., *The First Forty Years of Washington Society,* 186.

67. *Ibid.,* 186.

68. Adams, *Memoirs,* IV, 503-4.

69. Hunt, ed., *The First Forty Years of Washington Society,* 182-83, 186; Cooper, *Notions of the Americans,* II, 182-83.

70. Adams, *Memoirs,* IV, 502-3.

71. *Register of Debates,* House of Representatives, 18:2, 547.

72. Adams, *Memoirs,* IV, 497.

73. *Ibid.,* IV, 481.

74. *Ibid.,* IV, 489-90.

75. Clay to John Quincy Adams, February 11, 1825, *Clay Papers,* Vol. 4, 63.

76. Adams to Henry Clay, February 11, 1825, *Ibid.,* Vol. 4, 63.

77. Adams, *Memoirs,* IV, 508.

78. *Ibid.,* IV, 508.

79. Clay to Francis T. Brooke, February 18, 1825, *Clay Papers,* Vol. 4, 74. This letter outlines the pros and the cons discussed by Clay and his friends.

80. Clay to John Quincy Adams, February 17, 1825, *Ibid.,* Vol. 4, 72.

81. Adams, *Memoirs,* IV, 518.

82. *Ibid.,* IV, 519.

83. *National Intelligencer,* March 4, 1825, reprinted in *Albany Argus,* March 11, 1825.

84. Adams, *Memoirs,* IV, 519.

85. John Quincy Adams, Inaugural Address, March 4, 1825, *Messages and Papers,* II, 860-61.

86. *Ibid.,* II, 861-62.

87. *Ibid.,* II, 863-65.

88. *Ibid.,* II, 865.

89. Adams, *Memoirs,* IV, 519.

90. *Ibid.,* IV, 519.

91. Madison, Monroe, and Adams all became president after serving as secretary of state.

Chapter Two: The Crisis and Promise of 1824–1825 in Historical Context

1. The authoritative study of Adams's life and career remains Samuel Flagg Bemis, *John Quincy Adams and the Foundations of American Foreign Policy* (New York: Alfred A. Knopf, 1949) and the same author's *John Quincy Adams and the Union* (New York: Alfred A. Knopf, 1956). More recent and shorter accounts include Robert V. Remini, *John Quincy Adams* (New York: Times Books, Henry Holt and Company, 2002); James E. Lewis, Jr., *John Quincy Adams: Policymaker for the Union* (Wilmington, DE: SR Books, 2001; and Lynn Hudson Parsons, *John Quincy Adams* (Madison: Madison House, 1998).
2. *Register of Debates,* House of Representatives, 18:2, 212.
3. For more complete explication, see Bernard Bailyn, *The Ideological Origins of the American Revolution* (Cambridge, MA: Belknap Press of Harvard University Press, 1967), ch. III.
4. Adam Smith described how all this came about. See his *The Wealth of Nations* (New York: Bantam Classics, 2003), Book V, ch. III, especially 1156-76. See also James Macdonald, *A Free Nation Deep in Debt: The Financial Roots of Democracy* (New York: Farrar, Straus and Giroux, 2003), chs. 4-7, and Robert E. Wright, *One Nation Under Debt: Hamilton, Jefferson, and the History of What We Owe* (New York: McGraw-Hill, 2008), ch. 2.
5. Bailyn, *Ideological Origins,* 48-51. For the relationship between debt, corruption, and a strong national government, see Gordon S. Wood, *The Radicalism of the American Revolution* (New York: Vintage Books, 1991), 262-64.
6. Lance Banning, "Republican Ideology and the Triumph of the Constitution, 1789 to 1793," *William and Mary Quarterly,* 31 (April 1974), 174.
7. Smith, *The Wealth of Nations,* Book V, ch. III.
8. Bailyn, *Ideological Origins,* ch. IV.
9. Wright, *One Nation Under Debt,* 13.
10. The Constitution of the United States, Article I, Section VIII, and Article VI. A vast literature exists regarding the difficulties, financial and otherwise, of the Confederation era and the movement to establish a stronger national government. Interested readers may wish to consult some overviews of the period. Useful are the following: Richard B. Morris, *The Forging of the Union, 1781-1789* (New York: Harper & Row, 1987); Forrest McDonald, *E Pluribus Unum: The Formation of the American Republic, 1776-1790* (Boston: Houghton Mifflin Company, 1965) and *We the People: The Economic Origins of the Constitution* (Chicago: University of Chicago Press, 1958); Jack N. Rakove, *The Beginnings of National Politics: An Interpretive History of the Continental Congress* (Baltimore and London: Johns Hopkins

University Press, 1979). It is difficult to omit from this brief listing Charles Beard's classic *An Economic Interpretation of the Constitution of the United States* (New York: Macmillan Company, 1913). For contemporary critique of the Confederation era, nothing, of course, surpasses Alexander Hamilton, James Madison, and John Jay, *The Federalist,* which is available in multiple editions.

11. See Chapter I, note 40.

12. U.S. Bureau of the Census, *Historical Statistics of the United States, Colonial Times to 1957* (Washington, D.C.: U.S. Government Printing Office, 1960), 721. Hereafter, *Historical Statistics.* Funding and assumption were hotly debated for a number of reasons. One major objection concerned the fact that funding the bonds at par to the current holders denied the original holders—farmers, veterans, shopkeepers—any compensation but instead offered a windfall to wealthy speculators who had purchased them at a fraction of face value. Assumption too raised issues, especially the injustice to those states which had already met their debt obligations. Hamilton's program required them to help bail out the states that had not addressed their debt problems. The opposition finally accepted assumption on the pledge that the national capital would be relocated to the south, the reason why Washington, D.C. sits on the Potomac River. Hamiltonian finance has generated a huge scholarly literature. Useful overviews include John C. Miller, *The Federalist Era, 1789-1801* (New York, Evanston and London: Harper & Row, 1960), ch. 3; Stanley Elkins and Eric McKitrick, *The Age of Federalism: The Early American Republic, 1788-1800* (New York and Oxford: Oxford University Press, 1993), chs. II, III; Forrest McDonald, *Alexander Hamilton: A Biography* (New York and London: W.W. Norton & Co., 1979), chs. VII, VIII; Ron Chernow, *Alexander Hamilton* (New York: Penguin Press, 2004), 295-331 and *passim;* Wright, *One Nation Under Debt,* 125-60; Donald F. Swanson, *The Origins of Hamilton's Fiscal Policies* (Gainesville, FL: 1963). The most recent overview of early American finance is Thomas K. McCraw, *The Founders and Finance: How Hamilton, Gallatin, and Other Immigrants Forged a New Economy* (Cambridge, MA. and London: Belknap Press of Harvard University Press, 2012).

13. Report on Public Credit, January 9, 1790, Harold C. Syrett, ed., *The Papers of Alexander Hamilton* (27 vols.: New York: Columbia University Press, 1961-1987), VI, 106.

14. For discussions of the Bank of the United States see Miller, *Federalist Era,* ch.4; Elkins and McKitrick, *Age of Federalism,* 223-33; McDonald, *Alexander Hamilton,* chs. IX and X; Chernow, *Alexander Hamilton,* 344-61. More specialized studies include David J. Cowen, *The Origins and Economic Impact of the First Bank of the United States, 1791-1797* (New York: Garland Publishing, 2000); Robert E. Wright, *One Nation Under Debt,* 147-52; Carl Lane, "For 'A Positive Profit': The Federal Investment in the First Bank of the United States, 1792-1802, *William and Mary Quarterly,* LIV (July 1997), 601-12.

15. The literature on Jefferson and Jeffersonianism is not only huge but overwhelming. For brief but solid treatments, readers may consult Marshall Smelser, *The Democratic Republic, 1801-1815* (New York, Evanston, and London: Harper & Row, 1968) and Norman K. Risjord, *Jefferson's America, 1760-1815* (2nd. ed., Lanham, Boulder, New York, Oxford: Rowman & Littlefield Publishers, 2002). For Jefferson's views on public indebtedness, see Herbert E. Sloan, *Principle and Interest: Thomas Jefferson & the Problem of Debt* (New York and Oxford: Oxford University Press, 1995). For the impact of republicanism on the early national period, see Drew R. McCoy, *The Elusive Republic: Political Economy in Jeffersonian America* (Chapel Hill: University of North Carolina Press, 1980) and for Jefferson's vision of a debt-free America, especially pp. 185-86. Actually, the quote appears in the first sentence of Henry David Thoreau's famous essay, *Civil Disobedience,* first published in 1848.
16. Hamilton, "Final Version of an Opinion on the Constitutionality of an Act to Establish a Bank," Syrett, ed., *Hamilton Papers,* VIII, 63-134.
17. For the foreign crisis of the 1790s and party formation, see Elkins and McKitrick, *Age of Federalism,* chs. IX-XIII and Miller, *Federalist Era,* chs. 8, 9, 12. Still useful is Joseph Charles, *The Origins of the American Party System* (New York: Harper & Row, 1956).
18. *Historical Statistics,* 721.
19. *Ibid.,* 721.
20. *Ibid.,* 721.
21. *Ibid.,* 721.
22. Van Buren, *Autobiography,* 197.
23. Thomas Hart Benton, *Thirty Years' View* (2 vols., New York and London: D. Appleton & Co., 1854-56), I, 5.
24. James Madison, Annual Message, December 3, 1816, *Annals of Congress,* Senate Proceedings and Debates, 14:2, 15.
25. "An Act to Provide for the Redemption of the Public Debt," *Statutes at Large,* 14:2, 379.
26. *Annals of Congress,* House of Representatives, 14:2, 1032; Senate, 14:2, 205.
27. "An Act . . . for the Redemption of the Public Debt," *Statutes at Large,* 14:2, 379.
28. Arthur M. Schlesinger, Jr., *The Age of Jackson* (Boston and Toronto: Little, Brown and Company, 1945), ch. 3.
29. *Register of Debates,* House of Representatives, 20:1, 1130. See also John F. Devanny, " 'A Loathing of Public Debt, Taxes, and Excises': The Political Economy of John Randolph of Roanoke," *Virginia Magazine of History and Biography,* 109 (no. 4, 2001), 386-416.
30. John Taylor, *Tyranny Unmasked,* F. Thornton Miller, ed. (Indianapolis: Liberty Fund, 1992), Section 3, Part 2. Taylor's work was originally published in 1822.
31. On Macon's unalloyed republicanism, see Schlesinger, *Age of Jackson,* 26-28. For the relationship between Macon and Randolph, see Elizabeth Gregory McPherson,

ed., "Letters from Nathaniel Macon to John Randolph of Roanoke," *North Carolina Historical Review,* 39 (Spring 1962), 195-211.
32. Wilentz, *Rise of American Democracy,* 181, 214, 230, 237, 291, 344.
33. C. Edward Skeen, "Vox Populi, Vox Dei: The Compensation Act of 1816 and the Rise of Popular Politics," *Journal of the Early Republic,* 6 (Fall 1986), 253-74.
34. *Register of Debates,* House of Representatives, 20:1, 1392.
35. James Madison, Annual Messages, December 5, 1815 and December 3, 1816, *Messages and Papers,* I, 552-53, 561. For discussion of Madison's seeming flip, see John Lauritz Larson, *Internal Improvement: National Public Works and the Promise of Popular Government in the Early United States* (Chapel Hill and London: University of North Carolina Press, 2001), 63-69.
36. Madison, Veto, March 3, 1817, *Messages and Papers,* I, 569-70.
37. Monroe, Veto, May 4, 1822, *Ibid.,* I, 711-12.
38. *Annals of Congress,* Public Acts of Congress, 18:1, 3217.
39. Adams, *Memoirs,* VII, 509.
40. Clay to Francis T. Brooke, February 18, 1825, *Clay Papers,* 4:74.
41. Clay to Robert Walsh, Jr., February 18, 1825, *Ibid.,* 4:75.
42. See, for examples, the warnings in Amos Kendall to Clay, February 19, 1825, and in Francis Preston Blair to Clay, March 7, 1825, *Ibid.,* 4:77, 91.
43. Clay, "Address to the People of the Congressional District," March 26, 1825, *Ibid.,* 4:165. An unnumbered footnote refers to publication outside of Kentucky. For verification, see *Albany Argus,* April 5, 1825.
44. Clay, "Address to the People . . . ," March 26, 1825, *Clay Papers,* 4:165.
45. Clay to Charles Hammond, May 23, 1825, *Ibid.,* 4:387.
46. *Ibid.,* 4:408, 414, 427, 431.
47. Clay to Samuel L. Southard, June 17, 1825, *Ibid.,* 4:447.
48. Clay to James Brown, September 4, 1825, *Ibid.,* 4:618.
49. Adams, *Memoirs,* VII, 22-28.
50. *Ibid.,* VII, 27-28.
51. *Ibid.,* VII, 21-22, 37.
52. *Register of Debates,* House of Representatives, 18:2, 212.
53. Adams, *Memoirs,* VII, 16.

Chapter Three: The National Debt and the Failure of the Adams Administration

1. Adams, *Memoirs,* VII, 59.
2. *Ibid.,* VII, 61.
3. *Ibid.,* VII, 63.
4. *Ibid.,* VII, 64-65.
5. *Ibid.,* VII, 63.
6. *Ibid.,* VII, 71-72.

7. Adams, First Annual Message, December 6, 1825, *Messages and Papers,* II, 868.
8. *Ibid.,* II, 869.
9. *Ibid.,* II, 870.
10. *Ibid.,* II, 871-77.
11. *Ibid.,* II, 877.
12. *Ibid.,* II, 877.
13. *Ibid.,* II, 877-79.
14. *Ibid.,* II, 880-81.
15. *Ibid.,* II, 881-82.
16. *Ibid.,* II, 871.
17. Calhoun to Samuel Gouverneur (?), December 18, 1825, in Clyde N. Wilson and E. Edwin Hemphill, eds. *The Papers of John C. Calhoun* (Columbia: University of South Carolina Press, 1977), X, 57-58. The first two brackets have been added by this writer; the third is in the text. Hereafter, *Calhoun Papers.*
18. Richard Rush, Annual Treasury Report, December 22, 1825, *Register of Debates,* Appendix, 19:1, 23.
19. *Ibid.,* 24-25.
20. Report of the Committee of Ways and Means . . . on the State of the Finances, February 6, 1826, *Register of Debates,* Appendix, 19:1, 105.
21. *Ibid.,* 106-7.
22. *United States' Telegraph,* February 21, 1826.
23. *Register of Debates,* House of Representatives, 19:1, 862.
24. An Act for the Relief of Penelope Denny, May 16, 1826, *Register of Debates,* Appendix, 19:1, xx.
25. *Register of Debates,* House of Representatives, 19:1, 1327, 1346.
26. *Ibid.,* 2570.
27. *Ibid.,* 1151.
28. *Ibid.,* 1152.
29. *Ibid.,* 1152. Cocke was referring to the refinance bill of early 1825.
30. *Ibid.,* 1153.
31. *Ibid.,* 1153.
32. *Ibid.,* 1166-67.
33. *Ibid.,* 1167.
34. *Ibid.,* 1171.
35. *Ibid.,* 1186.
36. *Ibid.,* 1200.
37. *Ibid.,* 1205.
38. *Ibid.,* 1206.
39. *Register of Debates,* Appendix, 19:1, vii.; Also, *Statutes at Large,* 19:1, IV,149.
40. *Register of Debates,* Senate, 19:1, 4.
41. *Ibid.,* 4.

42. *Ibid.*, 20-21.
43. *Ibid.*, 29, 704-5, 710-19, and for the Cumberland Road see 350-64.
44. *Ibid.*, 726.
45. *Register of Debates,* House of Representatives, 19:1, 2554.
46. *Ibid.*, 2570.
47. *Ibid.*, 2570.
48. *Ibid.*, 2570.
49. *Ibid.*, 2655.
50. *Ibid.*, 2655.
51. *Ibid.*, 2655.
52. *Ibid.*, 2656.
53. *Ibid.*, 2656.
54. *United States' Telegraph,* September 30, 1826.
55. Reprinted in *Ibid.,* May 25, 1827.
56. The canal companies were Chesapeake and Delaware, Louisville and Portland, and Dismal Swamp. The omnibus internal improvement bill appropriated a total of $85,320. See *Register of Debates,* Appendix, 19:1, xiii, xx, xxiv, xxv.
57. See, for example, on this matter Van Buren, *Autobiography,* I, 196. Useful secondary sources are Wilentz, *Rise of American Democracy*, 251-265, 281-82, 293-300; George Dangerfield, *The Era of Good Feelings* (New York: Harcourt Brace and Company, 1952. Reprint by Elephant Press, 1989), Book 5, chs. 1-7; Remini, *Henry Clay: Statesman for the Union*, chs. 14-18.
58. Van Buren, *Autobiography,* I, 117.
59. Wilentz, *Rise of American Democracy,* 293.
60. Adams, Second Annual Message, December 5, 1826, *Messages and Papers,* II, 923.
61. Larson, *Internal Improvement,* ch. 5.
62. *Ibid.*, 150.
63. *Ibid.*, 165-66.
64. *Ibid.*, 166.
65. Reprinted in the *United States' Telegraph,* October 17, 1827.
66. Adams, *Memoirs,* IX, 253.
67. Quoted in George Dangerfield, *The Awakening of American Nationalism, 1815-1828* (New York: Harper & Row, 1965), 234, and also in Feller, *The Jacksonian Promise*, 53.

Chapter Four: The Accession of Andrew Jackson and the End of Internal Improvements

1. The most complete account of the election of 1828 is Robert V. Remini, *The Election of Andrew Jackson* (Philadelphia and New York: J. B. Lippincott Company, 1963).
2. For Jackson's characterization of Clay, see Andrew Jackson to William B. Lewis, February 14, 1825, in John Spenser Bassett, ed., *Correspondence of Andrew Jackson* (7

vols., Washington, D.C., Carnegie Institution of Washington, 1926-35), III, 276. Hereafter cited simply as Jackson, *Correspondence.*

3. On party development see Richard P. McCormick, *The Second American Party System: Party Formation in the Jacksonian Era* (New York: W. W. Norton & Co., 1966). Also valuable is Wilentz, *Rise of American Democracy,* chs. 8, 9.

4. Dangerfield, *Awakening of American Nationalism*, 240-41.

5. For an insightful contrast of Adams and Jackson, see John William Ward, *Andrew Jackson—Symbol for an Age* (London, Oxford, New York: Oxford University Press, 1953), 63-71.

6. The authoritative life of Jackson is Robert V. Remini's magisterial three-volume account: *Andrew Jackson and the Course of American Empire, 1767-1821* (New York: Harper & Row, 1977); *Andrew Jackson and the Course of American Freedom, 1822-1832* (New York: Harper & Row, 1981) and *Andrew Jackson and the Course of American Democracy, 1833-1845* (New York: Harper & Row, 1984). Remini's work is also available in a one-volume abridgment, *The Life of Andrew Jackson* (New York: Harper & Row, 1988). H. W. Brands, *Andrew Jackson: His Life and Times* (New York, London, *et al.*: Doubleday, 2005) is an important, more recent account of the Old Hero's life as is Sean Wilentz, *Andrew Jackson* (New York: Time Books, Henry Holt and Company, 2005), which, although comparatively brief, is rich in insight. For Jackson and the Creek War, see Howard T. Weir, III, *A Paradise of Blood: The Creek War of 1813-14* (Yardley, PA: Westholme Publishing, 2014). Also useful is Andrew Burstein, *The Passions of Andrew Jackson* (New York: Vintage Books edition, 2004, [original hardcover by Alfred A. Knopf, 2003]) but, alas, debt elimination is not counted among Jackson's "passions." A recent interesting overview of the entire Jacksonian era is William Nester, *The Age of Jackson and the Art of American Power, 1815-1848* (Washington, D.C.: Potomac Books, 2013). For works more tightly focused on the Jackson administrations, see Schlesinger, *The Age of Jackson* and Jon Meacham's Pulitzer Prize-winning *American Lion: Andrew Jackson in the White House* (New York: Random House, 2008). Other significant accounts include Harry L. Watson, *Liberty and Power: The Politics of Jacksonian America* (New York: Hill and Wang, 1990) and Donald B. Cole, *The Presidency of Andrew Jackson* (Lawrence: University Press of Kansas, 1993). It is impossible to overlook James Parton's *Life of Andrew Jackson,* not only because of the primary sources it contains but also because Parton interviewed people who knew and worked with Jackson.

7. Jackson to James W. Lanier, May 15 (?), 1824, Jackson, *Correspondence,* III, 251.

8. *Register of Debates,* House of Representatives, 21:1, 1147; See also Van Buren, *Autobiography,* 315.

9. Van Buren, *Autobiography,* 314.

10. Jackson, *Correspondence,* III, 451-52. This document is also available in Daniel Feller, *et. al.*, eds., *The Papers of Andrew Jackson,* (Knoxville: University of Tennessee Press, 2007), VII, 69-70. Hereafter simply *Jackson Papers.*

11. On Rachel's death, See Remini, *Life of Andrew Jackson,* 169-70 and Meacham, *American Lion,* 4-7.
12. Hunt, ed., *The First Forty Years of Washington Society,* 273, 295.
13. R*egister of Debates,* House of Representatives, 20:2, 350.
14. *Ibid.,* 350.
15. Hunt, ed., *The First Forty Years of Washington Society,* 273.
16. *Register of Debates,* Senate, 20:2, 18.
17. *Ibid.,* 18.
18. *Ibid.,* 18-28.
19. *Ibid.,* House of Representatives, 20:2, 378.
20. *Ibid.,* 378-82.
21. Hunt, ed., *The First Forty Years of Washington Society,* 292.
22. *Ibid.,* 291.
23. *Messages and Papers,* II, 1000.
24. *Ibid.,* II, 1000.
25. *Ibid.,* II, 1000.
26. *Ibid.,* II, 1000.
27. *Ibid.,* II, 1001.
28. *Ibid.,* II, 1001.
29. Hunt, ed., *The First Forty Years of Washington Society,* 295.
30. *Ibid.,* 287; Van Buren, *Autobiography,* ch. XXI.
31. See, for example, Thomas Ritchie to Martin Van Buren, March 27, 1829, Van Buren, *Autobiography,* 246-48.
32. For the scandal and its impact, see John F. Marszalek, *The Petticoat Affair: Manners, Mutiny, and Sex in Andrew Jackson's White House* (Baton Rouge: Louisiana State University Press, 1997). Van Buren's account is especially interesting. See Van Buren, *Autobiography,* ch. XXVI. For Peggy's side of the story, see *The Autobiography of Peggy Eaton* (New York: Charles Scribner's Sons, 1932). To close associates Jackson was quite frank regarding his views on Calhoun and Van Buren. See, for example, Jackson to John Overton, December 31, 1829, *Jackson Papers,* VII, 655-56.
33. Andrew Jackson, Annual Message, December 8, 1829, *Messages and Papers,* II, 1011-12.
34. *Ibid.,* II, 1012.
35. *Ibid.,* II, 1014.
36. *Ibid.,* II, 1014.
37. *Ibid.,* II, 1014.
38. *Ibid.,* II, 1014-15.
39. *Ibid.,* II, 1015.
40. *Ibid.,* II, 1015.
41. *Ibid.,* II, 1015.
42. *Register of Debates,* House of Representatives, 21:1, 637-38.

43. *Ibid.*, 646.
44. Van Buren to Jackson, May 4, 1830, Van Buren, *Autobiography,* 322.
45. Annual Treasury Report, December 14, 1829, *Register of Debates,* 21:1, Appendix, 70.
46. Oddly, Ingham did not make that error when recapping the finances for 1829. *Ibid.,* 66-67.
47. *Ibid.*, 67, 70.
48. Jackson to Van Buren, May 15, 1830, Van Buren, *Autobiography,* 322.
49. *Ibid.*, 322. This note to Van Buren, May 15, 1830, is also available in *Jackson Papers,* VIII, 265. Jackson took special pride in debt reduction. In September 1830, on returning to Washington, he wrote to John Overton: "I found every thing well and have just ordered two millions more of the national debt to be paid—This will make in all this year about 12 millions." *Ibid.*, VIII, 534.
50. Van Buren, *Autobiography,* 322.
51. *Ibid.*, 381, 323.
52. *Ibid.*, 323.
53. *Ibid.*, 323.
54. *Ibid.*, 324.
55. *Ibid.*, 324-25.
56. *Ibid.*, 325.
57. Andrew Jackson, Veto, May 27, 1830, *Messages and Papers,* II, 1046-51.
58. *Ibid.*, II, 1051.
59. *Ibid.*, II, 1051.
60. *Ibid.*, II, 1051.
61. *Ibid.*, II, 1051-52.
62. *Ibid.*, II, 1052.
63. *Ibid.*, II, 1052.
64. *Ibid.*, II, 1052-53.
65. *Ibid.*, II, 1056-57.
66. *Ibid.*, II, 1057.
67. Reprinted in the *United States' Telegraph,* May 17, 1830.
68. *United States' Telegraph,* June 3, 1830.
69. Speech in Cincinnati, August 3, 1830, *Clay Papers,* VIII, 244.
70. *Messages and Papers,* II, 1054.
71. Larson, *Internal Improvement,* 161-80.
72. *Messages and Papers,* II, 1054.
73. This result was not immediate but was clearly established by the time Jackson left office. A year after the veto, Congress passed—and the President signed—a river and harbor bill as well as an internal improvement measure. *Statutes at Large,* 21:2, 34-38. Apparently these undertakings met Jackson's conception of what constituted "national" projects. Ironically, as it turned out, Jackson's administrations spent more

on internal improvements than Adams's did. See Larson, *Internal Improvement,* 191.

Chapter Five: Jackson, the Bank War, and the National Debt

1. For the legislation chartering the second Bank of the United States, see *Statutes at Large,* Vol. 3, 14:1, 266-77. For the bank's organization and operations, see Ralph C. H. Catterall, *The Second Bank of the United States* (Chicago: University of Chicago Press, 1903) and Bray Hammond, *Banks and Politics in America from the Revolution to the Civil War* (Princeton: Princeton University Press, 1957), especially chapters 9- 11.
2. For more on Biddle, see Thomas P. Govan, *Nicholas Biddle: Nationalist and Public Banker, 1786-1844* (Chicago: University of Chicago Press, 1959).
3. Richard Rush to Nicholas Biddle, Nov. 19, 1828, in R.C. McCrane, ed., *The Correspondence of Nicholas Biddle* (Boston: Houghton Mifflin Co., 1919), 55. Hereafter, simply *Biddle Correspondence.*
4. Nicholas Biddle to Richard Rush, November 25, 1828, *Ibid.,* 57.
5. Richard Rush, Annual Treasury Report, December 6, 1828, *Register of Debates,* House of Representatives, Appendix, 20:2, 18.
6. Nicholas Biddle to George Hoffman, December 22, 1828, *Biddle Correspondence,* 62.
7. Andrew Jackson, Inaugural Address, March 4, 1829, *Messages and Papers,* II, 999-1001.
8. For a full discussion of this aspect of bank-administration relationships, see Robert V. Remini, *Andrew Jackson and the Bank War* (New York: W. W. Norton & Co., 1967), 49-60.
9. William B. Lewis to Henry Toland, November 11, 1829, *Biddle Correspondence,* 85. This letter suggests that Biddle had also used Toland as an intermediary.
10. *Ibid.,* 85.
11. Samuel D. Ingham to Andrew Jackson, November 24, 1829, Jackson *Correspondence,* IV, 91. For Ingham's analysis, see 86-91. Biddle's proposal is included as an insert. The plan is also reprinted in *Jackson Papers,* VII, 568-75.
12. Nicholas Biddle, Memorandum, between October 1829 and January 1830, *Biddle Correspondence,* 93-94. Biddle apparently added the dates sometime later and likely erred. Biddle, it seems, met the president in November, but precision is elusive. Van Buren later recalled that Biddle and Jackson met between November 17 and November 26. Van Buren, *Autobiography,* 619.
13. Biddle, Memorandum, *Biddle Correspondence,* 94. On this point Professor Remini wrote, incorrectly, that "the President had no intention of commending the Bank in his annual message to Congress. Quite the opposite." *Andrew Jackson and the Bank War,* 59. But Jackson did, in fact, commend the bank, although not in the way Biddle had expected. See Jackson's first annual message, December 8, 1829, *Messages and Papers,* II, 1014.
14. Samuel D. Ingham to Andrew Jackson, November 24, 1829, Jackson *Correspondence,* IV, 91.

15. Andrew Jackson, Annual Message, December 8, 1829, *Messages and Papers,* II, 1014.
16. *Ibid.,* II, 1025.
17. Alexander Hamilton to Nicholas Biddle, December 10, 1829, *Biddle Correspondence,* 88-89.
18. Nicholas Biddle to Alexander Hamilton, December 12, 1829, *Ibid.,* 91.
19. Nicholas Biddle to William B. Lewis, May 8, 1830, *Ibid.,* 99-100.
20. Nicholas Biddle to Josiah Nichol, August 3, 1830, *Ibid.,* 109.
21. For both reports, see Appendix, *Register of Debates,* 21:1, 98-133.
22. *Ibid.,* House of Representatives, 21:1, 921-22.
23. Andrew Jackson, Second Annual Message, December 6, 1830, *Messages and Papers,* II, 1091-92.
24. See, for examples, Joseph Hemphill to Biddle, December 9, 1830, and Robert Smith to Biddle, December 13, 1830; and John Norvall to Biddle, December 16, 1830, *Biddle Correspondence,* 117-18, 120.
25. Nicholas Biddle to Joseph Hemphill, December 14, 1830, *Ibid.,* 118-20.
26. *Register of Debates,* Senate, 21:2, 46.
27. *Ibid.,* 51, 53.
28. *Ibid.,* 54.
29. *Ibid.,* 75.
30. *Ibid.,* 75.
31. *Ibid.,* 75-76.
32. *Ibid.,* 76.
33. *Ibid.,* 76.
34. *Ibid.,* 78.
35. Memorandum, October 19, 1831, *Biddle Correspondence,* 128-31. See also Remini, *Andrew Jackson and the Bank War,* 72-73.
36. *Biddle Correspondence,* 131.
37. Andrew Jackson, Third Annual Message, December 6, 1831, *Messages and Papers,* II, 1121. According to Professor Remini, the fact that Jackson did not push the issue but left it instead to Congress meant that he lived up to his end of the bargain. *Andrew Jackson and the Bank War,* 73. This view should be contrasted with Bray Hammond's assertion that the president retreated from the agreement because of the influence of Roger Taney. *Banks and Politics in America,* 383-84.
38. Louis McLane, Annual Treasury Report, December 7, 1831, Appendix, *Register of Debates,* 22:1, 28-29.
39. *Ibid.,* 26-27.
40. Biddle was not the only one to smell a rat. John Quincy Adams, now a Massachusetts representative, also sensed that something was not right. As Chair of the Committee on Manufactures, he visited Secretary McLane on January 14, 1832, to transact committee business. Adams told McLane that he supported the admin-

istration's plan to eliminate the national debt in 1833. He added, however, that he "had not found a single other person in Congress" willing "to effect it by selling" bank stock earning seven percent to discharge debt costing three percent. McLane responded that he had "calculations to show that the bank stock might be sold to pay off the three per cents. not only without loss, but with profit to the public." Adams was incredulous. Such "calculations," he confided to his diary, were designed "to prove that five and two make three. I could not abide them." Adams, *Memoirs,* VIII, 456-57.

41. *Register of Debates,* Senate, 22:1, 53-54; House of Representatives, 22:1, 1502.
42. *Ibid.*, Senate, 22:1, 55.
43. Benton, *Thirty Years' View,* I, 235.
44. *Register of Debates,* Senate, 22:1, 113-44; 154-55.
45. *Ibid.*, 530.
46. *Ibid.*, 533.
47. *Ibid.*, 534-36.
48. *Ibid.*, 536-37.
49. *Ibid.*, 538.
50. *Ibid.*, 538-39.
51. *Ibid.*, 547-58.
52. Ibid., House of Representatives, 22:1, 1502.
53. *Ibid.*, 1502.
54. *Ibid.*, 1519-20.
55. *Ibid.*, 1520.
56. *Ibid.*, 1529.
57. *Ibid.*, Appendix, 127-28, 134, 139.
58. *Ibid.*, 143-48.
59. *Ibid.*, 147.
60. *Ibid.*, House of Representatives, 22:1, 1780. The proposed charter modifications aimed at appeasing critics like Benton. They included: Presidential appointment of at least one director at each branch bank; branch notes were specifically to state that they were payable at the office of issue; Bank of the United States annual reports would name individual stockholders, the amount of stock they held, and their states of residence; state legislatures would be permitted to tax real estate owned by branch banks as well as the "proprietary interest" of stockholders within their borders; new branch banks would not be established without congressional consent; the Bank of the United States would pay interest (unspecified) to the United States on the government's deposits; and the new charter would last for fifteen years, not twenty. There were several other modifications, including the doubling of the bonus to $3,000,000. *Ibid.*, 1781.
61. These resolutions are not recorded in *Register of Debates.* They are available, however, in Thomas C. Cochran, ed., *New American State Papers: Public Finance, 1789-1860,* (32 vols., Wilmington, DE: Scholarly Resources, Inc., 1972-73), vol. 23,

Banking and Currency, 37-38. Hereafter simply *NASP.*

62. *Ibid.,* 37-38. Biddle's response constituted a huge set of statements documenting a wide range of bank business.

63. Benton, *Thirty Years' View,* I, 236.

64. *Register of Debates,* House of Representatives, 22:1, 1846.

65. The charges included usury, illegal issue of branch bank notes, and other alleged violations of the bank's charter. *Ibid.,* 1874-75.

66. *Ibid.,* 1944-96.

67. *Ibid.,* 2082.

68. *Ibid.,* 2139-41.

69. *Ibid.,* 2160-61.

70. *Ibid.,* 2161. Other Bank of the United States opponents on the committee were Richard M. Johnson of Kentucky, Francis Thomas of Maryland, and C. C. Cambreling of New York. Bank of the United States proponents on the committee besides Adams were George McDuffie of South Carolina and John Watmough of Pennsylvania. See also Benton, *Thirty Years' View,* I, 241 and *NASP,* vol. 23, 578.

71. Appendix, *Register of Debates,* 22:1, 43-44.

72. *Ibid.,* 43-44.

73. *Ibid.,* 44.

74. *Ibid.,* 46. The latter linked debt extinction and the status of the bank to the concurrent dispute over tariff policy.

75. *Ibid.,* 68.

76. *Ibid.,* 71-72.

77. *Register of Debates,* House of Representatives, 22:1, 3453-55; 3507-8; 3835-51; 3852.

78. *Ibid.,* Senate, 22:1, 943 and *passim.*

79. *Ibid.,* 961.

80. *Ibid.,* 965.

81. *Ibid.,* 970.

82. *Ibid.,* 1040.

83. *Ibid.,* 1041.

84. *Ibid.,* 1073.

85. Andrew Jackson, Veto, July 10, 1832, *Messages and Papers,* II, 1139-54.

86. *Ibid.,* II, 1148.

87. *Ibid.,* II, 1149.

88. Jackson's veto of the recharter bill remains one of the most controversial issues of his presidency, and a voluminous literature exists concerning it. To sample this historiography, see Hammond, *Banks and Banking,* Remini, *Andrew Jackson and the Bank War,* and Schlesinger, *The Age of Jackson.* Also enlightening are: Charles Sellers, *The Market Revolution: Jacksonian America, 1815-1846* (New York and Oxford: Oxford University Press, 1992); Watson, *Liberty and Power,* Feller, *The Jacksonian Promise:*

America, 1815-1840 ; Glyndon G. Van Deusen, *The Jacksonian Era, 1828-1848* (New York: Harper & Row, 1959); and Richard Hofstadter, *The American Political Tradition* (New York: Alfred A. Knopf, 1948), ch. III.

Chapter Six: The Nullification Crisis and Debt Freedom

1. For both the Spanish Florida matter and the Jefferson Day dinner, see Meacham, *American Lion,* 135-36, 169-70.

2. Two brief but solid biographies of Calhoun are Margaret L. Coit, *John C. Calhoun: American Patriot* (Boston: Houghton Mifflin, 1950) and Richard N. Current, *John C. Calhoun* (New York: Washington Square Press, 1966).

3. For Jackson's characterization of a desirable tariff, see Jackson to James Hamilton, Jr., June 29, 1828, in Jackson *Correspondence,* III, 411. For Calhoun's hope that Jackson would pursue a revenue only tariff, see his speech on the Force bill, February 15 and 16, 1833, in *Calhoun Papers,* XII, 57-62.

4. For a collection of contemporary descriptions and characterizations of Calhoun, see Margaret L. Coit, ed., *John C. Calhoun* (Englewood Cliffs, NJ: Prentice-Hall, 1970).

5. Hofstadter, *American Political Tradition,* 87-88.

6. For the *Exposition* and *Protest,* see *Calhoun Papers,* X, 442-539.

7. Madison, still alive, repudiated nullification. Drew R. McCoy, *The Last of the Fathers: James Madison and the Republican Legacy* (Cambridge: Cambridge University Press, 1989), ch. 4.

8. *Calhoun Papers,* X, 489. For the Free trade argument and its several constructions, see William S. Belko, *The Triumph of the Antebellum Free Trade Movement* (Gainesville: University Press of Florida, 2012).

9. *Calhoun Papers,* X, 539.

10. *Messages and Papers,* II, 1000.

11. *Ibid.,* II, 1012.

12. *Ibid.,* II, 1013.

13. *Ibid.,* II, 1075.

14. *Ibid.,* II, 1086.

15. *Ibid.,* II, 1086-87.

16. *Ibid.,* II, 1086.

17. *Ibid.,* II, 1088.

18. For private comment on the matter, see, for example, Clay to Edgar Snowden, September 25, 1831, *Clay Papers,* vol. 8, 405.

19. Adams, *Memoirs,* VIII, 445. For comment on the frigid weather conditions, see M.A. DeWolfe Howe, *The Life and Letters of George Bancroft,* 2 vols. (Port Washington, NY and London: Kennikat Press, 1971) I, 193.

20. Adams, *Memoirs,* VIII, 446.

21. *Ibid.,* VIII, 446-47.

22. *Ibid.*, VIII, 446-47.
23. *Ibid.*, VIII, 448.
24. *Ibid.*, VIII, 448.
25. James A. Hamilton, *Reminiscences of James A. Hamilton; or, Men and Events at Home and Abroad, During Three Quarters of a Century* (New York: Charles Scribner & Co., 1869), 231.
26. South Carolina's Ordinance of Nullification is readily available. See, for example, any edition of Henry Steele Commager's *Documents of American History* or Google the ordinance at the Avalon Project: Documents in Law, History, and Diplomacy, Yale Law School, Lillian Goldman Law Library.
27. *Messages and Papers,* II, 1159.
28. *Ibid.*, II, 1160.
29. *Ibid.*, II, 1160.
30. *Ibid.*, II, 1160.
31. *Ibid.*, II, 1161.
32. *Ibid.*, II, 1161.
33. *Ibid.*, II, 1161.
34. *Ibid.*, II, 1161.
35. Jackson's Proclamation to the People of South Carolina, December 10, 1832, is one of his greatest state papers. For the entire text, see *Ibid.*, II, 1203-19.
36. *Ibid.*, II, 1205.
37. *Register of Debates,* House of Representatives, 22:2, 974.
38. *Ibid.*, Senate, 22:2, 55.
39. *Ibid.*, 416.
40. *The North American Review,* vol. 36, 78 (January 1833), 216.
41. H.R. 641, *Bills and Resolutions,* House of Representatives, 22:2.
42. *Register of Debates,* House of Representatives, 22:2, 962-1772 and *passim.*
43. *Statutes at Large,* 22:2, 629-31.
44. *Register of Debates,* Senate, 22:2, 477-78; *Calhoun Papers,* XII, 41.
45. Parton, *Life of Andrew Jackson*, III, 477.
46. *Ibid.*, III, 478-82.
47. *Register of Debates,* Senate, 22:2, 791-92; *Calhoun Papers,* XII, 138.
48. Van Buren, *Autobiography,* 553. Some historians agree with Van Buren's assessment. See, for example, Richard E. Ellis, *The Union at Risk: Jacksonian Democracy, States' Rights, and the Nullification Crisis* (New York and Oxford: Oxford University Press, 1987), 99-100.
49. *Clay Papers,* vol. 8, 622; Ellis, *Union at Risk,* 99-100.
50. Martin Van Buren to Andrew Jackson, December 27, 1832, Jackson *Correspondence,* IV, 507.
51. Joel R. Poinsett to Andrew Jackson, January 16, 1833, *Ibid.*, V, 7.
52. See Robert Y. Hayne to Frances W. Pickens, December 26, 1832, and James H.

Hammond to Hayne, January 23, 1833, in Robert Y. Hayne, "Letters on the Nullification Movement in South Carolina," *American Historical Review,* (July 6, 1901), 753, 763.

53. John C. Wormeley to James K. Polk, January 23, 1833, Herbert Weaver, ed., *The Correspondence of James K. Polk,* 2 vols. (Nashville: Vanderbilt University Press, 1972), II, 42.

54. William W. Freehling, *Prelude to Civil War: The Nullification Controversy in South Carolina, 1816-1836* (New York and Evanston: Harper & Row, 1965), ch. 3.

55. *Register of Debates,* House of Representatives, 22:2, 956.

56. For example, *Calhoun Papers,* X, 453-55. House and Senate debates concerning the tariff in 1828, 1832, and 1833 are characterized by these recurrent southern complaints. See the *Register of Debates* for both chambers during those years.

57. *Register of Debates,* House of Representatives, 22:2, 1071-72.

58. *Historical Statistics,* 711.

59. *Ibid.,* 8. The population data for South Carolina are, of course, available in the 1830 census but are conveniently accessible in Ira Berlin, *Slaves Without Masters: The Free Negro in the Antebellum South* (Oxford and New York: Oxford University Press, 1974), 398-99.

Chapter Seven: Awaiting Debt Freedom, 1833–1834

1. Allan Nevins, ed., *The Diary of Philip Hone,* (2 vols., New York: Dodd, Mead and Company, 1927), I, 72.

2. *Messages and Papers,* II, 1223.

3. *Ibid.,* II, 1224.

4. *Ibid.,* II, 1224.

5. Jackson, *Correspondence,* V, 35-37; Van Buren, *Autobiography,* 625.

6. Carl Brent Swisher, ed., "Roger B. Taney's Bank War Manuscript," *Maryland Historical Magazine* (September 1958), Part II, 233.

7. *Ibid.,* 233. On this matter see also Remini, *Andrew Jackson and the Bank War,* 120-21.

8. Swisher, ed., "Roger B. Taney's Bank War Manuscript," Part II, 233.

9. *Ibid.,* Part II, 233.

10. *Ibid.,* Part II, 234.

11. *Ibid.,* Part II, 234.

12. *Ibid.,* Part II, 230.

13. Messages and Papers, II, 1225.

14. *Ibid.,* II, 1225.

15. *Ibid.,* II, 1225-1229.

16. *Ibid.,* II, 1229.

17. *Ibid.,* II, 1229.

18. *Ibid.,* II, 1230.

19. *Ibid.*, II, 1230.
20. *Ibid.*, II, 1230.
21. *Ibid.*, II, 1230.
22. William Stickney, ed., *Autobiography of Amos Kendall* (Boston and New York: Lee and Shepard, Publishers and Lee, Shepard and Dillingham, 1872), 385.
23. Much of this is a familiar story and may be traced through most of the narrative histories of the period. For an analysis of the complicated politics involved in the removal of the public funds from the Bank of the United States and its aftermath, see John M. McFaul, *The Politics of Jacksonian Finance* (Ithaca and London: Cornell University Press, 1972).
24. The best treatment of the public lands issue is Daniel Feller, *The Public Lands in Jacksonian Politics* (Madison: University of Wisconsin Press, 1984).
25. The Virginia Land Cession is readily available in any edition of Henry Steele Commager, ed., *Documents of American History.*
26. An Act Making Provision for the Debt of the United States, August 4, 1790, *Statutes at Large,* 1:2, 144.
27. Between 1789 and 1795 the public lands generated no revenue. Over the next two decades, 1796-1815, they grossed $9,430,000, an average of $471,500 per year, a meager sum. *Historical Statistics,* 712. See also Lane, "For 'A Positive Profit': The Federal Investment in the First Bank of the United States, 1792-1802," 608-11.
28. For a thorough examination of these matters, see Feller, *The Public Lands in Jacksonian Politics,* chs. 1-6.
29. *Messages and Papers,* II, 1015.
30. *Register of Debates,* House of Representatives, 21:1, 477.
31. *Ibid.*, 477-78.
32. *Ibid.*, 484.
33. *Ibid.*, 485.
34. *Ibid.*, 486.
35. *Ibid.*, 486.
36. *Ibid.*, 488.
37. *Ibid.*, 490, 496.
38. *Ibid.*, Senate, 21:1, 3.
39. For a full analysis of the sectional interests involved, see Feller, *The Public Lands in Jacksonian Politics,* 119-36.
40. *Register of Debates,* Senate, 21:1, 33-34.
41. *Ibid.*, 34.
42. *Ibid.*, 34-35.
43. *Ibid.*, 38.
44. *Ibid.*, 45.
45. *Ibid.*, 48.
46. *Messages and Papers,* II, 1077-80.

47. *Register of Debates,* House of Representatives, 21:2, 539-40; *Ibid.,* Appendix, lxxxvi-xcii.
48. *Ibid.,* 550-620 and *passim.*
49. United States Congress. Bills and Resolutions, 22:1, Senate Bill 179.
50. *Ibid.*
51. *Messages and Papers,* II, 1159-63.
52. *Ibid.,* II, 1163.
53. *Ibid.,* II, 1164.
54. *Register of Debates,* Senate, 22:2, 62-92, 114-15, 124-46, 158-70, 196-202, 232-36 and *passim.*
55. *Ibid.,* House of Representatives, 22:2, 1920-21.
56. *Ibid.,* Senate, 22:2, 809.
57. Clay to Biddle, March 4, 1833, *Clay Papers,* 8, 630.
58. Clay to Samuel L. Southard, April 22, 1833, *Ibid.,* 8, 639.
59. *Messages and Papers,* II, 1275.
60. *Ibid.,* II, 1276-80.
61. *Ibid.,* II, 1280.
62. *Ibid.,* II, 1281.
63. *Ibid.,* II, 1281-82.
64. *Ibid.,* II, 1282.
65. *Ibid.,* II, 1284
66. *Ibid.,* II, 1285.
67. *Ibid.,* II, 1285.
68. *Ibid.,* II, 1282.
69. *Ibid.,* II, 1285.
70. *Ibid.,* II, 1285-86.
71. *Ibid.,* II, 1286.
72. *Ibid.,* II, 1287.

Chapter Eight: Debt Freedom and the Meaning of Jacksonian Democracy

1. *Messages and Papers,* II, 1160.
2. *Ibid.*, II, 1326.
3. *Ibid.*, II, 1327.
4. *Ibid.*, II, 1327.
5. *Ibid.*, II, 1327.
6. *Ibid.*, II, 1327.
7. *Ibid.*, II, 1327.
8. *Ibid.*, II, 1327.
9. *Ibid.*, II, 1327.
10. *Register of Debates,* Appendix, 23:2, 55.

11. *Ibid.*, 56.
12. *Ibid.*, 56.
13. *United States' Telegraph,* December 12, 1832.
14. Quoted in Robert V. Remini, *The Life of Andrew Jackson,* 296.
15. Adams, *Memoirs,* IX, 197.
16. Hunt, ed., *First Forty Years of Washington Society,* 361.
17. Harriet Martineau, *Retrospect of Western Travel* (2 vols., London: Saunders and Otley, 1838), I, 197.
18. Simon A. O. Ferrall, *A Ramble of Six Thousand Miles through the United States of America* (London: Effingham Wilson, Royal Exchange, 1832), 234.
19. Stephen Davis, *Notes of a Tour in America in 1832 and 1833* (Edinburgh: Waugh & Innes, 1833), 94.
20. Michel Chevalier, *Society, Manners and Politics in the United States; Being a Series Of Letters on North America* (Boston: Weeks, Jordan and Company, 1839), 98.
21. Charles Lyell, *Travels in North America, Canada, and Nova Scotia with Geological Observations* (2 vols., 2nd ed., London: John Murray, Albermarle Street, 1855), I, 226.
22. This paragraph and the next fourteen were originally published in Carl Lane, "The Elimination of the National Debt in 1835 and the Meaning of Jacksonian Democracy," *Essays in Economic and Business History,* XXV (2007): 67-78. Many thanks to the Economic and Business Historical Society for permission to reproduce them here.
23. *Messages and Papers,* II, 1000.
24. *Ibid.*, II, 1000.
25. Daniel Walker Howe has reminded us that the term "Jacksonian Democracy" is "inappropriate" because the "Jackson movement" victimized non-whites and women. *What Hath God Wrought,* 4. Yet contemporaries were well aware of profound changes in American political culture, and the idea of Jacksonian Democracy has become deeply rooted in American historiography. In short, historians generally agree that the years 1824-1840 witnessed an upsurge of democracy, and they have explained it in a variety of ways: as the "era of the common man" resulting from almost universal white male suffrage and the emergence of mass political parties; as the triumph of the west over the eastern establishment; as a struggle between agriculture and industry for ascendancy in the American economy; as a conflict between capital and labor; as a victory of *laissez-faire* over government interventionism; as a period of social and moral reform; as a manifestation of religious and ethnic demography upon American politics; and as a dissatisfaction with the seeming loss of the values and traditions of the very early republic. To sample this rich historiography, see Van Deusen, *The Jacksonian Era*; McCormick, *The Second American Party System*; Frederick Jackson Turner, *Rise of the New West, 1819- 1829* (New York: Collier Books, 1962 [originally published in 1906]); Sellers, *The Market Revolution*; Schlesinger, *The Age of Jackson;*

Hofstadter, *The American Political Tradition,* ch. III; Watson, *Liberty and Power*; Feller, *The Jacksonian Promise*; Alice Felt Tyler, *Freedom's Ferment: Phases of American Social History from the Colonial Period to the Outbreak of the Civil War* (New York: Harper & Brothers, 1961 [originally published in 1944 by University of Minnesota Press]); Ronald Walters, *American Reformers, 1815-1860* (rev. ed., New York: Hill and Wang, 1997); Lee Benson, *The Concept of Jacksonian Democracy: New York as a Test Case* (Princeton: Princeton University Press, 1961); Marvin Meyers, *The Jacksonian Persuasion: Politics and Belief* (Stanford: Stanford University Press, 1957).

26. Thomas Jefferson, *Notes on the State of Virginia* (New York, *et al.:* Harper Torchbook, 1964), 157.

27. Benton, *Thirty Years' View,* I, 5.

28. The line that "The government that governs least governs best" is from Henry David Thoreau's essay "On the Duty of Civil Disobedience." See Thoreau, *Walden and Civil Disobedience* (New York and Toronto: New American Library: A Signet Classic, 1960), 222. See also ch. 2, note 15.

29. Lane, "For 'A Positive Profit': The Federal Investment in the First Bank of the United States, 1792-1802," 601-12.

30. See Treasury Department Reports for the years 1821-32 in Cochran, ed., *New American State Papers: General Reports.*

31. Report of the Committee on Roads and Canals, February 6, 1825, *Register of Debates,* House of Representatives,18:2, Appendix, 76.

32. Carl Lane, "Federal Investments in Private Canal Companies, 1825-1835." Unpublished paper presented at the annual conference of the Economic and Business Historical Society, Albany, New York, April 26, 2001. Digital and hard copy available at the Felician College Library.

33. *Messages and Papers,* II, 1072-73.

34. *Ibid.,* II, 1074.

35. Lane, "Federal Investments in Private Canal Companies," 12. Another possible exception is the Emergency Banking Act of March 1933, which allowed the Reconstruction Finance Corporation to purchase stock of publicly owned banks. During the recent Great Recession the United States wound up owning stock in AIG, GM, Fannie Mae, and some other enterprises, at least for a time, but those holdings were part of the "bail-out" effort as opposed to investment.

36. See Chapter 5.

37. For more on this subject, see Bruce H. Mann, *Republic of Debtors: Bankruptcy in the Age of American Independence* (Cambridge and London: Harvard University Press, 2002).

38. A vast literature exists on the second Awakening. Interesting and insightful accounts include Nathan Hatch, *The Democratization of American Christianity* (New Haven: Yale University Press, 1989); Jon Butler, *Awash in a Sea of Faith* (Cambridge: Harvard University Press, 1990); and Mark Noll, *America's God* (Oxford and New

York: Oxford University Press, 2002). For the impact of the revival on one community, see Paul E. Johnson, *A Shopkeeper's Millenium: Society and Revivals in Rochester, New York, 1815-1837* (New York: Hill and Wang, 1978).

39. *Register of Debates,* House of Representatives, 22:2, 1094.

40. *Ibid.,* Senate, 22:2, 197.

41. *Ibid.,* House of Representatives, 22:1, 2139-41.

42. Myers, *Jacksonian Persuasion,* especially 3-15.

43. *North American Review,* 25(July 1827), 174.

44. Cooper, *Notions of the Americans,* I, 89.

45. Hamilton, *Reminiscences,* 176.

46. *Messages and Papers,* II, 1325. See also Chapter IX.

47. For the suffrage restrictions imposed on free blacks in the North during the Jackson era, see Leon F. Litwack, *North of Slavery: The Negro in the Free States, 1790-1860* (Chicago and London: University of Chicago Press, 1961), ch. III.

48. *Messages and Papers,* II, 1021.

49. *Ibid.,* II, 1021-22.

50. "An Act to provide for an exchange of lands with the Indians residing in any of the states or territories, and for their removal west of the river Mississippi," *Statutes at Large,* IV, 21:1, 411-12.

51. The literature on this subject is vast and growing. Essential is Ronald N. Satz, *American Indian Policy in the Jacksonian Era* (Lincoln: University of Nebraska Press, 1975). But see also Gloria Jahoda, *Trail of Tears: The Story of the American Indian Removals, 1813-1855* (New York: Wings Books, 1995).

52. Jackson to the Senate, May 6, 1830, *Messages and Papers,* II, 1042.

53. *Senate Executive Journal,* May 27, 1830, 111-12.

54. P. J. Staudenraus, *The American Colonization Movement, 1816-1865* (New York: Columbia University Press, 1961) remains the classic study, but much has been added to the body of scholarship on ACS. See especially Eric Burin, *Slavery and the Peculiar Solution: A History of the American Colonization Society* (Gainesville: University Press of Florida, 2005), ch. 1.

55. *Register of Debates,* House of Representatives, 14:2, 481-83.

56. Burin, *Slavery and the Peculiar Solution,* 18.

57. *Statutes at Large,* 15:2, 532-33.

58. "An Act Making an Appropriation for the Suppression of the Slave Trade," *Ibid.,* 20:1, 302.

59. Report of the Secretary of the Navy, December 6, 1830, *Register of Debates,* 21:2, Appendix, xix.

60. *Ibid.,* xix.

61. *Ibid.,* xix.

62. *Ibid.,* xix.

63. The ACS was always interested in securing federal dollars to help underwrite its operations. The approach of national debt freedom seemed to offer an opportune

moment to win congressional support. In 1827, for example, Senator Ezekiel F. Chambers of Maryland presented an ACS petition for assistance, touching off an angry reaction in the Senate led by Robert Y. Hayne of South Carolina. (*Register of Debates,* Senate, 19:2, 289-96). In the House much the same happened. In January, 1827, Representative John C. Weems of Maryland introduced a resolution to create a select committee to consider funding the ACS. It, however, was voted down by a "large majority." (*Register of Debates,* House of Representatives, 19:2, 635-36.) ACS supporters did not resign themselves to defeat. In the spring of 1830, as Congress was dealing with Indian removal, Representative John Fenton Mercer of Virginia introduced a bill authorizing the Treasury to pay the ACS $25.00 "for each and every native born free person of color" whom the ACS transported to Africa. The bill capped the total appropriation in any given year at $50,000. (*Bills and Resolutions,* 21:1, House Resolution 412, April 7, 1830.) Southern reaction, especially South Carolina's, was vigorous and vehement. (Freehling, *Prelude to Civil War,* 196-99). The Mercer bill was ultimately tabled, but the matter did not go away. Two years later, for example, Mercer introduced a petition from British subjects petitioning congressional support for colonization. The petition threw the House of Representatives into hot and angry debate. Mercer ultimately withdrew the petition, but it is interesting to note that some of the arguments against it anticipated the "gag rule" adopted by Congress a few years later to quash abolitionist petitions. (*Register of Debates,* House of Representatives, 22:1, 2332-50.) The petition itself, from Cirencester in England, made a significant concluding point relating debt freedom to colonization: "It appears that numerous offers of slaves for emancipation And colonization are made to the society, which, to the extent of its means, it eagerly embraces; but, for the purpose of so great an undertaking, the means of individuals, or of the society, are too limited. Happily for America, she is about to be exonerated from a public debt; and we venture respectfully to ask, to what better purpose can national resources be applied?" (*Register of Debates,* House of Representatives, 22:1, 2350.)

64. For more on this subject, see Judith Wellman, *The Road to Seneca Falls* (Champaign: University of Illinois Press, 2004).

Chapter Nine: Surplus, Distribution, and the End of Debt Freedom

1. Calhoun to Ingham, December 31, 1834, *Calhoun Papers,* XII, 377.
2. Calhoun to Ingham, January 9, 1835, *Ibid.*, XII, 381.
3. *Messages and Papers,* II, 1320. For an extended account of the French crisis, see John M. Belohlavek, *"Let the Eagle Soar!": The Foreign Policy of Andrew Jackson* (Lincoln: University of Nebraska Press, 1985), ch. 4.
4. *Messages and Papers,* II, 1321.
5. *Ibid.*, II, 1323.
6. *Ibid.*, II, 1324.
7. *Ibid.*, II, 1325.
8. *Register of Debates,* Senate, 23:2, 215-16. The Senate voted unanimously against

reprisals on January 14, 1835.

9. *Ibid.*, 23:2, 377.

10. For expression of this view see, for example, Calhoun to Littleton W. Tazewell, January 24, 1836, *Calhoun Papers,* XIII, 48-49.

11. *Register of Debates,* Senate, 23:2, 730.

12. *Ibid.*, 731.

13. *Ibid.*, 732.

14. *Ibid.*, 730.

15. *Ibid.*, 738.

16. *Ibid.*, 738-39.

17. *Messages and Papers,* II, 1375.

18. *Ibid.*, II, 1375-76.

19. *Ibid.*, II, 1376.

20. *Ibid.*, II, 1379.

21. *Ibid.*, II, 1380.

22. *Register of Debates,* Senate, 24:1, 106. Benton's speech on January 11 was not included in the *Register of Debates.*

23. *Ibid.*, 106.

24. *Ibid.*, 107.

25. *Ibid.*, 109-10.

26. *Ibid.*, 111.

27. *Ibid.*, 113-14.

28. *Ibid.*, 114.

29. *Ibid.*, 130-31.

30. *Ibid.*, 131.

31. *Ibid.*, 136.

32. *Ibid.*, 142-44.

33. *Ibid.*, 148-63.

34. *Ibid.*, 163.

35. *Ibid.,* 166-67; *Messages and Papers,* II, 1411. The *Register of Debates* does not include all thirteen documents but *Messages and Papers,* II, 1407–32, does.

36. *Register of Debates,* Senate, 24:1, 168.

37. *Ibid.,* 170.

38. Bankhead to Forsyth, January 27, 1836, in *Messages and Papers,* II, 1436-37.

39. Bankhead to Forsyth, February 15, 1836, in *Ibid.,* II, 1440.

40. *Messages and Papers,* II, 1434-35.

41. *Register of Debates,* Senate, 24:1, 48.

42. *Ibid.,* 48-50.

43. *Ibid.,* 48.

44. *Historical Statistics of the United States,* 712.

45. *Register of Debates,* Senate, 24:1, 1289.

46. *Ibid.*, 1290.
47. *Ibid.*, 1292.
48. *Ibid.*, 1300.
49. *Ibid.*, 1301.
50. *Ibid.*, 1302.
51. *Ibid.*, 1309.
52. *Ibid.*, 1356.
53. *Ibid.*, 1356-57.
54. *Ibid.*, 1362.
55. This was a peculiar line of argument. In his 1833 veto of Clay's bill Jackson had argued that the distribution would make the states mere appendages of the federal government. Senate critics in 1836 were arguing that the distribution would undermine the authority of the federal government.
56. *Register of Debates,* Senate, 24:1, 1396.
57. *Ibid.*, House of Representatives, 24:1, 2892.
58. *Ibid.*, 2893.
59. *Ibid.*, 2893.
60. *Ibid.*, 2899.
61. *Ibid.*, 2900.
62. *Ibid.*, 2900.
63. *Ibid.*, 2903.
64. *Ibid.*, 2904.
65. *Ibid.*, 2906-17.
66. *Ibid.*, 3584-3586.
67. *Ibid.*, 3552.
68. *Ibid.*, 3586.
69. "Remarks on the Treasury Surplus," February 17, 1836, *Calhoun Papers,* XIII, 79–85. The quotation is on p. 83.
70. Calhoun in the Senate, March 14, 1836, *Ibid.,* XIII, 112.
71. Calhoun in the Senate, March 17, 1836, *Ibid.,* XIII, 114.
72. Calhoun to Ingham, April 3, 1836, *Ibid.,* XIII, 137.
73. *Ibid.*, XIII, 137.
74. *Register of Debates,* Senate, 24:1, 1383.
75. *Ibid.,* 1579-84.
76. *Ibid.,* 1599-1604. He also asked obvious questions. How could those who voted for Clay's land revenue distribution bill also vote for Calhoun's bill? Was the same money being appropriated twice? The questions, of course, were moot. Although the Senate had passed Clay's bill, the House had not yet acted on it. Calhoun's bill, in effect, overrode Clay's.
77. *Ibid.,* 1618-1845.
78. *Ibid.,* 1845-46.

79. *Register of Debates,* House of Representatives, 24:1, 4379-80.
80. Jackson, it seems, considered vetoing it but changed his mind.
81. *Statutes at Large,* 24:1, V, 52.
82. *Ibid.,* V, 53.
83. *Ibid.,* V, 53.
84. *Ibid.,* V, 53.
85. *Ibid.,* V, 54.
86. *Ibid.,* V, 55. This interest provision represented a sharp departure from the federal government's longstanding relationship with banks. The public's deposits had always been interest free.
87. *Ibid.,* V, 55.
88. *Ibid.,* V, 55.
89. Specie Circular, July 11, 1836, *Register of Debates,* Appendix, 24:1, 107-8.
90. *Ibid.,* 107.
91. *Messages and Papers,* II, 1458.
92. *Ibid.,* II, 1459.
93. *Ibid.,* II, 1464.
94. *Ibid.,* II, 1460.
95. *Ibid.,* II, 1467.
96. *Ibid.,* II, 1468.
97. Treasury Department, "Apportionment of the Surplus," January 3, 1837, *Register of Debates,* Appendix, 24:2, 108.
98. *Messages and Papers,* II, 1501-2. See Attorney General Benjamin F. Butler's lengthy list of difficulties with the bill. *Ibid.,* II, 1502-7.
99. *Ibid.,* II, 1512.
100. *Ibid.,* II, 1513-18.
101. *Ibid.,* II, 1519.
102. *Ibid.,* II, 1521.
103. *Ibid.,* II, 1531.
104. *Ibid.,* II, 1532.
105. For the latest account of the Panic, see Jessica M. Lepler, "1837: Anatomy of a Panic." (Ph.D. dissertation, Brandeis University, 2007). Peter Temin's *The Jacksonian Economy* (New York: W. W. Norton & Co., 1969) remains an important analysis, deemphasizing the roles of the Specie Circular and the distribution and emphasizing instead the British financial connection. See especially ch. 4. Brief but sound coverage is available in a variety of sources. Recent commentary in overview studies includes Wilentz, *The Rise of American Democracy: Jefferson to Lincoln*, 456-65 and Howe, *What Hath God Wrought*, 501-6.
106. The quote, of course, is from Lerner and Loewe's classic Broadway musical, *Camelot.*

Epilogue: Then and Now

1. The debt inherited from the Revolution, once funded by Hamilton's program, generated wealth and economic development. See Wright, *One Nation Under Debt.*
2. For the traditional view that Jackson's bank and monetary policies triggered the financial crisis, see, for example, Hammond, *Banks and Politics in America.* For the international explanation, see Temin, *The Jacksonian Economy.* For the business culture analysis, see Lepler, "1837: Anatomy of a Panic."
3. Thomas Senior Berry, "What Was the GDP Then?," in Louis Johnston and Samuel H. Williamson, "The Annual Real and Nominal GDP for the United States, 1789-Present," Economic History Services, March 2004. All figures for late eighteenth- and early nineteenth-century America are estimates. According to the distinguished economic historian John J. McCusker, Berry's estimates "are not significantly different from the more recent estimates made by others." McCusker, "Estimating Early American Gross Domestic Product," *Historical Methods,* 33 (Summer 2000), 159.
4. *Historical Statistics*, 712.

BIBLIOGRAPHY

PRIMARY SOURCES

Government Records and Documents (All the following are available at the Library of Congress's American Memory website, http://memory.loc.gov/ammem/index.html. Of special importance is the *Register of Debates* of the House and Senate because the national legislature continually dealt with the national debt issue.):

American State Papers

Annals of Congress, 1789-1824

Bills and Resolutions of the House and Senate

Journal of the House of Representatives

Journal of the Senate

Register of Debates

Senate Executive Journal

Statutes at Large of the United States of America

Also useful but not available at the LC American Memory website are:

Cochran, Thomas C., ed. *New American State Papers: Public Finance, 1789-1860.* 32 vols. Wilmington, DE: Scholarly Resources, Inc., 1972-1973.

MAGAZINES AND NEWSPAPERS

Albany Argus

New-England Magazine

North American Review

United States' Telegraph

Books and Articles

Adams, Charles Francis, ed. *Memoirs of John Quincy Adams, Comprising Portions of His Diary from 1795 to 1848.* 12 vols. Philadelphia: J. B. Lippincott & Co., 1874-1877.

Bassett, John Spenser, ed. *Correspondence of Andrew Jackson.* 7 vols. Washington, D.C.: Carnegie Institution of Washington, 1926-1935.

Benton, Thomas Hart. *Thirty Years' View; Or a History of the American Government for Thirty Years.* 2 vols. New York and London: D. Appleton & Co., 1854-1856.

Chevalier, Michel. *Society, Manners and Politics in the United States; Being a Series of Letters on North America.* Boston: Weeks, Jordan and Company, 1839.

Coit, Margaret L., ed. *John C. Calhoun.* Englewood Cliffs, NJ: Prentice-Hall, 1970.

Commager, Henry Steele, and Milton Cantor, eds. *Documents of American History.* 10th ed., 2 vols. Englewood Cliffs, NJ: Prentice-Hall, 1988.

Cooper, James Fenimore. *Notions of the Americans: Picked Up by a Travelling Bachelor.* 2 vols. New York: Stringer & Townsend, 1850.

Davis, Stephen. *Notes of a Tour in America in 1832 and 1833.* Edinburgh: Waugh & Innes, 1833.

Eaton, Peggy. *The Autobiography of Peggy Eaton.* New York: Charles Scribner's Sons, 1932.

Faux, William. *Faux's Memorable Days in America, November 27, 1818-July 21, 1820,* vols. XI and XII in Thwaites, Reuben Gold, ed. *Early Western Travels, 1748-1846.* 32 vols. Cleveland, OH: The Arthur H. Clark Company, 1904-7.

Ferrall, Simon A. O. *A Ramble of Six Thousand Miles Through the United States of America.* London: Effingham Wilson, Royal Exchange, 1832.

Fitzpatrick, John C., ed. *The Autobiography of Martin Van Buren.* Annual Report of the American Historical Association for the Year 1918. Washington, D.C.: Government Printing Office, 1920.

Hamilton, James A. *Reminiscences of James A. Hamilton; Or, Men and Events, at Home and Abroad, During Three Quarters of a Century.* New York: Charles Scribner & Co., 1869.

Hamilton, Stanislaus Murray, ed. *The Writings of James Monroe.* 7 vols. New York and London: G.P. Putnam's Sons, 1898-1903.

Hayne, Robert Y. "Letters on the Nullification Movement in South Carolina, 1830-1834." *American Historical Review* 6 (July 1901): 736-65.

Hiatt, Joel W., ed. *Diary of William Owen from November 10, 1824 to April 20, 1825.* Indianapolis: Bobbs-Merrill Company, 1906. (This volume may also be cited as Indiana Historical Society Publications, vol. IV, no. 1.)

Hopkins, James F., Mary M.W. Hargreaves, and Robert Seager II, eds. *The Papers of Henry Clay.* 11 vols. Lexington: University of Kentucky Press, 1959-92.

Howe, M.A. DeWolfe. *The Life and Letters of George Bancroft.* 2 vols. Port Washington, NY and London: Kennikat Press, 1971. Originally Published in 1908.

Hunt, Gaillard, ed. *The First Forty Years of Washington Society in the Family Letters of Margaret Bayard Smith.* New York: Frederick Ungar Publishing Co., 1965. Reprinted from Charles Scribner's Sons 1906 edition.

Jefferson, Thomas. *Notes on the State of Virginia.* New York, Hagerstown, London: Harper & Row, 1964. (Introduction by Thomas Perkins Abernathy.)

Lyell, Charles. *Travels in North America, Canada, and Nova Scotia with Geological Observations.* 2 vols., 2nd ed. London: John Murray, Albermarle Street, 1855.

Martineau, Harriet. *Retrospect of Western Travel.* 2 vols. London: Saunders and Otley, 1838.

McCrane, R.C., ed. *The Correspondence of Nicholas Biddle.* Boston and New York: Houghton Mifflin Company, 1919.

McPherson, Elizabeth Gregory, ed. "Letters from Nathaniel Macon to John Randolph of Roanoke." *North Carolina Historical Review* 39 (Spring 1962): 195-211.

Meriwether, Robert L., W. Edwin Hemphill, and Clyde N. Wilson, eds. *The Papers of John C. Calhoun.* 28 vols. (at present). Columbia: University of South Carolina Press, 1959–.

Murray, Sir Charles Augustus. *Travels in North America during the Years 1834, 1835, & 1836.* London: R. Bentley, 1839.

Nevins, Allan, ed. *The Diary of Philip Hone.* 2 vols. New York: Dodd, Mead and Company, 1927.

Parton, James. *Life of Andrew Jackson.* 3 vols. New York: Mason Brothers, 1860. (Included here because Parton's work contains much primary material.)

Richardson, James D., ed. *A Compilation of the Messages and Papers of the Presidents, 1789-1897.* 11 vols. Washington, D.C.: Bureau of National Literature, 1896-99.

Rossiter, Clinton, ed. *The Federalist Papers.* New York: NAL Penguin, 1961.

Smith, Adam. *The Wealth of Nations.* New York: Bantam Classics, 2003. (Introduction by Alan B. Krueger; as edited by Edwin Cannan in 1904.)

Smith, Samuel B. and Owsley, Harriet Chappell, *et. al.*, eds. *The Papers of Andrew Jackson.* 8 vols. to date. Knoxville: University of Tennessee Press, 1980-2010.

Stickney, William, ed. *Autobiography of Amos Kendall.* Boston: Lee and Shepard, Publishers, and New York: Lee, Shepard, and Dillingham, 1872.

Swisher, Carl Brent, ed. "Roger B. Taney's 'Bank War Manuscript.'" Part I, *Maryland Historical Magazine* 53 (June 1958): 103-30, and Part II, *Maryland Historical Magazine* 53 (September 1958): 215-37.

Syrett, Harold C., *et al.*, eds. *The Papers of Alexander Hamilton.* 27 vols. New York: Columbia University Press, 1961-87.

Taylor, John. *Tyranny Unmasked.* Indianapolis: Liberty Fund, 1992. (Edited by F. Thornton Miller; originally published in 1822.)

Thoreau, Henry David. *Walden and "Civil Disobedience."* New York and Toronto: New American Library, Signet Classic, 1960.

Weaver, Herbert, ed. *Correspondence of James K. Polk.* 2 vols. Nashville: Vanderbilt University Press, 1969-72.

Weed, Harriet A., ed. *Autobiography of Thurlow Weed.* 2 vols. Boston: Houghton, Mifflin and Company, 1884.

Secondary Sources

Bailyn, Bernard. *The Ideological Origins of the American Revolution.* Cambridge, MA: Belknap Press of Harvard University Press, 1967.

Baker, Pamela L. "The Washington National Road Bill and the Struggle to Adopt a Federal System of Internal Improvement." *Journal of the Early Republic.* 22 (Fall 2002): 438-64.

Banning, Lance. "Republican Ideology and the Triumph of the Constitution, 1789-1793." *William and Mary Quarterly* 31 (April 1974): 167-88.

Beard, Charles. *An Economic Interpretation of the Constitution.* New York: Macmillan Company, 1913.

Belko, William S. *The Triumph of the Antebellum Free Trade Movement.* Gainesville: University Press of Florida, 2012.

Belohlavek, John M. *"Let the Eagle Soar!": The Foreign Policy of Andrew Jackson.* Lincoln: University of Nebraska Press, 1985.

Bemis, Samuel Flagg. *John Quincy Adams and the Foundations of American Foreign Policy.* New York: Alfred A. Knopf, 1949.

________. *John Quincy Adams and the Union.* New York: Alfred A. Knopf, 1956.

Benson, Lee. *The Concept of Jacksonian Democracy: New York as a Test Case.* Princeton: Princeton University Press, 1961.

Berlin, Ira. *Slaves Without Masters: The Free Negro in the Antebellum South.* Oxford and New York: Oxford University Press, 1974.

Berry, Thomas Senior. "What was the GDP Then?" in Louis Johnston and Samuel H. Williamson "The Annual Real and Nominal GDP for the United States, 1789- Present." Economic History Services (March 2004).

Brands, H. W. *Andrew Jackson: His Life and Times.* New York, London, *et alia:* Doubleday, 2005.

Burin, Eric. *Slavery and the Peculiar Solution: A History of the American Colonization Society.* Gainesville (and elsewhere), Florida: University Press of Florida, 2005.

Burstein, Andrew. *The Passions of Andrew Jackson.* New York: Vintage Books edition, 2004. Original hardcover by Alfred A. Knopf, 2003.

Butler, Jon. *Awash in a Sea of Faith: Christianizing the American People.* Cambridge, MA: Harvard University Press, 1990.

Catterall, Ralph C. H. *The Second Bank of the United States.* Chicago: University of Chicago Press, 1902.

Charles, Joseph. *The Origins of the American Party System.* New York: Harper & Row, 1956.

Chernow, Ron. *Alexander Hamilton.* New York: Penguin Press, 2004.

Coit, Margaret L. *John C. Calhoun: American Patriot.* Boston: Houghton Mifflin, 1950.

Cole, Donald B. *The Presidency of Andrew Jackson.* Lawrence: University Press of Kansas, 1993.

Cowen, David J. *The Origins and Economic Impact of the First Bank of the United States.* New York: Garland Publishing, 2000.

Cunningham, Noble E., Jr. *The Presidency of James Monroe.* Lawrence: University Press of Kansas, 1996.

Current, Richard N. *John C. Calhoun.* New York: Washington Square Press, 1966.

Dangerfield, George. *The Awakening of American Nationalism, 1815-1828.* New York: Harper & Row, 1965.

________. *The Era of Good Feelings.* New York: Harcourt Brace and Company, 1952. Reprint by Elephant Paperback, 1989.

Devanny, John F. " 'A Loathing of Public Debt, Taxes, and Excises': The Political Economy of John Randolph of Roanoke." *Virginia Magazine of History and Biography* 109 (no. 4, 2001): 386-416.

Elkins, Stanley and McKitrick, Eric. *The Age of Federalism: The Early American Republic, 1788-1800.* New York and Oxford: Oxford University Press, 1993.

Ellis, Richard E. *The Union at Risk: Jacksonian Democracy, States' Rights and the Nullification Crisis.* New York and Oxford: Oxford University Press, 1987.

Feller, Daniel. *The Jacksonian Promise: America, 1815-1840.* Baltimore and London: Johns Hopkins University Press, 1995.

________. *The Public Lands in Jacksonian Politics.* Madison: University of Wisconsin Press, 1984.

Freehling, William W. *Prelude to Civil War: The Nullification Crisis in South Carolina, 1816-1836.* New York and Evanston: Harper & Row, 1965.

Govan, Thomas P. *Nicholas Biddle: Nationalist and Public Banker, 1786-1844.* Chicago: University of Chicago Press, 1959.

Hammond, Bray. *Banks and Politics in America, from the Revolution to the Civil War.* Princeton: Princeton University Press, 1957.

Hatch, Nathan. *The Democratization of American Christianity.* New Haven: Yale University Press, 1989.

Hofstadter, Richard. *The American Political Tradition.* New York: Alfred A. Knopf, 1948.

Howe, Daniel Walker. *What Hath God Wrought: The Transformation of America, 1815- 1848.* New York: Oxford University Press, 2007.

Jahoda, Gloria. *The Trail of Tears: The Story of the American Indian Removals, 1813- 1855.* New York: Wings Books, 1995.

Johnson, Paul E. *A Shopkeeper's Millenium: Society and Revivals in Rochester, New York, 1815-1837.* New York: Hill and Wang, 1978.

Lane, Carl. "Federal Investments in Private Canal Companies, 1825-1835." Unpublished paper presented at the annual conference of the Economic and Business Historical Society, Albany, NY, April 26, 2001. Copy on file at the Felician College Library.

_______. "For 'A Positive Profit': The Federal Investment in the First Bank of the United States, 1792-1802." *William and Mary Quarterly* LIV (July 1997): 601-12.

_______. "The Elimination of the National Debt in 1835 and the Meaning of Jacksonian Democracy." *Essays in Economic and Business History.* XXV (2007): 67-78.

Larson, John Lauritz. *Internal Improvement: National Public Works and the Promise of Popular Government in the Early United States.* Chapel Hill and London: University of North Carolina Press, 2001.

Lepler, Jessica M. "1837: Anatomy of a Panic." Doctoral Dissertation: Brandeis University, 2008.

Lewis, James E., Jr. *John Quincy Adams: Policymaker for the Union.* Wilmington, DE: SR Books, 2001.

Litwack, Leon F. *North of Slavery: The Negro in the Free States, 1790-1860.* Chicago and London: University of Chicago Press, 1961.

Macdonald, James. *A Free Nation Deep in Debt: The Financial Roots of Democracy.* New York: Farrar, Straus and Giroux, 2003.

Mann, Bruce H. *Republic of Debtors: Bankruptcy in the Age of American Independence.* Cambridge, MA and London: Harvard University Press, 2002.

Marszalek, John F. *The Petticoat Affair: Manners, Mutiny, and Sex in Andrew Jackson's White House.* Baton Rouge: Louisiana State University Press, 1997.

McCormick, Richard P. *The Second American Party System: Party Formation in the Jacksonian Era.* New York: W. W. Norton & Co., 1966.

McCoy, Drew R. *The Elusive Republic: Political Economy in Jeffersonian America.* Chapel Hill: University of North Carolina Press, 1980.

________. *The Last of the Fathers: James Madison and the Republican Legacy.* Cambridge: Cambridge University Press, 1989.

McCraw, Thomas K. *The Founders and Finance: How Hamilton, Gallatin, and Other Immigrants Forged a New Economy.* Cambridge, MA and London: Belknap Press of Harvard University Press, 2012.

McCusker, John J. "Estimating Early American Gross Domestic Product." *Historical Methods* 33 (Summer 2000): 155-63.

McDonald, Forrest. *Alexander Hamilton: A Biography.* New York and London: W. W. Norton & Company, 1979.

________. *E Pluribus Unum: The Formation of the American Republic, 1776-1790.* Boston: Houghton Mifflin Company, 1965.

________. *We the People: The Economic Origins of the Constitution.* Chicago: University of Chicago Press, 1958.

McFaul, John M. *The Politics of Jacksonian Finance.* Ithaca and London: Cornell University Press, 1972.

Meacham, Jon. *American Lion: Andrew Jackson in the White House.* New York: Random House, 2008.

Meyers, Marvin. *The Jacksonian Persuasion: Politics and Belief.* Stanford: Stanford University Press, 1957.

Miller, John C. *The Federalist Era, 1789-1801.* New York, Evanston and London: Harper & Row, 1960.

Morris, Richard B. *The Forging of the Union, 1781-1789.* New York: Harper & Row, 1987.

Nester, William. *The Age of Jackson and the Art of American Power, 1815-1848.* Washington, D.C.: Potomac Books, 2013.

Noll, Mark. *America's God.* Oxford and New York: Oxford University Press, 2002.

Parsons, Lynn Hudson. *John Quincy Adams.* Madison: Madison House, 1998.

Perdue, Theda and Green, Michael D. *The Cherokee Nation and the Trail of Tears.* New York: Penguin Books, 2008.

Rakove, Jack N. *The Beginnings of National Politics: An Interpretive History of the Continental Congress.* Baltimore and London: Johns Hopkins University Press, 1979.

Remini, Robert V. *Andrew Jackson and the Bank War.* New York and London: W. W. Norton & Co., 1967.

______. *The Election of Andrew Jackson.* Philadelphia and New York: J. B. Lippincott Company, 1963.

______. *Henry Clay: Statesman for the Union.* New York and London: W. W. Norton & Company, 1991.

______. *John Quincy Adams.* New York: Times Books, Henry Holt and Company, 2002.

______. *The Life of Andrew Jackson.* 3 vols. New York: Harper & Row, 1977-84.

______. *The Life of Andrew Jackson.* Abridged ed. New York: Harper & Row, 1988.

Reynolds, David S. *Waking Giant: America in the Age of Jackson.* New York: HarperCollins, 2008.

Risjord, Norman K. *Jefferson's America, 1760-1815.* 2nd ed. Lanham, Boulder, New York, Oxford: Rowman & Littlefield Publishers, 2002.

Roseboom, Eugene H. *A History of Presidential Elections.* 2nd ed. New York: Macmillan Company, 1964.

Satz, Ronald N. *American Indian Policy in the Jacksonian Era.* Lincoln: University of Nebraska Press, 1975.

Schlesinger, Arthur M., Jr. *The Age of Jackson.* Boston and Toronto: Little, Brown and Company, 1945.

Sellers, Charles. *The Market Revolution: Jacksonian America, 1815-1846.* New York and Oxford: Oxford University Press, 1992.

Skeen, C. Edward. "Vox Populi, Vox Dei: The Compensation Act of 1816 and the Rise of Popular Politics." *Journal of the Early Republic* 6 (Fall, 1986): 253-74.

Sloan, Herbert E. *Principle & Interest: Thomas Jefferson & the Problem of Debt.* New York and Oxford: Oxford University Press, 1995.

Smelser, Marshall. *The Democratic Republic, 1801-1815.* New York, Evanston, and London: Harper & Row, 1968.

Staudenraus, P. J. *The American Colonization Movement, 1816-1865.* New York: Columbia University Press, 1961.

Swanson, Donald F. *The Origins of Hamilton's Fiscal Policies.* Gainesville, Florida [Publisher Not Listed], 1963.

Temin, Peter. *The Jacksonian Economy.* New York: W. W. Norton & Co., 1969.

Turner, Frederick Jackson. *Rise of the New West, 1819-1829.* New York: Collier Books, 1962. (Originally published in 1906.)

Tyler, Alice Felt. *Freedom's Ferment: Phases of American Social History from the Colonial Period to the Outbreak of the Civil War.* New York: Harper &

Brothers, 1961. (Originally published in 1944 by the University of Minnesota Press.)

U.S. Bureau of the Census. *Historical Statistics of the United States, Colonial Times to 1957.* Washington, D.C.: U.S. Government Printing Office, 1960.

Walters, Ronald. *American Reformers, 1815-1860.* Rev. ed., New York: Hill and Wang, 1997.

Ward, John William. *Andrew Jackson: Symbol for an Age.* London, Oxford, New York: Oxford University Press, 1953.

Watson, Harry L. *Liberty and Power: The Politics of Jacksonian America.* New York: Hill and Wang, 1990.

Weir, Howard T., III. *A Paradise of Blood: The Creek War of 1813-14.* Yardley, PA: Westholme Publishing, 2014.

Wellman, Judith. *The Road to Seneca Falls.* Champaign: University of Illinois Press, 2004.

Wilentz, Sean. *Andrew Jackson.* New York: Times Books, Henry Holt and Company, 2005.

_______. *The Rise of American Democracy: Jefferson to Lincoln.* New York and London: W.W. Norton & Company, 2005.

Wood, Gordon S. *The Radicalism of the American Revolution.* New York: Vintage Books, 1991.

Wright, Robert E. *One Nation Under Debt: Hamilton, Jefferson, and the History of What We Owe.* New York: McGraw-Hill, 2008.

Young, James Sterling. *The Washington Community, 1800-1828.* New York: Columbia University Press, 1966.

INDEX